How the World Makes Love

Also by Franz Wisner

Honeymoon with My Brother

Franz Wisner

HOW THE WORLD MAKES LOVE

... And What It Taught a Jilted Groom

ST. MARTIN'S GRIFFIN ★ NEW YORK

HOW THE WORLD MAKES LOVE. Copyright © 2009 by Franz Wisner. All rights reserved.
Printed in the United States of America. For information, address St. Martin's Press, 175
Fifth Avenue, New York, N.Y. 10010.

www.stmartins.com

The Library of Congress has catalogued the hardcover edition as follows:

Wisner, Franz.
    How the world makes love : . . . and what it taught a jilted groom / Franz
Wisner.—1st ed.
        p. cm.
    ISBN 978-0-312-34083-4
    1. Wisner, Franz—Travel.   2. Dating (Social customs).   3. Man-woman
relationships.   4. Travelers—Biography.   I. Title.

HQ801.W765 2009
306.7309'0511—dc22

                                                                    2008035453

ISBN 978-0312-60558-2 (trade paperback)

First St. Martin's Griffin Edition: February 2010

10 9 8 7 6 5 4 3 2 1

To Joyce and Bob Wisner,
a world-class love story

Contents

A Note to Readers

In the interest of storytelling, I:

- Changed some names, usually to much better ones.
- Consulted my bedraggled thesaurus far more than a decent writer should, "bedraggled" being case in point.
- Threw time lines into a blender and hit puree.
- Trusted my interviewees to be honest and my translators to be accurate.
- Tried and failed to arrange a wedding for my brother, Kurt, in India, though feel free to e-mail me with any suggestions.

The Professional Dumpee

Only in America can a person get dumped at the altar and turn it into a career.

I discovered this verity thanks to Jennifer Wilbanks, the wild-eyed Georgia bride-to-be who chose to put a twist on traditional prewedding festivities by shunning a simple rehearsal dinner in favor of a faked abduction and a cross-country road trip. The arctic-footed fiancée was picked up by New Mexico police after a nationwide manhunt and countless television stories featuring *Runaway Bride*'s Julia Roberts on a galloping horse. I was one of millions of Americans mumbling to Jennifer's fiancé, "You lucky SOB."

Then the phone started to ring.

We want you on our morning show to speak on behalf of jilted grooms, the television schedulers begged. Can you be in New York City tomorrow?

"Why me?"

"Franz," said one earnest producer. "You don't understand. You're the world's number-one authority on getting dumped."

My parents must be so proud. Four years of Tufts University, tutors and science kits and that thirty-volume set of encyclopedias my father lugged home—all so I could comment on failed engagements.

But so it was. The producer's words confirmed my fate. I had become a professional dumpee.

You see, several years prior, my fiancée had fled as well. She decided to do so just days before our large wedding at the remote coastal community of Sea

Ranch, California. With guests en route and the wine on location, I decided to go ahead and enjoy all the festivities of the weekend, pretending, with zero success, to forget about the whole bride part.

Of the 150 people invited, 75 showed up—my entire side of the aisle. We had the golf tournament on Friday, the rehearsal dinner on Saturday, and even a mock wedding ceremony on Sunday, complete with a seaweed-clad friend who filled in for my absentee bride.

And you know what? It felt all right, even meaningful at times. Okay, for the other twenty-three hours and fifty-seven minutes it felt like somebody took a battering ram to my stomach and unleashed a martini hangover ty-phoon in my brain. I was humiliated and miserable and shocked enough to know the feelings had yet to fully sink in.

The meaningful part was having everyone who meant something to me in the same place for a long weekend. I realized then how few times we gather our en-tire group of friends and family in one setting—twice, in fact: your wedding and your funeral. And it's tough to enjoy the latter. Sure, we speak of their impor-tance in monotone: "My friends mean everything to me." Really? Do we really feel their depth or embrace their warmth until we need them? That weekend, I needed them. My brother, Kurt, two years my junior, led the festivities. He jumped on the first plane from Seattle to California after I gave him the news.

When my fiancée dumped me, I pledged to marry my job, to become the workaholic's workaholic. Then, shortly after the nonwedding wedding, they demoted me. The two loves of my life, gone.

So I opted for the rational course—take Kurt with me on my prepaid hon-eymoon to Costa Rica. I told him about it the night before.

"C'mon," I said. "We're going on a honeymoon."

"With whom?" he replied.

"I have first-class plane tickets. I have honeymoon suites. I have cham-pagne."

"Whoa, whoa. I love you, man. And I really want to help you out. But hon-eymoon suites have one bed. And it's usually heart-shaped. And I'm sorry you got dumped and all, but there ain't no way I'm going to spend two weeks in a heart-shaped bed with you in Costa Rica."

After I assured him I'd sleep on the floor, Kurt and I took off. He was a year out of a divorce. He hated his job. So there we were, two brothers, both dumped, both in dead-end jobs, on my honeymoon in the tropics.

Now, honeymoons are a big deal in Costa Rica. Those hotel managers have their places spiffed up and flower-laden, eager to hand room keys and PRIVACY PLEASE signs to happy couples for a week of tropical bliss. One owner took pains to meet us curbside.

"Meeester and . . . Meeester Wisner?" he said with a scrunched face.

"You're not half as surprised as I am," I said.

That lump of gray matter I used to call my head continued to swirl with guilt and regret and embarrassment and a gnawing question of whether she'd cheated on me. *Aha!* The other man grew in stature and riches each day. *He must be a model. A Hilton heir. A tango expert with an American Express Black Card. I'll kill him.*

I hurt. I was in a deep, dark hole, gasping for air, praying only to stop the fall, far from the day when I could even envision pulling up to level ground. *Snap out of it,* I scolded myself before realizing nobody snaps out of pain. Instead, I struggled with equally devastating forces—attempting to figure out where our relationship went astray and realizing I'd never be able to do anything about it.

Meanwhile, Kurt and I did something we hadn't done in years—we talked. It wasn't as if there had been a big issue that separated us. It was simply that we'd drifted apart, like so many brothers and sisters in our society. We went to different colleges, moved to separate towns to begin careers, began love lives, and shoved our relationship to the bottom of the priority list. I believed the occasional phone calls and tidbits passed from Mom were enough. I was wrong.

I discovered this in Costa Rica, somewhere between the Arenal volcano and Tamarindo sunsets. Maybe it was better to take a honeymoon with a brother I barely knew than with a woman who obviously didn't love me the way I loved her. I wanted the conversations to continue, wanted to learn more about Kurt. I also longed for a change of scenery to clear my head and thought the road may be a potential healer. So after two weeks of brotherly bonding, I suggested to Kurt we lengthen the trip.

"Great idea," he said. "There's a golf course nearby. We could stay there for a couple days, play a few rounds, eat some more fish."

"You have no idea what I'm talking about," I said.

Over dinner that night I convinced Kurt to extend the honeymoon for two years and fifty-three countries.

Now, this was not exactly how I dreamed my honeymoon would go. But the two years offered a world of discovery, enlightenment, and renewal, as well as a strengthened relationship with a long-lost best friend who just happened to be my brother. The planet made me a believer in many things— optimism amid chaos, soccer as a legitimate sport despite the grade-school playacting, green tea, siestas, the power of faith beyond the pulpit, Eastern medicine, a father's right to improve the lives of his children across all borders. The world showed me the importance of living life with my heart rather than just my brain, the need in all of us to follow passion wherever it takes us. It made me prouder than I'd ever been to hold a passport with the words UNITED STATES OF AMERICA etched in gold, ever more so each time I met an aid worker with a Southern drawl or a villager whose dreams were fueled by a place he'd never see, a land I was lucky enough to call home.

This was the honeymoon of a lifetime . . . if you overlooked that whole runaway bride aspect.

There was one small problem. Herculean, as far as my mother was concerned. I'd spent two years traipsing around the world's most romantic destinations—Rio and Prague, African safaris and exotic islands—meeting affable women at every port of call, with ample time to invest in friendship and conversation and love. Somehow I'd managed to take this dream setup, one so laden with options even Borat could have filled a black book full of numbers, and come back single.

"Man, you're lucky," said my friends, most of them married. "You had the whole world to choose from."

"Are you kidding me?" I'd reply. "Have you been in the singles game in, say, the last decade? Don't you know how impossible it is to fall in love in our own country, let alone connect with someone in a place where everything is foreign—language, culture, fashion don'ts, political insults, or even what to order from the menu?"

How on earth do you meet someone? How, on this earth, do you fall in love? The questions rumbled around throughout the honeymoon with my brother, especially when we found ourselves in a romantic setting, at sunset, as real couples strode off for their sidewalk café dinners. I'd go to sleep in, say, Lake Como or Los Roques, look over at Kurt in the other bed, and think, "What in God's name am I doing here with you?"

As the honeymoon ended and I came back to California, I concluded love was unreachable for the masses, and especially for a sap who ate his wedding cake alone. Their love stories were just that, stories.

It's not that I didn't believe in love. I just didn't believe in the odds. It's like Powerball. We see people who win the mega-jackpots on television. They wear muumuus or cowboy hats. Played the same numbers for thirty-eight years. They hold five-foot checks and promise to buy houses for their children. We see them, but we don't know them. And we certainly aren't one of them.

I'd been afforded my single shot at love. I'd blown it. Just the way it is. I'd invested a decade. Not all investments pay off.

Truth is, I can't say my life was completely devoid in this arena. Humans are a creative species. Bedouins can sense water under a sea of sand. Pacific Islanders know when storms are coming despite cloudless skies. So, too, with love. If one source dries up, we'll find it elsewhere. The mind convinces itself time with friends and family will suffice. We get creative. We get pets.

Strangers in Paradise

(all-inclusive)

You know that ripcord feeling you get on a bad first date? That almighty urge to flee after your dinner partner launches into a lengthy explanation of failed loves, reincarnated lives, or infatuation with all things Ricky Martin? Out go the predictions that "you'll make a perfect couple"; in sets an overwhelming urge to decouple. Now. You speed through your ravioli and stare at her wine as if doing so will make it evaporate. No dessert or coffee, thank you. Just the check, please. We're in a bit of a hurry.

I set the world record for that feeling aboard an Air Jamaica red-eye en route to a couples-only resort in the Caribbean. On a first date. I should explain.

Midafternoon on an aimless Friday, I popped by the offices of *Coast Magazine* in Newport Beach, California, "popped by" being code for "no job and nothing better to do." The editor, Justine Amodeo, had a habit of throwing assignments to unemployed scribes who lingered by her door. I lingered, long enough for it to happen again. Could I go to St. Lucia the first week in March? Justine didn't have all the details, but a public relations representative would call.

Let's see. The junket would entail canceling a haircut and an afternoon of laundry, but, sure. The clothes weren't *that* dirty.

"Since the trip is to a couples-only resort, we want you to bring a love interest," explained the bubbly spokeswoman the following day.

Couples only? As in those full-page ads in airline magazines, the ones with happy Caucasian couples in neon-colored bathing suits splashing each other on the beach, though never so much that it tousles the hair? Couples only as in wristbands and activity directors and all-you-can-eat?

That's when the panic set in, and not because my wardrobe was devoid of anything tangerine. The destination was an escape for couples, pet-named, hand-holding, Jimmy Buffett–worshipping couples.

"Are you sure you have the right guy?" I said. "Franz is a popular name."

"You're fun-nee," she said. "Justine said you'd liven up the trip."

"That Justine. What a character to pick me for this."

Oblivious to my hesitation, she gabbed on about the romantic setting in St. Lucia and the endless stream of activities I'd enjoy with my significant other. Their brochures in the press kit explained: "Love Is All You Need."

That's exactly my problem.

"Can I bring my brother?" I said. "I took him on my honeymoon."

"That's hil-aaaaarious."

"Great."

"Oh, no. The Caribbean isn't really into that kind of thing."

She resumed her spiel about swim-up bars and his-and-her massages. I didn't register a word. I was too busy searching every corner of my brain for a living, breathing, preferably unrelated female who might possibly say yes. The feelers began immediately after our phone call. The results went something like this:

"That's nice, Franz, but I don't really see you that way."

"I swear it's nothing more than a free trip. I'd never in a million years lay a hand on you."

"Now I *really* don't want to go."

My girlfriends, as in girl *friends,* were working. They had obligations. They had aversions to buffets. They said no en masse. Could you blame them?

The assignment had seemed so idyllic when Justine handed it to me. Ocean swims and happy hours and pupu platters or whatever they called them in the Caribbean. I could do that. Spend a few days with a group of pampered travel journalists? No problem. Her call changed all. My island fantasy evaporated thanks to those two god-awful words: couples only.

No longer was this a free trip to an expensive resort. The assignment didn't occupy an atom of thought. This was now a trial, a highly publicized inquisition into the love life of a terminal bachelor. *That's it. Justine's doing this to*

mess with me. To force me into a relationship with someone, anyone. The pro-
ceedings began with my ego as the first witness.

I called my friend Martha, a documentary filmmaker and adventurous
soul, to see if she had any suggestions.

"Bullshit, Wiz," she said. "This sounds like some sort of a scam."

"I swear it's legit. I just need someone to hang beside me so they don't kick
me off the island. It's illegal to be single at a couples-only resort, you know."

"Libby has this friend. She might go. Careful, though. She's strong enough
to reject anything you might pull down there."

"Great. Just don't tell her about my whole getting-dumped-at-the-altar
thing. I don't want to scare her off."

Martha called back the next day.

"I gave Tracy my best sales pitch," she said. "Told her you guys would
laugh the whole time, and that you'd sleep on the floor."

"What did she say?"

"She said she'd meet you for coffee. When you get back."

Then, a way out. I was sure the resort would be a breeze for couples en-
amored with each other. But what about couples who weren't? Better
yet, how about a couple who didn't even know each other? How would it do
as the setting for a first date?

Yes! A journalistic coup. Bob Woodward never took a blind date to a
couples-only resort. I'd bring someone I didn't even know. Brilliant solution.
That, and the small fact it was my only option.

Cue Angela A. She's the brave-slash-reckless soul who answered an ad I
placed online offering a "Free Trip to the Caribbean" in exchange for letting
me write about the experience. Strictly professional, I assured all Craigslist
readers. And I meant it, kind of. "Please send picture."

Three days later, and stag I remained. Microsoft must equip its computers
with a virus protection for any contact with unemployed, thirty-eight-year-
old vagabonds. Then, a ray of hope in my inbox.

Angela sent me the first, and only, response. She included a picture, a
grainy black-and-white image that reminded me of a stern flight attendant on
Cathay Pacific. She looked pensive, with tweezed eyebrows arced in faux concern, and staged, her long brown hair pulled back to frame her Asian features. She looked like, well, the only person who replied.

I decided to meet her for five minutes at the Casbah Café in Silver Lake, both to assure her of my quasilegitimate scribe status and to make sure she didn't fit the chainsaw-murderer profile. At the front table she waited, an eight-by-ten glossy in hand, which she presented to me as if auditioning for a role. I shook her hand and looked for any ominous mannerisms, tics, or eye darts and such. She sounded sane. She didn't fondle the knives. Plus I decided it would be next to impossible to get a chainsaw through a metal detector. There was no love connection, no tidal wave of pheromones, but at least she seemed fun. *If you flake out on this, Justine will never give you another assignment.*

"Okay," I announced. "You got the part."

"Great!"

We flew to St. Lucia the next day.

O ver ginger ales, and Arizona, Angela informed me she was an actress "in the middle of a repackaging phase."

"I'm trying to reposition myself as the female Keanu Reeves," she said.

Keanu Reeves. Whoa. I had nothing against Keanu Reeves. But did I really want to spend a romantic weekend with his female impersonator? Couldn't she have chosen someone a bit more androgynous? Say, Orlando Bloom?

A 757, I now remembered, is a sealed metal projectile with no way out. The CALL ATTENDANT button wouldn't help, either. The date with Angela A., the female Keanu Reeves, had just begun. There would be no early exit.

Angela pulled a book called *Casting Director Secrets* out of her bag and handed it to me as proof of her quest. I was bored. I was trapped. I spent the next couple of hours reading her manual, the only upside being I now know never to chew gum or bring a pet to an audition.

A t the check-in desk in St. Lucia, I begged the manager for a two-bedroom suite. The man laughed, then nodded like he understood too well. Poor guy. He shrugged and handed me the key to the room.

Apparently there are no such things as separate beds at couples-only resorts. Bickerers beware. We settled for a room with a master bedroom, sitting area, enclosed patio, and dipping pool. While Angela unpacked, I checked the couch to see if it came with a foldout bed. Apparently there are no such things as foldout beds at couples-only resorts. I dangled my feet over the armrest and eyed the deck chair outside as Plan B.

After a quick dinner spent drinking Red Stripes and avoiding questions from other journalists, I told Angela I wanted to retire for the night. Though a teetotaler, she planned to stay with the group and tackle the bar. No worries, I said. I'd be asleep on the foyer floor.

I heard the shower at 3 A.M. Angela took another at 7 A.M.

Okay. No big deal. Maybe she's jet-lagged. Nothing wrong with a late night/early morning shower combo.

What jolted me wasn't the sound of the water but the sight of her outfit for the day when she emerged from the monsoon that used to be our bathroom: shorts, bathing suit, sunscreen, and the hotel shower cap.

"You're not going outside like that, are you?"

"They said it might rain today."

"It rains here every day."

"I don't want to mess up my hair."

I wanted to yell, to order her to yank that ridiculous Saran Wrap from her head. *No girlfriend of mine is gonna wear something like that outside. Take that freezer bag off your scalp!*

Then I remembered Angela wasn't my girlfriend. She wasn't a trophy bride or my longtime companion or significant anything. What did I care if people stared?

"Go for it," I said.

She smiled, victorious, and off we went to a breakfast of Sterno-flamed eggs and limitless papaya. Angela bypassed these options in favor of raw fish and whole garlic cloves. To ward off insects, she explained (not to mention vampires or any possible gentleman caller).

As Angela nodded her plastic dome to passersby, I thought about the millions of men and women out there who'd waged war over things like shower caps, remembering a few nasty skirmishes of my own. My former fiancée and I fought for a week over a clock she purchased, one of those artsy contraptions with no numbers and bent wires for hands. "What's the point of having a clock if you can't tell the time?" I argued ad nauseam. It felt so much better now to acquiesce. Forget shower caps. Perhaps the key to being a happy couple is just not to care.

This was her first journey to a tropical island, and she talked excitedly about the all-inclusive options. We chose to split up for the day. Angela preferred the catamaran sail to the nearby beaches and twin-peak Pitons, while I decided to poke around the capital city of Castries.

"We'll meet up this afternoon," I said. "Take notes."

Angela, Angela, Angela. I can't even imagine you trying to strike up a conversation with that goofy plastic on your head. They'll snicker and talk behind your back and . . .

I froze, then reversed path. Amid the tin-roof city blocks, I realized I was responsible for Angela. I'd brought her to this island on a promise and thoughtlessly shuffled her off on a catamaran full of happy, rum-soaked couples. Happy couples can be hell, after all.

So what if she was a little protective of her hair. We should all be a little more follicle-sensitive.

I also started to think about my own idiosyncrasies. Was I any less odd than Angela? What is odd? I didn't shower at 3 A.M., but I did towel off the exact same way every time I exited one. Hair first, then underarms, left leg then right, arms then torso. I didn't cover my hair with plastic, but I remembered many a morning in junior high, riding my bicycle to school with my head cocked into the wind at just the right angle to ensure the part down the middle of my scalp would remain chiseled in stone for the rest of the day.

I bought her a juice that afternoon, and we walked along the beach, past the couples-only limbo contests and paddleball games. We talked about her parents, and her sister who begged her not to go on a trip with a stranger. What if he tried to force himself on her? What if he was a chainsaw-wielding maniac? Why do all doomsday scenarios involve chainsaws? She told me she sent her sister several e-mails to reassure her I was a gentleman, if a bit weird.

"How's the career going?" I asked as we ambled. "You score any big roles?"

"Yes. I'm really psyched about it."

"Tell me."

"It's a voice-over in the video game Grand Theft Auto. All the kids play it."

"Cool. Let's hear something."

"Okay, okay," she said, steadying herself. "Here goes. Uhhhh!"

"That's it?"

"Well, they sample it. You can hear it over and over if you play the game."
Right there I bought into her dream. Who cared if her lines weren't even
words. This was big. Angela was on her way. I shifted to problem-solving-guy
mode and listed a dozen steps she should take to ignite her Hollywood career,
ignoring the fact I knew nothing about acting or Keanu Reeves. The more I
heard, the more I rooted for Angela. I began to feel for her. We bonded. Until dinner.

I haven't seen a scientific study to back this up, but I'm convinced a person's curiosity/nosiness increases exponentially after marriage. You have a
co-conspirator. You have time to hatch theories. How else do we explain the
bombardment of questions that ensued whenever Angela and I shared a meal
with betrothed duos?

"So, are you married?" asked a sunburned wife from Alabama. "I don't
see a ring."

"How did you two meet?" chimed in a husband from New York while I
stammered to answer the first question.

Here, at a couples-only resort, I learned couples love to talk with couples
about their favorite subject: other couples. First dates, proposals, wedding
days, getaways—they cover it all. They dissect all that is coupledom all day,
every day.

They talked about being a couple so much I suddenly had couple envy.
Their courtships seemed so blissful and balanced, their quirks so cute. Not
once did someone mention an office affair or a Xanax binge. Their well-
scrubbed children, smiling at me from the school photos, looked like Mini-Me
mirror images of happy Mom and Dad. There wasn't a booger or tangled hair
in sight. Joint checking accounts, nicknames for body parts, he washes while
she dries—I pined for it all. I caved to the frenzy, convincing myself I was now
miserable being single. My butt wasn't "Mr. Cheeky" or "Milk Moons." The
only words I'd heard used to describe it in the last ten years were "lard ass," as
in "Hey, lard ass!"

I looked to Angela. Before the trip, I made her promise not to spoil my
ruse. I didn't want the kind people at the resort to think I was taking advan-
tage of their hospitality. I didn't want them to think I was, umm, *single*. Just
follow my lead, I told her; we'll duck the issue entirely and divert them to different subjects. At a couples-only resort, this is easier pledged than completed.

"When are you going to make an honest woman out of her, Franz?" pried a wife from Boston.

"Angela's very truthful."

"You know what I mean."

"How about those Sox, huh?"

On the third night I gave up. I was a gate crasher, not a member.

"How long have you known Angela?" asked another writer.

"About a plane ride longer than I've known you."

"I didn't *think* you guys made a great couple."

"Why?" I said, suddenly defensive. "What's wrong with us?"

"You don't ever look at her."

"Well, looking's overrated. It's what you feel on the inside."

"Now I know you're single."

That set off a rapid round of conversations. And I realized the favorite topic of conversation among couples isn't simply other couples, it's the problems with other couples. We were low-hanging fruit for their pop psychology counseling. Angela excused herself from the dissection.

"I'm going to the gym," she said.

"It's nearly midnight."

"That's the best time. There are no people there. I shower late."

"You're a sweetheart," I said. "But how on earth am I going to describe you in this story?"

"How about this?" she said without pause. "An up-and-coming actress with a creative flair."

"Have a good workout," I said to the up-and-coming actress with a creative flair.

Angela adjusted her iPod and made her way through a crowd of couples. I didn't notice the waitress standing next to me.

"Would you or your wife like any coffee?"

"I'm . . . single," I said. "Very single."

The Accomplice

LOS ANGELES

Don't get me wrong. Los Angeles is a wonderful place. They have fish tacos, after all. Also Griffith Park, KCRW, and hungover movie stars without makeup at your neighborhood supermarket. In all aspects of life except for dating, it's fine.

But when it comes to love, Los Angeles is, and this is a scientific fact, the worst place on earth. Look it up. If for no other reason, how can you fall in love in a city where nobody looks anybody else in the eye?

Restaurants, encounters at the park, optometry appointments—it doesn't matter. You start talking to people in Los Angeles and the first thing they do is glance over your shoulder to see if anyone better has arrived. Ladies and gentlemen, the Hollywood Gaze. Mmm, they'll say, bobbing their head back and forth to stare behind you. Right. Even red carpet hosts interviewing the most well-groomed and fabulous people on the planet have the Gaze, thinking there's bound to be someone even more well groomed and fabulous pulling up in a limo soon.

The Gaze is more than a by-product of Los Angeles. It *is* Los Angeles. Beyond anywhere else, Southern California is rapt by the next big thing, the new "it girl," the next wave. Purchased a new Mercedes? You should see the hybrid coming out. The Skybar? Forget the Skybar. Go to the Standard. Chai is fine, but have you tried yerba maté? Is it good? It's going to be huge. But is it good?

In the workplace and during casual conversations, the Gaze is annoying yet tolerable. You learn not to take it personally and to stop glancing over your own shoulder during conversations. Everyone is more important than you. Accept it. This was not a tough argument with me.

On a date, though, the Gaze becomes deadly, sucking the life out of any potential love connection. Dating in Los Angeles is like doing Shakespeare amid a cast with ADD.

Of course, I made matters worse. I didn't exactly have the right points of connection with Los Angeles. I cheered against the Lakers and Dodgers, had never shared beds or drugs with anyone who reads *Variety,* and had no astrologers or herbalists on speed dial. My wardrobe, devoid of anything Von Dutch, lingered in the fashionista DMZ, several years out of style, yet not so old it became cool again like my father's mail-order corduroy coats. I didn't even have a car for the first six months after Kurt and I rented a Craftsman house in Los Feliz, a neighborhood our landlord described as "half Bohemian, half Armenian."

Los Angelinos, when asked what they do, tend to tell you about their hobbies. "I'm a wind surfer working on a screenplay." I love that about them. Unfortunately, my hobby, honeymooning with brothers, didn't exactly constitute the best pickup line. "That's odd," they'd say. When a Californian tells you something's odd, it's *odd.*

I'm done," I said.

"You're home early," said Kurt, only half listening.

Kurt stared in a trance at the golf tournament on television, his runner's body, long and lean, stretched up and over the sofa armrest. He needed a haircut, and I thought about telling him so. Then I remembered I was his older brother, and those sorts of comments didn't always go over so well. As Mike Myers (a.k.a. Linda Richman) would say on *Saturday Night Live:* "Your friendly suggestions are neither friendly nor suggestions. Talk amongst yourselves."

"It's impossible to have a conversation in this town," I said. "Let alone a relationship."

"I thought she was going to make you dinner with some friends?"

"She did."

"What did she serve?"

"Ecstasy . . . in Pez dispensers."

"You think she digs you?"

"Kurt, she was on ecstasy. She was nice to the litter box."

Try as I might, and Lord knows I tried, I just couldn't see a way out. We'd signed a lease. I was stuck in Los Angeles, single, declining X from the head of Popeye, without a female prospect in sight. Opening the refrigerator to grab a Corona, I paused.

There are moments in life when a man needs to wage the impossible fight, casting aside improbable odds and dire surrounds like used wads of Kleenex. Shackleton on Elephant Island, Willis Reed in Game 7, Al Pacino in *The Godfather: Part III.* This was not one of those moments.

I'm out."

"Where ya going?" he asked, still fixated on golf.

"What's the one thing that everyone asked us about our travels?"

"Did you get diarrhea."

"Try again."

"Malaria."

"Love."

"Love."

"Yeah, did you meet anyone? Did you fall in love in Rio? Did you hit on any women in burkas?"

"Nobody ever asked me about burkas."

"When we go to a foreign country, and we meet people, what do we end up talking about?"

"Soccer," he said.

"Love lives! It's the most interesting thing about travel, and completely missed by the guidebooks."

"Don't go off on another guidebook rant."

Kurt, at last, glanced up from the television.

"How many happy couples did we meet out there?" I asked. "People who didn't live in McMansions or serve X in Pez dispensers?"

"Tons."

"Exactly. What are their secrets?"

"I don't think they have Pez in those places."

"You want to keep traveling, right?"

"Yes."

"What if we picked one country on each continent, anywhere. We go there for a month and learn what we can about love. Young, old, gay, straight, Arabs, Hindus. Vegans. What are we doing here that's more important than love?"

"Wow," he said, turning toward me. "I never thought you'd take X."

"I didn't take X. I'm serious. You, we might learn something. Strengthen our game here at home."

"How do we pay for it?"

"LaRue."

The most inspiring person on the two-year, fifty-three-country honeymoon with my brother was a ninety-eight-year-old cancer survivor who painted red birds on china and playfully chastised neighbors if they started to use a walker: "I'll give you just one more day on that thing, Peggy." She lived not in an exotic locale but in a pink stucco retirement home in Carmichael, California. She was special; she was our stepgrandmother, and her name was LaRue.

We had told LaRue about our crazy plans before we told our parents. "Guess what? We're going to quit our jobs, sell our homes, give away our clothes, and keep honeymooning around the world for a couple of years."

"Splendid," she replied without pause.

She'd take the journey with us, in fact. All this required was a world map, a box of red pushpins, and a postcard or letter from each port of call.

"I'll share the postcards with the rest of Eskaton," she said. "We'll all go with you."

And to a person they embraced the trip.

"I wish I did more of that when I was your age," they said. "I have the time and the money, just not the body. My brother's passed away."

"You never regret travel," summed up LaRue. "Only the trips you don't take. And you certainly never regret time with family. Don't let those times slip away."

Kurt and I held her hand during those final days in the hospital room. Above the IVs and monitors rested our photos and postcards from abroad, smiling children in Africa, a sunset over Iguaçú, me holding a guinea fowl that had flown through our bus window in Malawi. I never explained that shot to LaRue, but I don't think I had to. She was with us at every step along the way. In her will, she left us some money to keep traveling.

What better way to spend it?" I asked Kurt. "LaRue was the embodiment of love. Let's go talk to the LaRues of the world."

Convincing Kurt to embark on another adventure didn't take much longer than the golf match. His love life had foundered as well, so much so that he'd started talking seriously about doing volunteer work at the hostels. "That way I'd meet a bunch of internationals, people who like to talk about travel. We could swap road stories for hours." He dropped the plan when I reminded him he used to wash his underwear in hostels.

Kurt's only prerequisites were that we go to India at some point and delay the trips until he finished his career as a competitive golfer. A coach at the local community college had convinced him to reenroll in school despite his having graduated from the University of Oregon a decade earlier. He had two years of athletic eligibility, after all. So Kurt spent his days taking Spanish and documentary film classes with eighteen-year-olds and competing at public links in the afternoons. I walked his dogs.

My agent called a few weeks later with the good news. Our publisher had agreed to accept our wholly half-baked take on international relations. Somehow (half nelson, I'm guessing) she convinced them to help fund trips to seven foreign countries—Brazil, Egypt, India, the Czech Republic, Panama, New Zealand, and Botswana—to talk to locals about love, dating, romance. Sex.

In the book proposal, I assured our publisher that the countries comprised a representative array of the world's inhabited continents, a cross-sampling of religions and races, wealth and topography, chosen by sociologists and scientists who worked in labs with Bunsen burners. I lied. There were no Bunsen burners, only a conversation with Kurt that began, "Where do you want to go?"

The world seemed so wise on matters of love. I craved that knowledge. To me, the planet was the anti-L.A. It helped me forge a new relationship with my brother and reinvent my life after getting dumped at the altar. Better than any self-help book or 12-step program, it remained my healer. If anyone could help recast my love life, it was the world.

During our travels we'd met countless happy couples in the third world, locals holding hands, talking to us from their lean-tos and huts, smiling sincerely and ceaselessly, the smiles of experience and cognition. They were on to something, secrets I hoped they'd share.

Better still, I now had a furlough from the misery that is the Los Angeles dating scene. I could try my hand around the world, in theory, at least. Was there an easier way to approach someone in a foreign country? "Excuse me, miss, but I'm writing a book about love. Would you mind sharing a cup of coffee?" Okay, that was kind of creepy. We could work on it.

And with a bit of luck, make that a lot of luck, I'd have an ending. Author Completes World Search, Marries Best Woman on Planet! European royalty, a South American novelist, an Australian surfing champion!

Or maybe I'd make it fiction.

Love Is Dead

I don't know how to define it, only that it should be dead. Love, that is. *Amour*. Eros. That nonsensical force that convinces two otherwise sane adults they should discard all rational reasons to the contrary and attempt to spend the rest of their lives together. By any measure or cursory analysis, love on our planet should top the list of extinct species. Done. Over. Buried among dodos and DeLoreans. Just take a look at what we've done to the poor thing.

Pick a hundred couples from around the world at random. All kinds— young or old, gay or straight, rich or poor, spooners or spoonees.

About half would be married. Half of the half would soon be divorced, higher still if your sampling skewed toward countries like Belarus, the United States, or the pristine Maldives, a remarkable place in that it is both a honeymoon haven and a divorce hell. Arab men can divorce their wives just by saying the word three times. In Cuba, a split will cost you four dollars and a half hour of paperwork at a notary office, roughly the price of a Cuban cigar and the time it takes to smoke it.

In much of the world, alimony is AWOL and child support from Dad means bouncing Junior on his knee when he happens to be around. Men flee and women are left to raise the kids on their own and on their own wages. It's a devil's choice for any woman in a bad marriage. They can't afford to stay, and they can't afford to leave.

So they turn their heads from their husbands' indiscretions, and they often partake in a little side action of their own. How many of our partners would cheat? An easier question: How many wouldn't? Surveys say at least half of all American men stray. Then again, why do we poll on this subject at all? Why would we ask people who aren't truthful if they've been truthful?

Americans seem vestal compared to the rest of the world. Half? Ha! They've got that figure beat by breakfast. Russians boast of infidelity rates of 75 percent and higher, with the other quarter polishing up their pickup lines in hopes of joining the masses. The Czech Republic, Brazil, Costa Rica, Kenya, and other testosterone-dominated countries around the globe see cheating as an ingrained benefit of being a virile man.

Whatever the infidelity rate, the world puts up with it. Most people in the United States view cheating as immoral, wrong, and harmful to a relationship. The vast majority of American women see no excuse for the one-night stand. This, of course, hasn't stopped generations of American men from trotting out ill-thought rationales that include Las Vegas bachelor parties, too many dirty martinis, or "it was just sex." The relationship can survive, they plead as their partners freeze their bank accounts and take measurements for house-arrest bracelets.

The majority of our hundred couples would view infidelity the same way they view droughts, government corruption, and *Baywatch*—as a constant in life to be tolerated rather than changed. Two-thirds of Peruvian women believe infidelity is justifiable. You'll find similar rates of excusers in the rest of Central and South America. In former Eastern Bloc countries, societies where secrecy has been the government-inspired norm for generations, women go to extraordinary lengths to adapt to infidelities, even befriending their husbands' lovers to better track the shenanigans.

Tell your friend in America her husband is having an affair, and you'll both spend days plotting his slow, painful demise, preferably to be televised on the *Jerry Springer* show. Tell a friend in Europe her husband is cheating, and you'll lose the friend. Of course her husband is cheating. It's Europe.

How does the planet curtail cheating? Simple: By not calling it cheating. That implies an offense, a crime. In France, it's merely an affair. So much more fun and frivolous that way. Botswana refers to it as *o ratana le mongwe,* or "he's going with someone else." Going where? There is no word in the Setswana language for infidelity.

Prostitution is legal or tolerated in a robust and growing United Nations quorum. Western countries like Germany and Australia joined the pimp's club recently, proclaiming paid sex is no longer immoral, it's taxable. Germany even imported tens of thousands of prostitutes from neighboring countries just to accommodate demand during the 2006 World Cup. I guess that's one way to handle the hooligans.

Dozens of other nations, while officially prohibiting prostitution on paper, decriminalize the practice and allow paid sex to flourish in red light districts and homemade brothels. Regardless of the region, our hundred couples would include many johns, and a few Dear Johns once their wives found out.

If infidelity has you down, you could always move to a place like Saudi Arabia or Nigeria or Yemen, where those secret trysts are punishable by death. American women should take note, however: The victims do not get to administer the sentence.

We've beaten love. Literally. Severely. More than a third of the women in our sample would be victims of physical, sexual, or emotional abuse. These are the ones who've dared come forward. Don't forget about the silenced millions, the women with no options and no support, the ones with heavy makeup and dark veils to hide the beatings. The World Bank estimates domestic violence injures or kills more women than traffic accidents and malaria. Combined.

Alcohol is an accessory to the crimes. If you see a black eye, there's often a bottle nearby. One in seven Americans experiences problems related to alcohol. We're the teetotalers. The rates are much higher in Japan, for example, where all-night booze fests and slurred versions of "Danke Schoen" at the karaoke bars are considered prerequisite steps for corporate advancement. But the Japanese are social drinkers compared to the Russians. Surveys claim half of Mother Russia has a drinking problem. Cynics who've been to Russia conclude the other half must have been sleeping it off.

Pornography is another assault, especially via the Internet, where a world's supply of liquor store porn racks can be summoned by the click of a mouse. America may not be the world leader in population or land mass, but we are the kings of pornography. And queens. And princes, dukes, footmen, and jesters. According to a recent *60 Minutes* segment, we produce three-quarters of the world's pornography supply, and devour it just as fast, to the tune of $10 billion a year.

Almost makes you feel bad for McDonald's. Critics cite them as the prime example of trashy American consumerism. Yet there are three times as many outlets to purchase pornography in our country as there are places to buy a Big Mac.

Nothing new, you say. India has its Kama Sutra. European museums are filled with Rubenesque orgies. Yes, but the chapters we add to the world history of sex will have titles like "Lust of the Mohicans," "Shaving Ryan's Privates," "Flesh Gordon," and "Yank My Doodle, It's a Dandy." Or so I have read.

Religion may be the opiate of the masses, but it only bolsters the argument against love. Look at the main texts. They're filled with stories of child brides and incest, rape, and murder—and that's among the protagonists and main prophets. Their authors are cold realists who tell us repeatedly and in graphic terms that love among humans is forever flawed, while love with our maker is our only salvation. They've given up on love between two adults in favor of a relationship with a partner who doesn't talk back.

Our poor sample. Would any of our couples love each other? We've taken an ideal—innocent, powerful, pure—and done everything possible to destroy it. We've penned it in, with restriction after restriction placed on any who dare fall in love. Go! Embrace! Love, we tell our children. Just choose within this religion or that sect. Pick only from this class, that caste, this race, that shade. Think America is more enlightened on this front? Before you answer, think about how many of our friends marry outside their race or tax bracket or even their MySpace links. We don't need government restrictions on love in America, thank you. We do just fine placing them on ourselves.

We've taken love for granted, fled from it, and trashed it behind its back. We've exploited it, distorted it, ignored it, politicized it, and closeted it. We've also framed it to some ghastly music.

Some people have tried to fill the world with silly love songs. What's wrong with that? Plenty. Balladeers in the seventies implored us to Love the One You're With, to understand Two Out of Three Ain't Bad, and be inspired by the virtues of Muskrat Love. The little critters, by the way, can produce three litters a year with multiple partners, mating just days after giving birth. But I digress.

We soured a tad during the eighties, convincing ourselves Love Stinks, Love Bites, Love Is a Battlefield, and Love Will Tear Us Apart. By the end of the century, we threw in the towel. We ditched the champagne and roses, and wanted only to F*** You Like an Animal or have a Zoom-Zoom-Zoom and a Boom-Boom. Is it any wonder Andrea Bocelli, the world's bestselling troubadour, has given up on new love songs?

"In my view, we're experiencing a serious crisis in creativity," said the Italian tenor to *The Times* of London. "Why should we insist on recording new music when it lacks true inspiration, that fundamental honesty which is the only thing that can touch people's hearts?"

What about love's role models? Yoo-hoo! Anybody home? Brad and Angelina? Bill and Hillary? Larry Craig and any poor guy who has to use the john? Charles and Camilla? J.Lo and what's-his-name? The world's most famous and celebrated love stories stream not from the inkwells of poets but from the sewer lines of tabloids. It's a sad day when, by all appearances, the most loving and functional high-profile couple on the planet today is Ozzy and Sharon Osbourne. Oh, we've strayed, people. We've strayed.

In our television dens, we embrace emergency rooms and forensic investigations, wannabe idols and has-been celebrities. We applaud desperate housewives, terminal bachelors, and kids who must somehow cope with it all. Absent is the popular television program where love, simple love, is the central theme. Sorry, the soap operas don't count.

No longer do we pen love letters; we text. Gone are the serenades and windowsill musicians; we karaoke. Dead are dating and courtships; we hook up.

Forget global warming and nuclear proliferation. We need a global summit on love! Just not in Las Vegas.

Possibility

BRAZIL

I knew the first stop without consulting Kurt. Brazil. Just the name evoked fantasy and escape. Over and over I said it. *Brazil. Brah-SEE-ooo. Braaaa-aahhhhhh.* I might not return.

I'd been to Brazil several times since the honeymoon, roaming the shores of Bahia and Santa Catarina, meandering through Curitiba and Manaus, exploring the Amazon and Rio de Janeiro, always Rio. After each trip I kicked myself for discovering the country at such a late stage in life. Why on earth did I waste those college summers eating Nutella on stale bread and taking hand showers in European train stations when I could have fallen in love each day in Brazil? I might not have been in my current predicament.

On all matters love-related, the planet needs Brazil. It is our muse, our guiding light. It's our inspiration to get off our duffs and pay a little more attention to our hearts. With a sway and a gaze, Brazil beckons and tells us yes, love is possible. For you too, gringo. You just need to be open. You need to dance.

All areas of the world have their role. Switzerland chose chocolate. The Cayman Islands opted for money laundering. Branson, Missouri, went with Mickey Gilley and Yakov Smirnoff. Brazil chose love and sexuality. You tell me who picked wisely.

Sure, Brazil has problems. Crushing ones. Eight-year-old drug runners and crooked cops who shoot at them. Indentured farmworkers who will labor their entire lives and never escape debt. Corrupt politicians who promise change, then shuffle goodwill off to foreign bank accounts.

But Brazil has forces far greater. Hope. Belief. Hope so great it seeps past its shores and off to the rest of us. Maybe, just maybe, we say as we look to Brazil, we can, too. Brazil inspires in a way the rich nations cannot, carving brilliant, all-encompassing love from nothing.

Forget appearance. You want to know Brazil's dirty little secret? It's not the world's beauty queen. Sure, there are hordes of gorgeous men and women straight from the pages of a glossy Coppertone ad campaign. Among them stand the pimpled and frumpy and plain. The rest of us. We tend to see Brazil like we see past relationships—remembering the highs and passions, forgetting the 2 A.M. fights over utility bills.

It's not the appearance, it's the attitude. Brazil's attraction lies not in the way it looks but in the way it stands. It never hesitates to strut. The land of *Ordem e Progresso* wakes with neither, pulls its dime-store outfit from the closet, and sports it like couture. Brazil is that smiling size-14 woman on the beach in the *fio dental* swimsuit. It's the factory worker who spends a year's time and a month's wages fashioning a Carnival outfit. It's that purred riff on traditional Portuguese to give words a pillow-talk edge. *Beeeh-jhos. Sow-daaah-geeee.*

Most of the planet makes relationship decisions based on practical considerations—family, dowries, cattle, checklists on eHarmony. Brazil still cedes affairs of the heart to the heart. Brazilians don't talk as much about the sensible when describing their ideal match. And that makes the rest of us feel alive and hopeful.

The more times I visited, the more I saw Brazil as our opposite, my opposite—sweaty sambas to our staid line dancing, Mondays at the beach to our Sundays in the office, decisions of the heart to our to-do lists. Brazilians made the most basic chore seem like foreplay, like the way they wrapped their arms around the handrails on the buses or how they'd accentuate conversations with shoulder sways and hair flips.

Even the Rio airport announcer oozed seduction. I felt the tension drain from every synapse when I first heard her voice again over the loudspeaker. "Now booaaahhrding, Vahhh-rigeeee flight number threeeee-ssssseeero-ssseeero." For four decades Iris Lettieri has set the mood for her country. With her calm cadence and ability to make simple numbers seem like a come-on, she's lit the candles and slipped into something a little more comfortable for the arousal of every jet-lagged traveler lucky enough to feel her presence.

Actually, the locals confided, Lettieri's voice was honed not through whispered sweet nothings but years of chain-smoking. And by the way, they said, she's been married to six different husbands. I ignored them. The separations were obviously the husbands' fault. Iris was too good for them, perfect and beautiful in every way, damn it.

If I was ever going to rekindle love, ever pick those winning lottery numbers, I'd need Brazil.

The country's draw also had a more personal explanation. Deborah. Deborah with the sleepy-eyed smile and four-part last name that took me a year to pronounce correctly. We met the previous year when she accepted an important role in Brazilian dating culture: safety friend.

Kurt, God bless him, arranged a double date for us with two Brazilians we met at a Rio nightclub. When we showed up at the outdoor café the next day for lunch, though, Kurt's Marina was there, but I found another in my date's place, a young woman, slender and shy, her knees touching like a schoolgirl's. Deborah. I stewed as we ordered steak sandwiches. Was this how they did things in Brazil? Did I say something offensive at the club? Did I forget to brush my teeth?

By the time the food arrived, I had noticed something about Deborah. With her dark mane and porcelain skin, she seemed to be in black and white, like one of those studio actresses from the 1940s, the kind GIs and prisoners would pin to their walls for inspiration. Just substitute Havaiana flip-flops for stiletto heels and long straight hair for all those buns and beehives. She smiled and joked about how American men waxed their bodies and tried to look like women while the women wore baggy khakis and strove to look like men. She could dish. I liked her more and more with each bite.

"How did a Brazilian get to be so pale?" I asked.

"I'm not pale!"

She was pale. And here I discovered "pale" is a dirty word in Brazil, somewhere between the B-word and the ones that begin with letters later on.

As Deborah picked at her plate of fries, I discovered something else. She and Marina barely knew each other. Once Marina learned her friend wouldn't come, she scoured her Rolodex for someone who could spend a few hours humoring a gringo, or at least pretend to laugh when he made clichéd comments about the girls from Ipanema. A classmate suggested Deborah, who'd spent a year in the Washington, D.C., area on sabbatical with her family. Deborah didn't think the request odd, nor would most of her countrymen. Brazil abhors the fifth wheel. When invited, they go.

It was a wonderful trait, I thought as Deborah and Marina chatted in rapid-fire Portuguese. We spend too much time safeguarding and not enough doing. Deborah and her fellow Brazilians made me realize how many of my favorite times involved the least amount of planning. I made a mental note to say yes more often at home.

Deborah attended marketing classes in Rio during the day. Not that there were any job prospects for the Deborahs of Brazil, even with her A average. The bulletin boards at school advertised women-only positions. She rode the bus to class and swapped clothes with her sisters to make her wardrobe seem bigger.

In America, she fell in love with Target, the red-and-white bull's-eye variety. She marveled at the wide aisles, cheap prices, goods stacked to the ceiling. In her eyes, Target embodied everything her country was not—methodical, responsive. Fair. Above all, she longed for a management training slot at Target or a big-box retailer in the United States. She wanted a job with benefits and opportunity. She wanted out of Brazil.

When she wasn't dreaming of red vests, Deborah found joy in small things. Four-cheese lasagna, window shopping at Zona Sul, nights at samba school preparing for Carnival, the weekly crafts fair in Ipanema. She had a crush on George Clooney and CNN's Jonathan Mann.

"Jonathan Mann?" I asked.

"I like the way he talks."

I liked Deborah. We ended up sharing many an enjoyable day together during that trip and the others that followed. In my mind, and in my state, I saw our relationship as, if not serious, at least honest and fun. I'd fly down, rent an apartment in Rio, drink banana shakes from the *botecos,* and write for large chunks of the day. At night, after she finished her classes, we'd go to dinner or out to hear music. I'd ask questions and she'd answer.

"What's a *viado*?"

"Gay. A homosexual. Did someone call you that?"

"No. Of course not."

"My sweet *viado*."

"What do they call a Brazilian wax?"

"A wax."

"What's over that pretty hill?"

"*Favelas*. Slums. More slums."

"I clipped this newspaper article out of *O Globo*. Will you read it to me?"

"I wish you spoke Portuguese."

I wish I did, too, though I don't think it would have been enough to change our relationship. Travel friendships tend to stay travel friendships, even when you dress them up with sex and shared secrets. That much I'd learned on the road. Return flights are also grand excuses to avoid those questions every budding couple should ask. You talk in the future tense, about the days left in country or the next time you'll see each other. I patted myself on the back for having managed to keep the conversations clear of words like "girlfriend" and "commitment." Love. I hadn't overpromised. *But you returned.*

"Do you have *saudade*?" she'd ask on the phone, using Brazil's unique word for missing someone so much you ache inside and everywhere.

"Sure I miss you."

"That's not *saudade*."

Still, I was eager to see Deborah again. Her nonchalance was starting to grow on me. Maybe this relationship could grow, too. I'd have more time this trip. We'd see.

We planned to meet where everyone meets in Rio, at the beach. Arriving early at Ipanema, Posto Nine, I haggled with a beach vendor before agreeing to rent a couple of umbrellas and chairs for the equivalent of three dollars. C'mon, he signaled, leading me to a patch of sand adjacent to a group of attractive young women. You tip extra for this, his smile seemed to say. Deborah spotted my salt-and-pepper head from the peeling tile sidewalk that frames the Rio shore.

"Fararanzo," she said, giving me a kiss on each cheek. "My George Clooney!"

"Just without the money," I said, kissing her in return. "Or the Lake Como estate."

After he finished adjusting the umbrella, the vendor spat a few words toward Deborah.

"What did he say?" I asked.

"Nothing."

"C'mon."

"He said I'm whiter than you."

"See."

"Shh!"

The tan in Brazil is a uniform, a way to establish rank in the all-important hierarchy of leisure. A person with dark skin must spend inordinate amounts of time at the beach, the country reasons. This person must be a master at avoiding work and maximizing fun. They salute the cocoa and tease the pale.

"I'm part black, you know."

"Which part?" I asked.

"My grandmother was black. On my father's side."

More than other countries, Brazil largely embraces its mixed-race past, dating back to the country's intimate and active relationship between Portuguese landowners and their African slaves and native *indios*. So what if we're the products of affairs and intermingling, Brazilians say. Who cares if we haven't re-created stuffy European class confines on our shores. This isn't a source of shame. This makes us more harmonious and strong, boast many, a blend of the best of all worlds. It also makes us more attractive. We don't limit sex appeal to a single look, a set color. In Brazil, we think everyone is sexy. Thank *Dios* our grandparents cheated and stirred.

Yet Brazil was the last country in the Western Hemisphere to abolish slavery; and the inequalities remain, visible and deep. You see them in the shantytown *favelas,* where dark-skinned Brazilians struggle to exist in lean-tos with cardboard walls and plastic roofs. They're in the corporate boardrooms and state capitals, still dominated by Brazilians of European descent. You'll find them in the pages of Brazilian fashion magazines, where hair is straight, noses are thin, and the Gisele Bündchens greatly outnumber their counterparts with more melanin.

Despite her skin tone, Deborah stayed clear of our umbrella. Cariocas don't use *guarda-sóis.* They're for gringos. Same for sunscreens more than SPF 2, long sleeves, swim shirts, robes, or wraps. She stretched her colorful sarong *kanga* in the direct sun and tossed her bag to the side. Like her countrymen, Deborah knew not to carry anything of value. She'd seen too many petty thieves descend from the *favelas* to gather as much loot as they could during mass sprints to snatch purses on the beach.

We idled and talked, and ordered refreshments from the stream of salesmen who hawked their wares in ninety-degree sun. She drank Mate Leão, a drink similar to iced tea, and snacked on doughnut-shaped Biscoito Globo air biscuits, which, according to the periodic table of the elements, most closely resemble, in taste and texture, Styrofoam packaging kernels.

A group of young men hovered nearby, all clad in Charles Atlas–style briefs. They kicked a soccer ball while standing in a circle, sprinted to the ocean for ten-minute body surfing sessions, and readjusted their *cacetes* more often than a Little Leaguer wearing a cup for the first time. Behind me, I heard the conversation heat up.

"Out of curiosity," I asked, "what are these women over here talking about?"

She listened for a minute.

"What every woman here talks about—how bad their boyfriends or husbands treat them."

Brazilian women love to hate Brazilian men. Even if they don't, it's required to say they do. Just a few innocent words like "tell me about the men here" will provoke a tirade. You'll hear it all—cheaters, sloths, or, the ultimate Brazilian insult, Argentines.

"It's good to be back," I said. "I feel so energized when I'm down here."

"This is a tough county, Fararanzo. It's different for the tourist. You don't see the pain."

As she said it I noticed a faint new wrinkle on the corner of her young eye. Crow's-feet and worry lines do big business in the third world.

"If anyone can conquer this place, you can."

"I have a job interview next week. With an American company."

"Great."

"There are five hundred people who've applied."

"You'll get it."

"You know what I'm doing? Brazilian eBay. I'm selling sunglasses on the Internet."

"You making any money?"

"A little. But I'm up all night responding to people. They want to tell you their life story. They're so lonely."

"C'mon," I said. "Cheer up. I'm taking you out tonight."

Brazilian nightlife doesn't begin until after the soap operas conclude around 9:30 P.M. Deborah arrived at the bar in Rio's Leblon neighborhood that evening raving about the latest episode of *The Clone.* She lost me after a few tortured explanations involving plastic surgeries, Morocco, and evil twins.

Though the exposed brick walls and leather couches were straight from a Greenwich Village nightclub, the bar felt far less standoffish, the patrons more open to chance meeting. They talked with strangers. The crowd looked young urban American, only tanner and without the rolls of ATM twenties. Then I noticed another difference.

"I don't remember this from before," I said.

"You're not listening to me."

"Everyone is making out."

She turned her head to one side and back.

"Kissing is big," she said matter-of-factly.

"I see that."

"It reveals a lot."

The lips around us appeared to have a life of their own. They'd meet with a peck, spit out a few words, then fling themselves together like superconductor magnets. Some clung together throughout the night; others tasted the offerings and parted ways. Nobody turned to stare. Except me.

"They're trying to decide if they want to sleep with each other," she explained.

Smack, smack. Gurgle, gurgle. Slosh, sip, slurp.

"What if the woman doesn't like his kissing?" I asked.

"She'll tell him *'Te ligo.'*"

Or, I'll phone you. This means the same as it does in the United States: "You kiss like a gecko. Don't wait by the phone."

"It's better than Match.com," she said.

According to Deborah and her compatriots, you'll learn more about your partner in three minutes than you would on three long dates. Do it in public, in front of the world. Who knows, maybe the crowd will give you some pointers on your technique.

Indeed, the scientists support their conclusion. Kissing partners swap much more than saliva; they trade genetic messages to signal compatibility and even the likelihood of conception. Male smoochers may also transfer trace amounts of testosterone, a natural aphrodisiac, albeit a sloppy one. At the very least, kissers learn about halitosis.

"I want to go somewhere with you," she said. "Outside Rio. It's too depressing here."

"I thought all Brazilians were optimists. What with all the sun and Carnival and such."

"You don't live here."

"Okay. Where do you want to go?"

"A beach town. Isla Grande, Paraty or somewhere. Not too far. We'll take a bus."

"Only if you let me pay for it."

"No. I've been saving. With the sunglasses."

"C'mon."

"We'll split it."

The crowd swelled, and the dance music began upstairs.

"You see these guys in here now?" she said. "You know why they meet their girlfriends at eleven P.M.?"

"Soccer."

"They say this, but half of them don't watch. They just don't want to pay for dinner. They can't afford it. Everybody eats at home with their parents."

"Well, I'm hungry. Let's get something to eat."

"I ate at home. With my parents."

As she said it, I had this overwhelming desire to kiss her. I glanced around the room before tilting my head toward hers and allowing our lips to touch for a beat.

"Don't stop," she said.

"I'm sorry. I feel like I'm at one of those parties my friends threw in junior high after they got their braces off. Bunch of thirteen-year-olds fumbling next to each other on a couch."

"Let's go."

Now, when Brazilians meet the smoocher of their dreams, it's a great feeling . . . then a miserable one. The minute they decide they want to sleep with each other, they'll remember they have no private spot to do so. Again, like at the junior high parties, a bunch of hot and heavy fondlers with no place to go.

What to do. It depends on the size of your wallet. Brazilians who live in the villages and urban *favelas,* two-thirds of the country according to the government accountants, will know each contour of vacant space within walking distance. They'll recite the working schedules of every able-bodied adult in the neighborhood, those with shacks or yards that may be free.

Brazilians of all economic tiers pride themselves on their ability to improvise. *Jeitinho,* the locals say, the craft of jettisoning problems away. This is especially true of poor Brazil. Find yourself at the end of a long line at the post office? No problem. With chitchat or an offered favor you can talk yourself up to the front. Brazilians believe that countrymen who pay traffic tickets aren't the worst drivers, they're just the worst at *jeitinho.*

The skill is honed to its sharpest the moment a Brazilian man meets a woman who likes his kissing prowess. He'll talk to his friend with a car to see if he can borrow the backseat for a couple of hours. He'll call the affable doorman at an apartment complex to ask if he'd accept a few Brazilian reals for use of an empty room. He'll find a way, all the while assuring his partner-to-be that everything's been meticulously planned for their amorous rendezvous.

More affluent Brazilians have other options, and other hurdles. If they're single and under thirty, they'll reside with their parents and a live-in maid who monitors all action in the house and reports back to Mom and Dad. Doormen, too, are notorious for gossiping and exposing the sins of all those who don't tip them regularly. Young apartment dwellers resort to back doors and diversions to keep them at bay. True schemers even coax their friends to pose as paramours just to give the doorman something to report.

T his isn't a good idea," said Deborah, as we entered the lobby of my hotel. "I thought you said you liked my kissing."

"They don't want me here."

"Who?"

"Them. The men at the desk. See, they're talking."

"Who cares? It's my room."

Cubed and thin like a stack of LEGOs, the hotel tried to expand its appearance through mirrored walls in the entryway and foyer. Deborah sat down in a lounge chair by the automatic door while I went over to the three men in short-sleeve business shirts and faded black ties.

"Wisner. Room two forty-two, please."

"Two forty-two," repeated the bald one of the three.

"Deborah. C'mere."

He paused before handing me the key.

"Sir," he said. "I must warn you against . . ."

"She's my girlfriend," I said in a hushed tone so Deborah wouldn't hear.

"Of course. But safety is . . ."

"Please. The key."

As Deborah made her way to the desk, the bellman said something that made her look away.

"If she is going with you, she must fill out these forms," said the manager, pushing two cards toward her.

"That's insane," I said. "She's just going to be here for an hour. Or two. Two."

"I'm sorry."

He chanted a few brusque words at Deborah, prompting her to pull identification from her purse.

"You're treating her like a prostitute," I said. "She has every right to come up with me."

"C'mon, Fararanzo," she whispered. "Let's go."

"No. I paid for this room."

"We have had problems in the past with guests being robbed," said the manager. "It's for your safety."

"That's bullshit. If I rented a room for her, would she get hassled like this?"

"No," said Deborah. "Please."

"I am sorry," said the manager, sounding anything but.

Deborah grabbed my hand to go. She held on as we walked outside.

The ACLU would be all over that one," I said. "I can just see some aggressive trial lawyer getting turned away."

"They would have been much ruder if I was alone."

"Fuckers."

"Thanks for standing up for me."

"I'm surprised they even knew you were Brazilian with that pale, I mean, pearly skin of yours."

"Hey!" she said, slapping my arm.

I slapped her back, on her rump.

"Kiss me," she said. "Nobody is looking."

This time it didn't feel as awkward. So I did it again. *No wonder Brazil kisses in public places; the private ones are all off-limits.* Deborah started to laugh.

"What?" I asked.

"I have an idea," she said.

The taxi driver seemed like he wanted to chat. Deborah answered in staccato bursts, wiping away his smile. He turned up the *forró* music and lowered his head toward the road. Along the Ipanema shore we sped, past the vacant lifeguard stations and ten-foot sand sculptures of mermaids and European castles. Loud crowds and plastic cups piled outside neighborhood *botecos* that morphed from juice bars to beer stands once the sun retired. At the end of the beach, a few industrious souls conducted their nighttime workouts at a makeshift gym of pull-up bars and concrete weights. Our driver turned on Avenue Niemeyer, pointing toward a large complex overlooking the water. Deborah's voice directed him to a smaller building nearby.

"Where are we going?"

"A motel," she said.

"I have a motel."

"No, you don't."

He edged the car into a driveway and barked into the intercom, prompting the gated door to slide open on a chain-driven rail. I paid the man, now grinning anew, and followed Deborah on foot to a darkened, bulletproof ticket window with a wall menu posted beside. The options read like a two-star tour of the cradles of civilization: Garden of Eden. Pharaoh's Kingdom. Graceland. Thirty dollars on up for six hours. A few more reals for a few hours more.

"A *motel*," I said.

"I like the Valentine's Suite."

"You've been here."

"No. My friend Livia told me about it."

"Naughty, naughty, Livia. I'm going to talk to her about this."

"You don't even know Livia. Her English isn't that good anyway."

Despite my doubts about Deborah's preference—*How do you have sex on a heart-shaped bed? Where do you put your legs?*—I said nothing as she asked the faceless voice behind the tinted glass if the Valentine's Suite was available. But this was Saturday. The rooms with cupids and evil serpents were occupied by randy Cariocas, locals. We could enjoy a standard suite or, for eighty dollars, the Presidential.

"Whose president?" I asked.

Deborah grabbed the key and shuffled me across the carport to one of a dozen private garage doors. A German car inched past us and into a separate unit, a repeat patron with a woman half his age. More than machismo or absence of manners, the women of Brazil complain loudest about the philanderers. Ask a Brazilian woman her ideal qualities in a man and hear "faithful" at the top of her answer. *Chifrar,* they label cheating: to gore with horns.

And if they could, they just might. In other male-dominated reaches, women often cede the inequity and grumble among themselves. In Brazil, they itch to fight. They want to drag that no-good boyfriend/husband/lover up onto Dr. Phil's couch and sit back as he castigates the man for his sins.

The men? The men don't see the problem. Victors with the spoils seldom do. Few even mention fidelity. They'll swear their girlfriends are faithful in the same breath they admit they themselves are not.

"Men like to taste the cookies," said João, a man I met in Curitiba. "We need to sample before we select one. That way we won't get divorced."

Brazil loves its cookies. The fidelity exemptions for both sexes come during Carnival, a period when relationship rules and restrictions explode like the fireworks above the parades. Ask Brazilians how many lovers they've known and you'll often hear an answer that begins with "Well, not counting Carnival . . ."

I led Deborah up the stairs to a darkened apartment. At last we'd be alone. It had been a while.

"This is nicer than I thought it would be," I said, flipping on the lights.

"A Jacuzzi. Let's take a Jacuzzi."

"Ewww, tank skank."

"What?"

"Forget it. Okay. After."

"I can't wait to tell Livia."

The unit came with two beds. *Two?* Deborah slipped off her jeans and eased her thin calves into the water. From behind I stared at her legs, pink where they entered the pool, her thighs splayed on the fiberglass edge.

"*Gustosa,*" I whispered. "Let's make love."

With a thud we landed on the industrial-strength mattress, a dentless, humorless creature, battle-tested and ready for more. The box spring had neither box nor spring, and the linen thread count could be totaled on one hand. On the nightstand and headboard, in the bathroom, and by the door I saw condoms, dozens of condoms. *Damn Brazilians. They make the rest of us seem so pedestrian.* Turns out the motels are required to provide an assortment in each room. They call this *Lei da Camisinha,* or Law of the Little Shirt. Brazilian men tend to go shirtless as much in the bedroom as they do on the beach.

None of this seemed to distract Deborah.

"Kiss me. Like you mean it," she said.

"I mean it."

"Shhhh."

Try as I might, I couldn't get the images of past occupants out of my mind. This never bothered me in a standard hotel. I'd just convince myself that anyone who'd checked in prior to me was either a nun or a nerd. Not here. This was the mecca of sexual aerobics, a love motel in the most amorous city in the most sensual country on earth. Samba queens, capoeira masters, beach all-stars, and soccer studs all honed their sweaty techniques within these walls. Oh, the flips and dismounts. The soccer players probably didn't even use their hands. It wasn't that I was grossed out by all that. I was just intimidated as hell.

Focus, focus. I looked up at the plastic-tubing lights edging the corners of the ceiling. This was what I wanted, wasn't it? To get back down to Brazil and spend a few weeks with one of its storied beauties. To learn something about love; to be inspired. White the lights turned, then green to purple to ahhh. Deborah rested her head on my chest and closed her eyes. I'd just made love in the back of a giant limo.

I looked at the clock. A grand total of twenty-four minutes had elapsed. *That's it?* I realized I was stuck for another five hours, thirty-six minutes. There was no way we could leave early. What would the manager think? Even if I couldn't see his face, he knew an American had entered the premises. This wasn't just about me now. I was here on behalf of a nation.

So I did what anyone does who wants to kill time in a stretch Town Car—I started to play with the buttons. The black remote turned on radio static, and the other powered up television porn identical to the American brand except with better music and in darker hues. *Now I see why they need the two beds.* "Hey, Deborah." Slumbering she remained. I reached for the brass switches on the wall, the third initiating a whirring sound, though I couldn't pinpoint where. Only when I lay back did I see the sunroof parting to a black-purple sky of whisked cloud and constellation.

What *in the world are you doing?*
  "Um, look around. Isn't it obvious?"
You know what I mean. And quit playing with those buttons.
"What's the problem? She's the one who suggested this place."
You plan on spending the rest of the year like this?
"No."
Really.
"Just the next six weeks."
Stop it with the buttons! You'll break something.
"Leave me alone. I'm an adult, having fun with an adult."
You're a teenager who's just learned to unhook a bra.
"I've made no promises to this woman. Zero. I've told her I date people in America. I've told her there is no future in this thing."
And you've flown down to Rio to tell her this. Relayed these heartfelt sentiments in a sex motel after your fifteen minutes of fun.
"Twenty-four."
What are you accomplishing on this trip besides a temporary escape from your shortcomings?
"I'll talk to her."
You're supposed to learn something on this gig. So learn something.
"I will."
Just not here.
I forgot about everything and drifted to sleep.

It's funny how a mood can reshape scenery. Brazil didn't feel as hopeful after those six hours. She now looked aimless and at times insecure, appearing so at the last place I'd imagine, astride the nation's catwalk, on the sands of the Ipanema shore. Grandfathers stretched out for their morning runs; mixed-race beauties unfolded their *kangas*. *Futevôlei* ringers, sun-stained acrobats who played volleyball without using their hands, paired up for the first matches of a daylong display. On the tips of the surrounding hills stood the *favelas,* lean-tos and wire jumbles, the city's crown with tines of corrugated steel.

I'd always seen the beach scene as a healthy endeavor, Brazilians energizing their lives and soaking up their country's attributes. Yet now it flashed another side. The beachgoers all seemed on a fruitless quest, searching for a darker tan, a toned muscle, a flirt session and a phone number. The problem with searches is that they usually lead only to additional searches. Brazil and the rest of the world held up Ipanema as the height of desire, but did it ever achieve more?

So I left the beaches and walked inland, to the working-class neighborhoods of Botafogo and Gávea, and to the *favelas* on high. I talked with carpenters and hairdressers about the image of their country as the epicenter of love, yet how difficult it is for the locals to capture and sustain.

Love is not a day at the beach, they said. Love in Brazil is hard, like everything else. Men here cheat because they can, because they saw their fathers stray without consequence. Women harden because they must, ever protective of their children. On top of it all, there are few jobs and fewer decent schools, large disparities between rich and not, black and white, and the constant chorus that someday things will change. We are a nation fueled on potential. The odds are we will not reach it. And in all likelihood love will fail.

But, they said, before you give up hope, forget about the surroundings and the long odds. The possibility for love remains. Love, it can happen. They all brightened at the word, the street sweeper and housewife, juice vendor and student. We burn for love, they said, shape our entire lives around this possibility. Crazy, perhaps. Rash, definitely. What's important, what's essential to the Brazilian approach to love, is that day after day we remain open to it despite the odds. We go to the beach, we iron that dress, we exchange phone numbers and think maybe, just maybe, this may be the time.

Away from the beaches, Brazil showed me her vulnerability and her *saudade.* Then she revealed her ability to stow away those emotions and continue her strut. This made her even more attractive.

Prior to coming, I'd spent hours, days, convincing myself to give Deborah a chance. I now knew this to be an elaborate self-con. I wasn't opening myself to this relationship. I wasn't opening myself to any relationship. I was fleeing from them. What good were Brazil's lessons if I wasn't ready for them? I'd come because the country from afar seemed everything I was not—convinced, confident, open to love. Yet the longer I stayed, the more depressed I became. Each Brazilian strut made me realize that I did not.

I'd deal with Deborah first. We'd seen each other less and less in recent days. A heavy load at school kept her occupied, but she still wanted to go away with me for a weekend. Perhaps a change of scenery would prompt other changes, she seemed to hint. I knew it wouldn't, but at least we could talk.

Deborah fashioned a new plan as we checked into our posada in Paraty, a gentrified port town a few hours south of Rio. She wore a ring on her left hand and tried to convince the manager we were engaged. I slid my arm around her waist to bolster the tale and handed him a credit card. We settled for a smaller room in the back of the compound.

"I hate my country," she said.

"It is weird. We have this vision of Brazil as ultrapermissive."

"It's just about the money. Always. If they can make money, they will act moral. If not, they don't care."

"Do you think it'll ever change?"

"The thing about Brazilian men is that, down deep, they know they should change. They're smart. They know. But they just can't do it. They see their fathers, their friends, and they stay the same."

"Sounds like the States."

"In America, men have more role models. You can be a lot of things. It's fine. Here you have one role model—machismo."

"Are you hungry? May I treat you to a gourmet dinner? I'll make sure we get a man to wait on us."

She smiled.

"I'm going to take a shower," she said.

Overlooked for decades, Paraty had reshaped itself from a gold and diamond port to a quaint escape for foreigners and middle-class families from Rio and São Paulo, restoring the stone streets and whitewashed colonial buildings with their arched doorways of red and blue to convince visitors they tasted the riches of old. The UNESCO World Heritage designation kept cars out of the town center and prevented high-rise buildings like the ones that lined Ipanema.

Deborah lingered in galleries looking at native art she couldn't afford and stopped to sing along with the street musicians. This song is about *saudade,* she'd say. Every song in Brazil is about *saudade.*

As we rested at an outdoor table, I told her that this trip to Brazil would likely be my last for a long time. She didn't seem surprised or even especially hurt, talking instead about her plans for the future. I sensed my words had been factored in far before I conveyed them, the way stock prices don't necessarily fall when a company delivers expected disappointment. I started to explain, searching for gentle answers and finding few. I was honest. Our relationship was through. She ordered another *caipirinha.*

On Saturday we chartered a small boat and took naps on the bow. Deborah complained about her stomach, and I worried I caused the pain. The captain pulled the craft to a small island inlet and dropped anchor so we could swim.

"I'm sorry," I said.

"Don't be."

"I haven't led you on, have I?"

"No. I just don't understand you. How you can be so detached."

"Guarded."

"You're not Brazilian. We would have had a big fight or something."

"You would have won."

"I feel sorry for you, Fararanzo."

"Don't."

"You don't believe in love."

"It's not that."

But was it? Was it her or everyone? I thought the honeymoon with my brother had gone a long way toward healing my heart. In the old port city, Deborah reminded me that some healing comes with scars.

We returned to Rio and spent a week more apart than together. Some nights we'd meet for *churrasco* or music. We'd agree on times, but she came later and later. When she did arrive, we'd smile and ask about each other's day, going through the motions, knowing this was the denouement. The food doesn't taste as good in the denouement.

One night I suggested a restaurant/club in Barra da Tijuca, a middle-class neighborhood south of Rio, a bus ride past the *favelas* that crisscross the city. Deborah said she'd try to make it, which now meant she would not.

The club pulsed for a Wednesday, with the office crowd finishing their meals and younger Brazilians swarming in after dinner. The dance floor filled and swayed, an amoeba threatening to engulf anyone who walked by. A voice from the masses shot straight toward me.

"Hey, I know you," yelled a raven-haired woman in black Lycra workout pants.

Her face dipped with the beat, then turned back to mine.

"On the airplane," she continued. "You were on my flight."

"I remember. Extra pillow."

This, the pillow we had in common, was enough to propel me into the throng, past the dancers who knew what they were doing.

"Franz."

"Vivian."

"You're not Carioca," I yelled.

"What?"

"You're not from Rio."

"Puerto Rican. But I live in Miami."

She may not have been Brazilian, but she more than held her own, bumping and twisting to match the locals while I shuffled around just to face her.

"You're definitely not Carioca," she said.

"True. Californian. With a name from the Hapsburg Empire."

"Who?"

"Forget it."

"Where in California? I fly there."

"L.A."

The song slowed, and I adjusted my leg spasms to match her sway. Dancing. It had been a while. Did people still try to move in sync with partners, or was I showing my age? The crowd seemed split on the question, about half on their own.

"I switched because I . . . you," she said.

"I can't hear you."

"I said I switched assignments on the plane because I wanted to talk to you."

"Well, why didn't you talk to me?"

"You were asleep the whole time."

"Oh. Right. I do that."

As soon as her flirtation registered, I suggested we take a break on the patio outside. There she told me she split her routes between the Brazil flights and domestic ones, and that while the rest of her crew slept in the hotel she and a steward liked to dance all night. *All night? Really?* In the light I guessed her age close to mine. All the dancing must keep her in shape. She had the confidence of an athlete, arching her feet on her toes as we talked. They bounced like they wanted to return to the dance floor.

I stalled her with another round of drinks, but Vivian soon dragged me back to the music. My resistance to dancing didn't stem from worrying about appearances. Even the best dancers could look silly doing it. Brazilians included. And I didn't mind the wailing synthesizer/siren music or the vocabulary-challenged singers who tended to prefer repeated child reprimands for their lyrics. "Listen, listen, listen. Do it, do it, do it. Get up, get up, get up." What I disliked about dancing in any country was the talking.

"I love this place," she yelled.

"Yeah."

"Are you married?"

"Am I very?"

"Married."

"No," I yelled, holding up my ring finger. "Single."

"That doesn't mean anything."

"You're right. The men don't really wear rings here."

"Dating?"

I slowed to a standstill as she said it.

"Listen," I said. "I should probably head back."

"Really?"

"Yeah. I have some stuff I need to do."

"Okay."

"Do you want to meet at the beach or something?" I asked. "Before you fly out."

"Sure, I guess. Call me at the Caesar Park."

"I'll call you."

I leaned in to give her a kiss, which she accepted without much emotion before turning back to the bobbing mob.

In the morning I called Vivian's hotel only to find out she'd gone. Or maybe she'd never come home. I ordered a *cafezinho* at a stand near the Caesar Park and wandered down to the beach. Perhaps she'd stroll by.

With a stretch and a yawn, the beach ecosystem slowly sprang to life. Umbrellas popped open like colorful mushrooms. Schools of surfers waited together offshore. Dozens of dark-skinned salesmen carried their goods in ant colony procession. Walrus-sized Europeans flopped their bodies on the warm sand. I finished my coffee and decided to walk on. Despite the din, the beach felt lonely.

Maybe Brazil wasn't such a great idea. It served to highlight my flaws, not correct them. How many people came to Brazil for love inspiration and walked away feeling worse? I'd probably set some sort of medical record this trip.

For the rest of the day I ambled around the neighborhoods of Rio, watching the entire city rub it in. They kissed each other by the *lagoa* and at the beach cafés, walked arm in arm on the shopping streets of Leblon, stroked and caressed and waited for their apartments to become vacant so they could have great sex all afternoon.

I called Deborah to say good-bye, then flew back to California that night.

A year later, I received an e-mail from Deborah. She was engaged to an American, living in the Midwest. And, I read with a smile, she was working for a big-box retailer.

Acting Lessons

LOS ANGELES

This woman is a-*maz*-ing," effused my friend Martha in her best Hollywood agent impersonation. "You said you'd go to coffee with her, remember? She's perfect."

"They're all perfect."

"She's beautiful."

"They're all beautiful."

"Smart."

"Ditto."

"My friend Libby is living with her right now. She was over for dinner and we both just had this aha moment."

Then I remembered my vow in Rio. I needed to be more Brazilian, minus the banana-hammock Speedo, that is. They walked with nothing save sun and pronounced all right with the world. They said, "Go. Seek love. Make love." Even if that confidence was at times fleeting or forced, they still said yes. They were ready for love at all times. Just look at how they greeted one another. *Tudo bom?* Everything good? *Tudo bem.* Everything.

"Okay, I'll do it. What's her name again?"

"Tracy. Tracy Middendorf. You can see her on TV tonight. She's on a movie of the week. Amber Frey in *The Laci Peterson Story*."

No, no. Not a thespian. Especially not one who plays Amber Frey. Please not another up-and-coming actress with a creative flair. They're weird. *Sorry, Angela.* There's no other word for it. They're different. They do things like "repackage" themselves. They drink teas named after moods, Passion and Serenity and such. They're superstitious and emotional and use words like "inner self" and "diaphragm."

Plus they talk and analyze. They bloviate over teeth and posture. I didn't want to think any more about my posture. I liked my posture just fine, thank you. *Do you like it more than being alone?*

"This is the same woman who rejected the blind date to the couples-only resort?" I asked.

"Wiz, they all rejected you."

"Okay. I'll do it. For you. I'm on the road right now, but give me her e-mail and I'll shoot her a note."

> *Tracy—*
>
> *Your Larchmont Fan Club (a.k.a. Martha and Libby) gave me your e-mail and permission to say, "Happy Tuesday." I'm their vagabond friend, Franz. [You can insert your best Hans and Franz joke here.] Anyway, the ladies sing your praises to the hilt. And I'm sorry I haven't had a chance to meet you. I'm back in town next week and would love to do so.*
>
> *Cheers,*
> *Franz*

To our date, Tracy wore black. I wore indifference. That's why I didn't suggest a change of venue when we entered the creole restaurant in Glendale, empty save an elderly woman at the bar who sipped a Manhattan and clipped coupons from the local newspaper. My time in Brazil convinced me to agree to the date but did little to stoke my enthusiasm. Tonight was a promise fulfilled to Martha, a favor even. That's how I mustered the necessary resolve to go through with the evening. She'd owe me.

I brightened when I saw Tracy. She was gorgeous, emerald-eyed and gorgeous, though the soft curves of her cheeks and chin made her beauty feel comfortable rather than intimidating. She wore her champagne-colored hair up, more schoolteacher than aristocrat. And I gazed and drifted and concluded there was no possible way a woman this attractive could be single. The flaws must be elsewhere. *Deep ones. This is the last time I listen to Martha.*

"Reservation for two," I said to the hostess while she chatted on her cell phone and held up a finger. "Wisner."

As we waited, I offered to remove Tracy's knee-length sweater, a massive garment that succeeded in masking every curve underneath, a fuzzy American burka. I wrestled the fabric from her shoulders and lingered a beat too long glancing at her backside. Tracy turned and caught me with her eyes, forcing mine to shoot to the floor. The date would be over soon. *NBA scores, here I come.*

Once seated, I added to the evening's issues by opting for a curry appetizer with chili grown in jet fuel. She nursed an oversized glass of sauvignon blanc, while I gulped my water, wondering the entire time if my tongue, now five sizes inflated, made my speech incomprehensible to anyone but the most experienced dental hygienist. Every first date begins with limitless possibility. This one proved possibility is fleeting.

"How'd you get your thhh-start?" I asked.

"The soaps," she said with an exhalation. "I got hired out of college for *Days of Our Lives.* It's frustrating, but people still know me as Carrie Brady."

"Have you tried a repackaging?"

"Excuse me?"

"I just know actrethh-ses reinvent themselveths from time to time."

"Here," she said, pushing her water glass toward me. "Though you're just washing the spice around. You should order milk. Or better yet, yogurt."

"I'll be fine. Thankths."

The stage—that was her passion. She'd won two best actress awards for Los Angeles theater, which sounded impressive before I remembered I'd yet to see any plays in Los Angeles. She won for *Summer and Smoke* and as that Marilyn Monroe character in *After the Fall.* I saw blonde but no Marilyn over dinner. Tracy seemed less obvious, which of course made her more interesting.

Sucking on my eighteenth ice cube, I learned she grew up in the languid hills of northern Georgia, amid the marble quarries and Dairy Queens, Augusts around the a/c. The acting school in Miami and a decade of television roles washed Pickens County out of her accent. I saw flashes of Georgia in her actions—the genteel "thank you," the way she allowed me to hold her chair, her propensity to shift the conversation away from her life and back to mine.

No, not Marilyn. Naomi Watts, maybe. I do like her blond widow's peak. And those cheeks.

Finally my mouth settled into a range approaching normalcy.

"So, I hear you have a book coming out," she said. "Something about honeymoons?"

"A book."

"Yes, what exactly is it?"

With that, our "potential" excused itself from the meal, threw a few twenties on the table, and hailed the next cab outside. What's the worst thing you can do on a first date? Talk about your ex. Exactly right. There's no bigger red flag. Someone starts talking about her former boyfriend or husband on that initial encounter, you signal the waiter for the check right then. The evening's over.

I did the gentlemanly thing. I dodged. Tracy asked again. I parried. And right back at me. There were few options—avoid, shift, or play deaf. Cornered, I chose to explain.

She did smile as I detailed my mixed-up tale, tossing in a few questions that now seem obligatory. I wouldn't have known what to make of it in her position. Was it admirable a guy took a two-year honeymoon with his brother, or just pathetic? Irrespective of the light under which you hold the vagabond, to any woman with a dash of good sense, a honeymooning brother would hardly seem the relationship type. A pause followed my explanation.

"But you're done with that," she said.

"Yes. The honeymoon's over."

"So what are you working on now?"

What's the second worst thing you can do on a first date?

"Oh, just another project."

"Did you get dumped again?"

"No. That's funny. Do you want another wine?"

"I'm fine. So, your project?"

"Yes."

"Is it travel?"

"Well, more or less."

"Where are you going this time?"

"Seven countries. Brazil, India, Panama, Czech Republic, New Zealand, Botswana, and I can't remember the last one."

"Sounds like a lot of work."

"Egypt. That's it."

"Is your brother going with you?"

"I'm going to the Czech Republic and Botswana on my own, but the others, yeah. He's got golf obligations."

"What's the focus?"

"Um, love."

"Love around the world."

"Yes."

"Bring condoms."

"No, not me dating around the world. That would be a short book. It's a look at how people in different countries meet, fall in love, have sex. Maybe pick up a tip or two."

"For a year."

"Give or take."

On the plus side, she didn't fold her arms or look at her watch the rest of the evening. If she wanted to flee, she did a great job of masking it. Another reason to avoid the actors. We talked about perfectly ordinary subjects—family, food, the best way across town at rush hour, the fallback topic for Angelinos. We talked; we just didn't engage.

Of course not. You just told this woman you're going to spend the next year roaming the planet, crawling around bedrooms and pickup bars. I'd stick to traffic as well.

Tracy said nice things but at times seemed like she was engaged in two dialogues, only one of which involved me. For a flicker, she even appeared sad, though her smile extinguished the moments.

No, no, no. Don't go there. There are few things as dangerous as a pretty woman with a problem.

The ride home felt as feckless as the date, growing ever quieter with each stoplight. Shy, perhaps. No. I didn't believe so. Maybe she was tired. As I debated the reason for the silence, I felt a sudden urge to kiss her. The fewer the words, the stronger the desire. *I should pull this car over right now and plant a giant smack on those lips. That's what the Brazilians would do. I'd learn more about her in a few seconds than I have on the whole date. Think of all the time and money we'd save.*

I pulled the car to the front of her house but kept the motor running. She opened her door and started to walk off. I quickly followed, having killed the ignition.

"You don't have to walk me up," she said. "My dog will start barking."

"I don't mind. Kind of a dog guy."

"No, don't. It's okay."

"Thanks again for taking the time," I said. "Sorry about drinking all your water."

"No, thank you."

"Maybe we . . ."

And as I stalled on the words, she leaned toward me in what I swear was a can't-miss sign to kiss her. There. Brazil. Go. Yet miss I did as she instead reached for her keys. This put in me kissing purgatory, intentions exposed, lips out, looking for somewhere to land. Tracy, sensing my fall, jutted out her cheek and my mouth came to a crash landing on her ear. Purgatory to hell. Undaunted, I completed the act of affection with a multi-decibel smack, which, judging from the way she grabbed her left lobe, probably didn't achieve the desired result. She mercifully put the whole affair to bed with a hug and a pat on the back. Brazilian I was not.

Just as well, I thought as I drove home. I'd completed my obligation. Plus my breath still reeked of chili. I'd e-mail Martha in the morning and say her friend was sweet and brilliant and everything else she'd promised. Then I'd never see Tracy again. I'd continue on with my travels. *And avoidance.*

Instead, I e-mailed Tracy. I had a box at Santa Anita Racetrack the coming weekend. I invited her to cheer the ponies and prevent me from throwing all my money away on trifectas predicted through numerology, names, and which horses emptied their bowels closest to the starting gate. Her e-mail response included something about "juggling commitments."

The World's Worst Pickup Lines

1. *"Don't I know you from a past life?"* INDIA

2. *"What's a nice place like this doing around a woman like you?"* CZECH REPUBLIC

3. *"I would love to be a farmer and you to be my soil. Our crop would be bananas."* NICARAGUA

4. *"At what time does a* hurain *like you need to be back in heaven?"* EGYPT

5. *"You are smelling very nice to me."* BOTSWANA

6. *"Let's have* cafezinho. *I can call you or nudge you."* BRAZIL

7. *"My parents have already engaged us to be married. They just forgot to tell you."* INDIA

8. *"How would you like your breakfast eggs—scrambled or fertilized?"* NEW ZEALAND

9. *"This woman is Shi'ite. She a'right!"* EGYPT

10. *"Does your backside want my phone number?"* BRAZIL

11. *"Why don't we get you out of your wet clothes,"* said by a quick-tongued Brno resident after licking a woman's sleeve. CZECH REPUBLIC

12. *"So, you like music?"* LOS ANGELES

Actually this last one was used on me. By a man.

I hovered by a jukebox with my friend Anthony while we waited for a table at a neighborhood restaurant in Los Angeles. He suggested Otis Redding. I pushed for Beck, though neither of us settled the argument by fishing a few dollars from our wallet.

A man with a scraggly beard and a dude ranch shirt stepped between us. White trash or trendy? In Los Angeles, I could never tell the difference. He acted as if Anthony weren't there.

"So, you like music?" he asked with a grin.

I laughed.

"Did I say something funny?"

"No, I like the approach. Go for the lowest common denominator and build from there."

"Great."

"No, not like that. I mean, 'Wow, we have so much in common. We both like music.' I love the concept. I might use it."

"So do you want to have sex?"

"No. No, thanks. I'm with Anthony."

Commitment

INDIA

To be honest, I went to India to learn about love, but I also had a few questions about sex. This was the land of the Kama Sutra, after all, the planet's most sacred how-to sex manual. I purchased an edition with pictures and carried it on the plane to Delhi. As soon as the middle-aged Korean woman sitting next to me fell asleep against the window, I eased it from my backpack.

There had to be a tip or two in there, something that could help me navigate those awkward moments, like the one I'd had with Tracy. Maybe there was a secret area of her body, an elbow or earlobe, for example, a spot I could have stroked with my finger to make her instantly agreeable to every advance. In the darkened cabin, I turned on my overhead light and opened the book.

Okay, I was a bit leery once I discovered Vatsyayana, the author of the two-thousand-year-old-text, died a virgin. This couldn't be possible. I imagined a hermetic contortionist doing awful things to a straw pillow each night. But as I continued reading, I found the initial chapters, the ones that dealt with lifestyle, residence, and manners, to be pertinent and utterly doable. So to speak.

For instance, the masterpiece began by advising readers to "solve riddles, enigmas, oral puzzles with hidden meaning." Check. I tackled a crossword puzzle every morning. It also counseled "water sports, striking water to make rhythmic sounds, and diving in various poses; gambling and playing dice." Sounded like a Vegas weekend to me. So far, so good.

My bedroom should contain a "soft mattress, low in the middle, and covered with a clean white sheet." Jars for "perfumed ointments, sweet smelling flowers and garland, pots for collyrium and other fragrant substances" should ring the room. Note to self: Add collyrium Glade to shopping list. I should also have "ample pillows," "birds in cages," "a few books," and a "lute hanging from a peg made from the tusk of an elephant." This could all be found on eBay, no doubt.

A teenage boy on his way to the bathroom peeked over my shoulder, lingering to see the drawing of a turbaned and stoic maharaja pleasure a bevy of naked Indian beauties. I shifted in my seat, turning my back to the aisle to shield the X-rated drawings, and continued with my research. Avoid "lunatics; outcasts; those with a loose and viperish tongue," the Kama Sutra counseled. Also steer clear of women "who cannot keep a secret; who have an inordinate sexual urge difficult to satisfy; who are unsightly and unclean, and those who have lost the glow of youth." I guess that meant Pamela Anderson was out.

The juicy stuff came next, chapters on kissing, embracing, biting, scratching, and "congress." Congress. Such a better use of the word. Plant your lips on the "forehead, eyes, cheeks, throat, bosom, lips, and the interior mouth." This could be done in many forms, including a Straight Kiss, Throbbing Kiss, Turned Kiss, Pressed Kiss, Kiss That Kindles Love, or Fighting of the Tongue. Got it. Can do, though the Fighting of the Tongue thing brought back memories of an overly aggressive junior high prom date with sharp braces.

When my encounters became heated, it would be time for "pressing the other's body with nails or scratching with them." The Kama Sutra took a good ole white trash approach to bites and love marks. The more the merrier. Who says hickeys are lowbrow? "The love of a woman who sees the marks of nails on the private parts of her body, even though they are old and almost worn out, becomes again fresh and new."

There are sixty-four dexterous sex positions outlined in the Kama Sutra, many difficult for even a rag doll with a lifetime of yoga lessons to re-create. That poor pillow of Vatsyayana's. I thought about it for the rest of the flight as he described the Blow of a Boar, Crab's Position, or Congress of a Herd of Cows, ancient India's version of an after-hours party at the Playboy Mansion. Animal names are big in the Kama Sutra. I like animals. I don't like *that* many animals. I prefer, say, three animals.

A flight attendant surprised me with the drink cart. I waved her by and went back to the book. Chapters on courting, marriage, "behavior of a king," and assembling a household of courtesans followed. Then came a section for adherents of Warren Jeffs or Billy Bob Thornton called "Senior and Junior Wives." Seemed a bit cost-prohibitive to me.

It wasn't until the end pages that the Kama Sutra lost me, in a final chapter called "Regarding Virility." To increase my stamina, I was advised to "drink milk, in which the testicles of a ram or a goat have been boiled and mixed with sugar." Or, "to enlarge the *lingam* and make it strong, a variety of insects with irritating hair on their bodies, like the *kandalika,* a type of caterpillar, are removed from trees on which they thrive, and vigorously rubbed on the skin and prepuce of the phallus, which results in painful swelling."

Umm, no.

After landing in India, I tucked my Kama Sutra back in my backpack and began to ask people about Pair of Tongs and Sporting of the Sparrow. I tried to do this in a tactful way, always away from others. Yes, I knew these weren't the questions they normally received from American tourists, but I was dying to know. Surely they had a few thoughts on the masterpiece or, better yet, a field pointer or two. Maybe they put a modern-day twist on the trysts—energy drinks with ancient aphrodisiacs (except the testicles, preferably) or Kama Sutra workouts at the local gym. I readied my pen . . .

Then never used it. In India today, the Kama Sutra is kaput. Dead. It's a punch line rather than a reference guide. It's a gag gift at weddings, something your jokester uncle would present with a wink. Copies sit unopened on bookshelves, usually hidden from public view.

"We don't read the Kama Sutra," said Rajiv, a student from Hardwar. "But we have seen the movie."

I asked hundreds of Indians in all corners of the country. Not one of them could offer any insight. The horror. This was devastating to me, puncturing every preconception of Indians as masters in the bedroom. It was like going to Memphis for the first time and discovering nobody listened to Elvis.

"Kama Sutra is just a book," explained Happy, a businessman from Rishikesh. "It is not important for life. Sex is a part of life, not an end for life."

"Don't you think it could give me, I mean, you some good tips?" I asked.

"You are sitting in the dark, and you eat something. You know it's food. You don't need to practice chewing."

"So, what did you do on your wedding night?"

"I watched a lot of pornography before. All Indian men do."

Enter Suresh, all one hundred and twenty pounds of him, handlebar mustache included. Suresh restored my faith in Indian sexuality. He knew the Kama Sutra.

Fittingly, we met him in Khajuraho, home of the raciest Hindu and Jain temples in India, thousand-year-old structures sure to make every tourist redden and exclaim, "Oh, my." The Kama Sutra temples. They're like giant Mormon Tabernacles of stone, covered with thousands of X-rated carvings featuring party-going gods and commoners doing things Larry Flynt didn't know were possible. Think Cirque du Soleil meets Caligula. Khajuraho—the party epicenter, drawing Hindus to pray. Enter. *Namaste*. And remember, tantric sex will bring you to closer to Nirvana. Just make sure to stretch out first.

We met Suresh at the only remaining Khajuraho temple not taken over by the tourists. He invited us to a Hindu ceremony at sunset in which he banged a metal skillet drum with a ball peen hammer for fifteen minutes. This gave his words, and everything else for the next few days, an added ring.

Walking outside, Suresh explained that Khajuraho raged until a couple of guests turned on the lights and buzz-killed the entire affair: the pious Mughals and pompous Brits. Like bringing an imam and a member of Parliament to a toga party. The Mughals, who were busy attacking Hindu carvings and statues across the country, spared only twenty-two of eighty temples at Khajuraho, while striking graphic aerobic sex from the favored practice list. The Brits of the Raj, unable to cover the remaining temples in a giant bathrobe and slippers, just built a proper English garden around them. This had the same effect.

"But the temples are very good for learning," he said as we made our way to a dirt courtyard. "Many scenes to loving here."

"So this is where you learned how to have sex, by looking at the carvings?" I asked.

"Yes. Khajuraho, Kama Sutra. Also the Internet."

"I can't believe it. I finally found a man in India who knows the Kama Sutra. Can you give us any pointers?"

"Men talking about sex number one. More than cricket!"

"Got it. Anything more tactical?"

"Some wives liking sex with oil."

"The Kama Sutra touched on that."

"Yes. Lots of oil."

"Anything else?"

"Come to my house," he said, grabbing my wrist. "I will show you. You will meet my wife."

Kurt turned his head to cover his laugh.

"That's very kind of you. I think we'll walk around for a bit. Check out the temples some more."

"No. Sir. Please. My wife, she would very much like to meet you."

His grip tightened. I thought about the contortionists in the book.

"I think there's a light show here at night, no? Better stick around."

"My house is not far. Five minutes."

"Kurt. Kurt?"

"We are walking."

The next thing I knew, we were sitting on the sagging bed of a one-bedroom apartment behind a small sundries shop. They'd punched nails in the plaster walls to hang clothes and five calendars, three chronological, one astrological, the other I had no idea. A brass Buddha gazed down at us from the shelf. Cooking pots were stacked in the corners. From an alcove, Suresh grabbed a large photo album and slapped it onto my lap. Someone stirred in the adjoining kitchen. I did not.

"My wife, she will be out in one minute."

"It's fine, really."

"Go, go. Open."

Slowly, I pulled back the front cover to reveal hundreds of photos of Suresh and his wife, all taken in the same room, at the same angle, in the same pose. Dressed in wedding white, he smiled like a candidate during a debate, enough to show confidence and amusement, never baring any teeth. She looked identical in each snapshot as well—mortified.

"Arranged marriage?" I asked.

"Yes. Her cousin suggesting this to our parents."

"What was going through your head?"

"I think she is good nature and her family is very good. We are the same caste."

"A good match."

"Also she is beautiful," he said, as if her looks were an ancillary benefit, the potato slicer to go with the Ginsu set.

"She is very beautiful. Very beautiful."

"Yes."

"Don't take this the wrong way, but she looks a bit solemn in the photos. Is she okay?"

"Her father, he died this time. Five days before the wedding."

"I'm sorry."

"She is very sad this day."

"Did you think about postponing the wedding?"

"No. Never. The astrologers say this is the auspicious day. We cannot change."

Suresh called out again, and from the kitchen his wife emerged, glancing quickly at us before shooting her eyes to the floor.

"In wedding she is skinny," he said. "Now she is fat!"

"No, no, no," I said.

His bride, at least fifty pounds heavier than she appeared in the photos, nodded her head in approval.

"She is pregnant!" he said.

"Of course. I mean, congratulations."

"Water?" she said.

"Thank you, yes," said Kurt.

She returned to the kitchen and came back out with a small glass of water, which she gave to her husband. Suresh tilted his head back and poured half in his mouth without letting the glass touch his lips per Indian custom. Kurt followed, pouring half of his half on his shirt. He'd need to work on this before sharing hot tea.

"You don't have a copy of the Kama Sutra," I said.

"No. But I know this. The animals' positions and kissing. Take your time. This is the most important. And don't forget the oil."

"As you mentioned."

"Very important."

"I see."

"Prepare. Make this an event."

"No hidden places or secret spots?"

"We get pregnant right here," he said, slapping the bed.

"No, I mean places on the body."

"I like sex every day, but my wife is no."

His wife reentered the room just then, and again she nodded her head in agreement.

I admired Suresh, and his wife, and the Indian honesty. They answered the questions. Even so, there is a natural aversion to some matters, claimed V. S. Naipaul in his book *India: A Wounded Civilization.*

"It is less easy for Indians to withdraw and analyze," he wrote. "The difference between the Indian and the Western ways of perceiving comes out most clearly in the sex act. Western man can describe the sex act; even at the moment of orgasm he can observe himself. Kakar [Dr. Sudhir Kakar, a psychotherapist] says that his Indian patients, men and women, do not have this gift, cannot describe the sex act, are capable only of saying, 'it happened.' "

Even with the Internet and MTV, Naipaul remains on target. The definition of "painful" is to talk to an Indian man about sex, the meaning of "impossible" to do so with a woman. Ask a sex-related question and they'll squirm. They'll joke. They'll blush. They'll flag down the nearest rickshaw.

Rare are the parents who talk openly and regularly to their children about sex. Equally sparse are the sex education seminars in public schools. The federal government reentered the debate during our time in India, urging individual states to incorporate sex and AIDS education in their curricula. They distributed pamphlets to teachers. They sent PG-rated visuals. And the states thumbed their noses. Too risqué, they said; the government drawings will encourage our youngsters to run outside and have sex with the first person they see. They did what we do in America—blamed Bollywood (Hollywood) for it all.

Enough, I said. I gave up. Indians are incapable of giving counsel on how to have sex. But they sure can tell you where. Ask any man how he manages to make love to a wife or girlfriend amid the congested homes and nosy neighbors and he'll give you a detailed geography lesson on the area's most secluded natural environs.

"Take the third dirt trail up the hill, around the rock quarry, past the cows.

Park your scooter and hike three kilometers down to a hidden cave. Just don't go on Thursday afternoon when Sanjay is there."

Indians, we discovered, are also experts on when to have sex.

"Midnight until two o'clock," stated Yogi, a hotel operator.

"Midnight," said Kapil, a medical student.

"Midnight," echoed Suresh.

"Midnight." His wife nodded.

"Is this because of some astrological harmonic convergence?" I asked.

It is when the others are asleep, they all said.

It's hard to utter the word "India" these days without tacking on the affiliate "change." India today dances with more dynamic upheaval and alteration than any other nation on the planet. Ancient rituals and age-old social norms are pureed daily with global economies and Western tastes.

India today is the televised yoga master leading breathing exercises while stock prices stream underneath. It's the mix of *sherwani* jackets and *salwar kameez* outfits with Radiohead T-shirts and iPod holders. It's the highways, shared by Mercedes-Benz sedans, oxcarts, puttering rickshaws, and Technicolor trucks with the words HORN PLEASE emblazoned on their back ends (as if any driver here needs encouragement). Ice cream vendors sell Bart Simpson pops and chilled coconuts. Goat herders bring their animals to graze on the grounds of five-star hotels. The ripples overflow to all reaches, including relationships.

Yet throughout the subcontinent, all matters of love and marriage still begin and end with the parents. They are the double helix of society, the core of life measured and sustained. The relationship between man and woman begins first with the one between boy and mom, girl and dad. Most Indians live at home until they are married, and many continue to do so after they wed. Under this living arrangement, parents permeate and influence all aspects of personal life.

In other words, it's a suspended-adolescence nightmare. Think about all the awkward conversations you had with your parents, the off-the-wall prom date suggestions or how you should apply deodorant properly "now that you have hair under there." Amplify those cringes and extend them throughout your entire adult life. That's hell. That's India. Here's the difference.

"My parents know better about life," said Sugandha, a student from Jaipur.

Come again? Kids who believe their parents have a valid point of view? Yes, say most young Indians. Without a smirk or a chuckle, I might add. For all the proximity and bickering, there is an all-encompassing emotional attachment between parent and child.

Children, a categorization in India that lasts for a lifetime, don't just try to please their parents, they strive to become their parents, to maintain the honor and reputation of the family name. Ask any Indian man his ideal qualities for a bride and he'll include phrases like "someone who respects and takes good care of my parents" somewhere in his answer.

Traditionally, parents made the arrangements for every stage of the relationship—meetings, courtship, proposal, wedding, married life. Often they condensed the process to one day, with couples meeting for the very first time at their wedding. Don't chuckle. Most of the time, the marriage worked. Or at least lasted. India's divorce rate has risen of late but remains less than a third of ours.

Most marriages in India are still arranged, though couples are given more and more say in the matter, expanded opportunities to veto or suggest, and additional time to court or explore the relationship before it is joined. Greater numbers of Indians are opting for Western-style unions, or "love marriages." It's a curious term in that most Indians will tell you love is not an explosion at first sight but something that can only come with cultivation.

Oh, times are changing. Bollywood movies, which a few years ago would never have shown a couple touching lips for fear of censorship and protest, now feature actors au naturel. There are pickup bars in Delhi and Mumbai. There are Web sites for one-night stands (list caste and religion, please).

More shocking than all of this is the fact that staid and conservative parents are adapting and, in places, even adopting it all. Not so much the one-night stand part, but the increased involvement of single sons and daughters in the matter. Yes, they applaud the simplicity and success of the old-fashioned arranged marriage. Sure, they blame Western-style dating and "love marriages" for the recent rise in divorce rates. And of course they bristle when their child swoons over a "bad boy" or a "fast girl." For the most part they go along—until their son or daughter praises a non-Hindu, that is. Those are the all-night conversations.

Kids who gravitate toward Americanized rules of dating know the dance is a delicate one. They burn inside for a greater say in the process, but nine times out of ten they'll suggest someone likely to meet Mom's and Dad's approval—same caste, same religion, good job, good family, and, most important, an auspicious astrological chart. When young Indians do manage to wrest greater leeway from their parents, they rarely challenge social confines set generations prior.

Across the poorer reaches of India, couples meet each other through family ties or community bonds. More affluent Indians frequently encounter their mates for the first time in high school or at college. In the larger cities, "love" couples meet at work, though this is a finesse game with perilous consequences. Rarely would a woman approach a male colleague with anything more than a business memo. To flirt and be rebuffed would jeopardize both job and reputation. In Indian offices, the man would have to make the first move. Even then, the approachee would take steps to minimize the risk.

"If a guy from the office asked you out, you would only go somewhere during the day," said Huma, a Delhi office worker. "Women are not free to go where they want, especially at night, when you need to tell your parents."

Pickup lines don't work in India. Come to think of it, pickup lines don't work anywhere. If a person warms to your lines, you'd have to question her judgment. So even when they succeed, they fail.

"What's your sign?" doesn't cut it here, though the nation is consumed with astrological approval for all major (and minor and minuscule) events in life. Deep in the Indian psyche runs a cultural aversion to pickups in general, along with a deathly fear of rejection. There is also a strong Indian comfort with the literal.

"If a man said to me, 'Don't I know you from somewhere?' I would ask myself if he did," said Aparna, a woman from Delhi.

In the land of caste and category, preparation and everything planned, even a more subtle approach usually fails.

"If someone smiled at me or my friends, we would immediately question why he is smiling," said Aparna's colleague Mona.

* * *

Kurt and I were interested in how Indians meet each other, but on our tenth day in country we were trying our hardest to avoid them. We'd made our way to the sacred city of Hardwar, a community of *sadhu* holy men and soul seekers on the banks of the Ganges in northern India. The Beatles journeyed near here four decades ago. Then they recorded *The White Album* and convinced the planet that the drugs in India must be pretty wild. The drawstring pants crowd has been coming ever since.

The Hardwar locals were fine with the influx. They sold energy bars and *lassi* yogurt shakes to the visitors. They bowed hello and swept their doorsteps each morning and on nearly every day of the year remained peaceful. We chose to visit the town on the one day they did not: Holi.

Like everything in India, Holi has a lengthy and conflicting origin. Some say it involves Lord Shiva incinerating the god of carnal love, Kamadeva. Others swear it stems from the relationship between Lord Krishna and the beautiful Radha.

How do Indians choose to celebrate Holi these days? With toxic dye and cannabis leaves. On a full-moon day each winter, Indians grab bags full of dried paint—magentas and tangerines and nuclear reactor greens—and bombard anyone who comes near, turning the entire nation into a Day-Glo Jackson Pollock painting. To ensure the body art is really abstract, Indians loft paint while chewing a cannabis leaf derivative called bhang. This gives their eyes a glow equal to their clothes. They do this all day and night.

Now, normally Kurt and I are all for the local celebrations in any country. We try to dive in and revel. Something important prevented us from doing so this time.

"It's my T-shirt," said Kurt as we looked at the city below us from the lofty Mansa Devi temple, debating how we'd get from the mountaintop to our hotel on the other side of town. "I don't want to ruin it."

He had a point. This wasn't any T-shirt. This was a replica of the jersey worn by Sachin Tendulkar, the captain of the Indian national cricket team, the Master Blaster, the man who would lead the native squad to sure greatness in the World Cup competition that would begin the following week. On a greatest hits list of the country's beloved icons, Tendulkar would rank somewhere between Ganesh and Gandhi. Kurt's T-shirt had proved an invaluable icebreaker in initiating conversations. Ahhh, you know Tendulkar. To mar such a vestment with Rorschach splotches of fuchsia and aquamarine would seem sacrilegious.

"So take it off," I said.

"Only the *sadhus* go without shirts," he said. "I feel like I'd be violating some kind of holy code. Plus I think we can do it."

"Look at the rooftops. You see all those kids with the Super Soakers and paint balloons. We'll get pounded."

"C'mon. We'll zigzag our way up the street and duck into any store that's open for protection."

With that we began a charge down the mountain and a sprint up the narrow streets, Butch Cassidy and Sundance on that final counterattack. The result was the same. *Pooof!* Kurt took a direct strike of royal blue on the back of his head. *Thwap!* A pint-sized sharpshooter drenched me with a water balloon. *Zimmm! Zshhhttt! Zappp!* The barrage came from all sides.

"What happened to the whole nonviolence thing?" Kurt panted.

"It's turned to cyan."

We redoubled our pace, zigged more and zagged less, and continued on.

How'd I do?" asked Kurt when we reached the hotel lobby.

I told him to turn around.

"Like somebody vomited Otter Pops on your back."

"Shit. I'm going to go see if I can get this stuff out."

The hotel staff nodded and grinned at our rookie status as we strode past in bright lavender and cranberry. An Indian family milled near the front desk.

"So how do you like our Holi?" asked the bespectacled father.

"Great," I said.

"And you know Tendulkar."

"Please don't tell him about Kurt's jersey."

The clan chuckled as Kurt bounded up the lobby stairs.

"So what brings you to India?" he asked, voicing the common Indian impulse for explanation and order.

"Love," I said.

"We, too, are here for love. My son is getting married."

"Congrats. Where's the lucky bride?"

"We don't know yet. We've just arrived from California to find her."

"Good-looking guy like this, you should have no problem."

"You should try it. Arranged marriage is very good."

"No, no," I said. "No offense."

"Why?" he asked. "It works."

I paused.

"Heather Elms."

My mother, on a weekly basis from preschool until I left the house for college, tried to pair me with Heather Elms. She and Heather's mom played tennis together. Heather served in student government. She played the cello. She took AP classes while I toiled in prerequisites. She had long brown hair and reminded me of Ali McGraw. She was perfect. And because my mother suggested her, she was doomed.

Of course, Heather Elms and all the other suggestions from my parents are now CEOs and tenured professors, über-moms who run ten miles with their kids in high-tech jogging strollers, stunning and sweet women who never complain when their partner forgets to pick up the dry cleaning. What angered me more than my mom's meddling was the fact she was right.

I thought about all the moms and all the Heather Elmses out there, about 50 percent divorce rates in America and all the mismatches that could have been prevented with a few words of wisdom. Is it insane to involve parents, the sane ones at least, in the matchmaking business?

Fewer than one in ten Indian marriages end in divorce. If Americans made a computer that broke down half the time, while Indians produced a model far more reliable, we'd sprint to Asia to copy their design or at least adapt it to fit our ways. Why do we not do the same for the most important product of all?

Learned love is one main reason. In American relationships, we focus on what works from the start rather than what we can create in the long run. We make decisions of the heart on such fleeting criteria as tan lines or time-shares. We act on crushes, tastes that change with the season, gut feelings. Too often we see wedding days as a culmination rather than a beginning. Half the time we fail.

I once ended a relationship over salt. The execution took place at a breakfast diner on a Saturday morning. My new girlfriend had spent the night at

my house, our third evening together. She ordered fruit; I wen|
rancheros as the best option to cure a mild hangover. As the wai|
the plate on the table, I grabbed the saltshaker and loaded my ⌐ ₋ₐₛy meal
with an extra dose of sodium to sop up the cobwebs in my brain.

"Franz!" she said, grabbing my wrist. "Enough with the salt!"

Despite my haze, I saw the future right there—relentless nag sessions over toilet time and Sunday afternoon football, gripes about underwear choices and e-mails. And salt. I've never loved salt more than I did at that moment.

"I think we should see other people," I said.

Her fingers released their clutch.

Okay," I told India. "I see the benefits of an arranged relationship. I can see how my parents' judgment might have been a bit more farsighted than mine. They probably would have avoided the salt Nazi. But even if I capitulated to an arranged marriage, to do so in my country would be impossible. American-style love is too ingrained. We're power shoppers. We demand specific cell phone ringtones and particular mineral waters. How can we then defer on the most essential decision? I just don't think we could ever get our heads around the concept of learning to love a stranger."

But you already do, the Indians replied. You didn't choose your siblings, and yet you learned to love them. Your parents shoved you in a room and said, "Get along." And you did. You found the good in each other. You discovered that the more respect, caring, and altruism you added to the relationship, the stronger it grew. When you didn't, the bond suffered. Is it crazy to think the same concepts can be applied to romantic love?

Ah, very auspicious day," announced Ali as we met in the hotel driveway. He'd been up since dawn, polishing his prized Hindustan Ambassador taxi, a rattling pug of a car first made in 1957 and not dramatically altered since. Taxi drivers like Ali referred to their rides as they would a spouse, coaxing, arguing, praising when need be, threatening violence if she got out of line. "My Amby and I have been together for twenty-two years!" He'd already popped the first of many *paan* chewing tobacco packets into his mouth, reddening his lips and moistening his rolled mustache.

Ali preferred to start and end his rides as early in the day as possible, regardless of the distance. This didn't jibe with our preference to have a few cups of coffee, read the morning paper, and take a look around. We'd hired Ali to drive us to several cities in northern India: Rishikesh, Hardwar, Mussoorie, and today back to Delhi.

"Let's leave at noon, Ali," Kurt would suggest.

"Oh no, no, no, no," he'd counter. "Too much this driving. Six."

"In the morning?"

"India best at first light."

This would begin an intricate bargaining session over the hour of departure, where we'd stop for lunch, how many smoking breaks he would take, and anything else Kurt could think to throw in. The end result this morning being we were up at dawn.

"Big, happy day," said Ali.

"To you, too, my friend," I said. "Freezing, though."

"Mussoorie is hill station. Hill station very cold," he said, referring to the dozens of old colonial retreats for the British army leaders of the Raj.

"I see that. The whole hill thing threw me. Kind of an understatement, don't you think? Now if they called it a snow-capped mountain station, I suppose I would have brought a jacket."

Ali tore open a second *paan* packet with his teeth, and off we crisscrossed down the "hill," the temperature rising like a taxi meter. By the time we reached the first village in the valley below, I realized what Ali meant about "auspicious." This was a wedding day, a moment prescribed by the nation's astrologers as an ideal time to get hitched. Wedding celebrations and lead-in festivities would overtake the country that Thursday. Delhi alone would host more than fifteen thousand.

Rare is the married couple in India whose union has not been blessed by a star watcher. Even if all other prerequisites for the marriage align—same caste, similar incomes, same religion, friendly in-laws, favorite Bollywood actors—wedding plans are canceled immediately if the astrologers raise objections. Without question. There are a billion other options, Indians shrug. Why not find one celestially attuned.

Narrain, a man married for four decades, canceled four engagements for his son after the astrologers advised him to do so. He didn't think twice about it. His wife and son readily agreed.

"Nobody minds it," he said forcefully when I expressed surprise that people acquiesced so readily to the stars. "We have taken all the precautions. I have done my duty."

"After three cancellations, didn't you think about changing astrologers?" I asked.

"No. There are plenty of boys and girls out there. Why take a chance?"

Indians cite history, science, religion, medicine, and Mom when justifying the practice. Their answers are long and complicated, vary from family to family, and often involve sketches of constellations. They talk about "chromosomes" and "natural order" and "universal symmetry."

Not everyone in India believes in astrology. Younger generations talk about heeding the stars to please their parents. Muslims claim it isn't as big a deal in their communities. Indians with degrees from Western universities dispute its scientific basis. They'll laugh and tell you their country is obsessed with the stars, then finish the thought by admitting they, too, consult the family astrologer from time to time. Not everybody in India believes in astrology, but few are adamant enough to challenge it.

For the rest of the day, and in every town on our route, we witnessed jaunty crowds gathered in vacant lots and in front of hotels, brass bands blaring, men dancing and waving rupees, women in their most colorful saris, looking embarrassed about the men. This was the pregame tailgating; the main ceremonies would come that evening.

"Ali," said Kurt. "Pull over here. This looks like a good one. I'd like to get some shots of this wedding."

Ali, on a mission to get us to Delhi in record time, pretended not to hear.

"Ali. Smoke break."

"Okay," he said, pulling the car to the side of the road.

Kurt hopped out and aimed his camera at the clustered parade revelers, a mass of men circling one another with their hands in the air, dancing to a high-pitched Hindu love song on concert speakers that rattled in the back of a flatbed truck. Not wanting to miss anything, I shuffled out as well and looked on from behind the Amby. That's when the shouts began. "Hey!" "You, sir!" At first I thought they wanted us to keep moving, but soon understood they wished us to join in. Kurt begged off by holding up his video camera, leaving his older brother to embarrass the family name on yet another dance floor, this one outside, for a never-ending stream of motorists to witness, honking their horns in approval.

After swearing at Kurt, I sauntered across the road and joined two hundred sweaty men as they bobbed and shimmied around a nervous young groom atop a rented steed, holding the reins with both hands as if the ride were his first. The whole event had a Sigfried and Roy feel with all the sequined jackets and grand-marshal sashes of the trumpeters, a jeweled headdress on the groom, dancing young men, and a blasé-looking beast. A lead partier grabbed me by the wrist and held it in the air like a referee awarding a bout to a prizefighter.

"Welcome," he said. "Please."

A teenager thrust his arm toward me, mouthing the music as if I were his bride.

"I'm sorry," I said. "I don't know the lyrics."

I shuffled and smiled, and after a few minutes started to enjoy myself, especially when I realized their dancing was as aesthetically challenged as mine. The men hugged and bowed, and the groom nodded in appreciation, still looking uncomfortable on his horse. Go get my brother, I motioned to a particularly energetic rollicker.

We repeated this scene a handful of times during the ride to Delhi. Kurt filmed, I watched and sometimes danced, Ali chewed *paan* and smoked. The celebrations coated the country. Come, they yelled. Join. Celebrate. At the end of the journey, I concluded the movie *Wedding Crashers* must not have done very well here. In India, there is no such thing.

The largest ceremony of the day, more than a thousand people strong, took place at our Delhi hotel, a preferred venue for modern-day Indian couples. Ali pulled our car into the driveway and we instantly found ourselves in the middle of the *baraat,* the massive procession of guests making their way to the main ballroom. This parade of people snaked its way through the parking lot and into the streets, shuffling to the beat of a dozen drummers leading the way, making it impossible for Ali to speed off. Kurt and I gave our bags to a bellman and entered the fray.

By this time, I was fully wrapped up in the Indian wedding. They draw you in like no other. The warm-up celebrations throughout the day only served to heighten the mood. We'd savored them all day and now found ourselves at the main feast.

Without warning the crowd parted and a young groom (which, in India, is almost redundant) sauntered in on a muscular white horse with a braided mane. The steed, led by two handlers in dark business suits, was a head taller than any we'd seen earlier in the day. The groom sported a glittering white turban laden with costume jewelry and a full-length white coat with cream piping and embroidery from the collar to the knee. On his lap sat a grade-school boy, most likely a young brother or cousin. Boys are supposed to bring good luck, a sign the marriage would soon produce more young boys. This lad brought what most American kids bring on long rides—requests to go to the bathroom.

All around us the women waved, their hands covered in henna tattoos of flower designs and geometric patterns and the occasional swastika. *You sure you want to celebrate the blessed union with the sign of the Third Reich?* Relax, they seemed to say, we've got Hitler beat by a couple thousand years. I saluted the mind-set—the bastard shouldn't get away with everything. I felt the same way about Donald Trump trying to patent the phrase "You're fired."

The drummers united with the tubas and trumpeters in front of a band cart full of brass speakers and neon, intensifying their march as the crowd edged closer to the ballroom. With their black jeweled suits and flashing lights, they reminded me of Dick Van Dyke's group in *Mary Poppins,* minus the penguins. Penguins, like other colonists, don't do well in India.

I looked across the hotel foyer to the bright palette of saris, aquamarines and chartreuses, apricots and lime greens. Americans are given a mega-sized box of Crayolas at birth, and we usually choose to go gray. Indians are handed pencil shavings and somehow explode in Technicolor.

At last the *baraat* made its way to the entrance. The band quieted, and several older guests waved to us all to stop. The partygoers continued to nod their heads at us, never questioning why a pair of vagabonds would want to witness the wedding of a couple they didn't know. Of course we were welcome, they said. This was India.

The groom left his horse outside and joined his parents and family at the doorway. There they waited as an older brother announced their arrival. After a few minutes, the bride, swathed in red and gold, emerged with her family, all walking arm in arm. The closer they got to their future in-laws, the tighter they clung. "No, don't take our beautiful daughter," they protested as if onstage. Her mother wailed, and a sister teared up.

"I love these faux protests," I said to the bald and white-bearded man standing next to me. "They really make it seem as if they don't want their daughter to marry him."

"Actually, they don't want him to marry her. Different caste."

But in India, there are few runaway brides. Marriage issues have been settled long before. Perhaps not to everyone's satisfaction, but they have been settled.

The groom's family offered their new daughter-in-law flower garlands to make peace. The lotus and jasmine leis seemed to do the trick, silencing the wails. Flowers can do that.

The crowd focused their attention on the couple every step of the way to the ceremony, but as soon as we all filed into the cavernous ballroom, they completely forgot about them. The food seemed to be a prime culprit, a buffet of puris and chutneys and tandoor pots stretching the length of the room, overflowing breadbaskets, towering sculptures of fruit, and every sweet imaginable. Just no onions or garlic, explained a portly elder. "Bad for the breath."

We grabbed a small plate of chocolates, fruit, and cashews.

"These people look like they haven't slept in a week," said Kurt.

"That's because they haven't slept in a week. That man over there told me he'd been to five parties for this couple."

"Maybe that's why nobody seems to be paying attention to the newlyweds. Look at them over there. All alone."

"You wanna see another reason why nobody pays attention to them? Look at the large woman in the yellow sari to your left."

"Got her."

"Look at her son beside her. The guy with the unibrow. She's been introducing him around since the minute we got here. Working this room harder than a cash-starved politician."

"Many matches to be made here."

"Forget the couple. Seems like the real purpose of the Indian wedding is more Indian weddings."

I heard a man bark orders near the front door and looked over to see a mini commotion. A small group of mannish-looking women pushed to enter the party, only to be restrained by a few male guests and escorted outside for a heated discussion.

"What's going on?" I asked the man who told me about the onions and garlic.

"Eunuchs," he said.

He explained they were the only unwanted guests at a wedding and there-fore, as in all cultures, the most likely to attend. Discarded by society and their government, India's gender-neutrals have banded together in the big cities and formed their own public works program. They show up at wed-dings, births, and other family milestone celebrations, demanding money in exchange for a blessing and a promise not to flash their nongenitalia or inflict bodily harm on the attendees.

Eunuchs are the Indian equivalent of the large men in New Jersey who knock on your door and promise protection. The difference is they come in pink saris and lipstick instead of sweatsuits and stubble. Also like the mob, the richer the constituent, the tighter the squeeze. Author William Dalrymple described the eunuch as "halfway between a talisman and an object of ridicule," which fits the mafia goon as well. I wondered how much they'd get off this family.

In the morning we accepted another invitation, this one from a very polite woman who'd read *Honeymoon with My Brother* and e-mailed us to say, "If you're ever in India . . ." I say she was polite because Priya didn't e-mail us back with a police restraining order when Kurt and I responded: Thank you, and, in fact, we would soon be in Delhi, and, yes, we would love a place to stay. An Indian American raised around the world, she was staying in Delhi for a few months with her mother, stepfather, and grandparents. None of them looked too shocked when we showed up at their doorstep.

We were becoming bigger and bigger fans of the blind invitation when visiting abroad, convinced that the world is far more hospitable than we perceive. What better way to see and experience the country than to para-chute into a local's existence. Within a few meals and conversations, you get past the tourist attractions and dive deep into the area's news, customs, jokes, and, in our case, love. I explained the purpose of our journey over breakfast.

"You should talk to my grandparents," said Priya. "They'll be down soon. My grandmother is finishing her morning prayers."

Surendra joined the table first. He said hello and reached for a cup of chai tea, letting the rest of us talk about the morning's news headlines. I looked over at him, his gray hair matted and parted on the side, blue oxford buttoned to the top, looking at his granddaughter with attentiveness, and I could feel a calming influence on the discussion though he'd yet to utter a word.

Saraswati came shortly thereafter, welcoming us with her palms together in prayer. *Namaste.* She wore a muted flower sari and a gray cardigan and had a knowing presence as well. *When I get old, I want to be Indian.*

The meticulous *bindi* between her eyebrows cut a perfect circle, maroon in hue as if it had matured from a bright red on her wedding night into the color of a seasoned merlot. Saraswati applied the mark each morning, a sign to the world she was secure in marriage.

The West opts for bright lipsticks and push-up bras, drawing a stranger's attention to the most suggestive parts of the body. The Arab world conceals as much as possible, preferring you wouldn't look at all. Indian women, with their nose rings and *bindis,* draw you in immediately, then just as quickly defuse. Look, they seem to say, but don't stare. See that I am content. See me for my status, for my being rather than my beauty.

After polishing off a few pieces of wheat bread toast and marmalade, we moved to the sofa and chairs in the living room. Fifty-nine years they'd been married. Fifty-nine years. They met on their wedding day.

"Were you nervous?" I asked.

"I was so excited," said Saraswati. "Though I had a hard time seeing him across the room with all the guests milling around."

"Very happy, fulfilled," added Surendra. "I was getting a life partner."

"Was it love you felt? Or something else?"

"A deep affection, I would say," said Saraswati. "Right away. You surrender to the process."

Surrender. That's an interesting term. We tend to see all forms of surrender as negative—war, sports, highway on-ramps. You'd never hear us describing a relationship as a type of surrender. But maybe we should. Is it wrong to cede the solo to the duet? Surrender doesn't mean you lose, only that you no longer wish to fight.

"This is a change of mind," said Surendra. "No two humans are alike. No two leaves are alike. Accept the differences, because they are superficial. We are still good human beings. Concentrate on the goodness in the other, rather than the difference."

Yes. I knew that sounded simple, but I realized how seldom it's said. We divide ourselves in every waking moment. Blond or brunette. Blue states or red. Then we define ourselves by the divides. We do the same with love.

As we talked, Saraswati grabbed her husband's hand without looking at it, resting their clasped fingers and her gold bangle bracelets on the cushion between them. Pulling it toward her would have suggested she was uncomfortable. But to leave it there in the divide, that said "we are one." Never had I wanted to hold a hand more than I did that morning.

"Love is much deeper than what we believe," Surendra said, paraphrasing J. Krishnamurti.

India has problems as long and lengthy as its borders. It is the world's largest contradiction—at once the most and least tolerant place on earth, at times brutal and at others the height of humanity. As Sarah Macdonald wrote in her book *Holy Cow,* "India is beyond statement, for anything you say, the opposite is also true. It's rich and poor, spiritual and material, cruel and kind, angry but peaceful, ugly and beautiful, and smart but stupid." Happily married couples like Surendra and Saraswati are a lit path in this terrain.

The more time we spent with them, the more I wanted to become one of them. They could spark even the most hardened cynic's belief in love. There on the couch I started to feel something inside, like a shot of single malt, first a jolt, then a slow creep to every finger and toe.

Inside I wanted to grasp every bit of knowledge they'd culled and put it to use in my own life. I wished I could download their experiences and load them into my brain. However, if there was one thing I'd learned in India, it was the fact they are hesitant to preach. Indians have meditated on love for millennia, yet they are the last to stand on a dais and tell the rest of us how to do it, the contemplative guru to our televangelist.

"Listen inside," said Surendra. "The answers are within. We are all the same."

"But if you could change something to strengthen Western relationships, what would it be?" I asked.

"Think less as an individual," he said. "More as one."

"And think less of the money," added Saraswati.

Westerners consume, they and others in India told me, though they rarely said it in a resentful way. It's the nature of accumulation; more breeds more. Indians we met stressed that wealth was a reward for magnanimous deeds in a past life. Good karma. No, Indians don't disparage Western wealth. They just don't believe we see the consequences, including the impact on love.

Money fashions a culture of individuals, they said. Money divides. Money runs counter to the forces needed for relationships to thrive. It distorts, confuses, and makes our criteria for love, well, bizarre.

What also struck me, sitting with Surendra and Saraswati, was something they didn't say—"I love you." In fact, never did I hear the words spoken in India, including as a good-bye or an aside. "Love is seen in the actions," explained an elderly man in Agra as he sat beside his wife. "You do not need the words."

"A Sikh man will never say 'I love you' in front of people," said Harbhajan, a man we met in Jaipur; his wife, Jaswant, nodded in agreement. "Especially elders or neighbors."

The women agree.

"I hope to teach my son to love by seeing his parents love each other, not by telling each other 'I love you,'" said Tanuja, a Jain from Udaipur.

I thought back to my previous relationship, and all the times I said the words wanting only to hear them in return. "Do you love me? Do you?" The days when I felt the least secure in love were the days I said "I love you" the most.

A run emerged from the hotel lobby restroom with wet hands. *Must be how all the palm readers do it. Don't want the paper towels to wipe away any clues.* Then I remembered I was in India. There weren't any paper towels.

I'd made arrangements to meet the astrologer/palm reader to learn more about a crucial step in all Indian relationships, the celestial blessing. In sickness and in health, in ventures business and romantic, before cricket matches and school exams, Indians rely to the core on the counsel of astrologists for "auspicious dates," "compatible partners," "opportune paths." They see them as a combination hair stylist/gossipy best friend/worldly uncle.

Hindu astrology dates back to the Vedas, the sacred compendiums of knowledge bestowed by Krishna to mere mortals more than five thousand years ago, millennia before Christ turned water into wine or Mohammed rounded up his armies. Indian astrologers have been kibitzing on life ever since, guiding good Hindus on whom to marry, what to eat, how to handle all those irate customer phone calls from people who "just want to talk to somebody who speaks American." Astrology, or *Jyotish,* the science of light, commands a large part of the all-knowing scriptures. And while Western astrology has gone in and out of favor (the buzz-kill of the Crusades, for example), Vedic astrology has forever been the house rule.

Certainly Arun looked competent. With pace and precision he said a quick prayer, unlocked his briefcase, and pulled out a camping flashlight, which he positioned like a microscope over my palm. He adjusted his glasses and took off his sweater vest.

"Now, why did you do that?" I asked.

"It's hot," he said.

"So it is."

Like most astrologers, Arun learned from a fellow practitioner. From the onset he sensed a knack for the craft. A string of pleased clients convinced him to quit his job as a shopkeeper and devote his hours to palms and signs.

"Everything in the universe is governed and controlled by astrology," he explained. "Hinduism goes hand in hand with astrology. Instead of planets it is the lines of the hand. So in astrology we have Saturn, and in palm reading we have the line of destiny. The results are the same."

"I've heard stories about the subtle techniques parents use to shape the outcome of a reading," I said. "Things like saying, 'My wife and I really like this guy and hope everything is auspicious.' Or they talk about inviting the astrologer to the wedding parties should 'everything be compatible.'"

"Sometimes there is pressure, but if you compromise on the basis of pressure, you compromise the profession."

"Well, no pressure from me," I said. "Let 'er rip."

He began by staring at my nails, which I'd cut to the nub earlier that day. I didn't want Arun to see the levees of dirt around each cuticle. He then made thirty-one dots with an executive's pen on the palm side of my right hand and drew a two-inch line below my middle finger. He jotted nine pen dots on my left palm, three on my ring finger, and one on the finger I often used to convey sentiment on Los Angeles freeways, then drew a similar line extending down from that finger. He retraced the dots with the pen, squeezed the soft tissue, and gave my hands a five-minute aerobic workout, bending them forward and back.

"Your lucky number is seven," he said as he pulled on his sweater vest.

"Cold?"

"The air-conditioning. This line is your emotional life," he continued. "It shows a very passionate behavior and satisfaction. This satisfaction is there in life until the relationship ends. You are not the type of person who will continue with a girl if you are not satisfied."

Actually, I got all the way to the altar and would have gone further. I decided not to challenge him on this.

"At twenty-nine or thirty and thirty-three or thirty-four, at these times there was a relationship that could not continue."

My fiancée and I first separated when we were both twenty-nine. She dumped me at the altar when I was thirty-three. He hedged on the dates but nailed this one.

"The complete in your love life begins at age forty-three. This relationship is going to be very good. Because your life line and your line of destiny are very strong."

"Sounds great. Do continue."

"From forty-three to forty-nine, this will be the golden part of your life. You must be married, and professionally you will do something great. This time should be utilized maximum."

"Perfect. I can dicker around for another couple years."

"After forty-nine, it's stable. You are more adjusted, suited for relationships. Around people, you are more happy. Very sensitive. Good heart. And continuous desire to live a full life."

"Swell."

"Your brain nerves are under stress. It should be lowered down. You will die at seventy-six to seventy-eight."

"Whoa. Weren't we focusing on my love life?"

"This is part and the same."

"Is there anything I can do about the dead-at-seventy-six thing?"

"Take life with less intensity. If the intensity is down, you will be in good health until then."

"And live longer."

"No."

"Oh."

"You are the person who gets easily hurt," he continued. "It's a combination of two aspects—on the one hand very cheerful, on the other very serious. Whenever we see this combination, it shows a successful career.

"You love to dominate. One is aggressive. The other is submissive. With you it is the case of submissive domination. If your domination is accepted, you will be very happy. If not, you will withdraw yourself."

"Are you saying I'm passive-aggressive? I'm not passive-aggressive! Am I?"

"Your palms say so."

"Can we get back to the love life?"

"I see your relationship will flourish with satisfaction. And longevity. It is not the case of divorce. This woman will provide you with all sorts of success and happiness in this relationship."

"Sounds optimistic."

"But this is a lady who cannot be tackled by domination. If there is anything you disagree with her, please explain your feelings rather than try to force her. She cannot be forced."

I thanked him for his insights and shelled out fifty dollars. Arun promised to e-mail my full chart reading in a couple of days. He never did. I guessed he didn't foresee any bad karma.

There was no love in India during our final days. We'd made our way south from Delhi, through Jaipur, Jodhpur, and Udaipur, on rickety buses and countless rickshaw rides. We explored our fair share of temples, but when we reached Mumbai we struck out on a quest for a different place of worship—the restaurant owned by cricket star Sachin Tendulkar. The World Cup matches in the West Indies would begin that night, and we wanted to cheer India to victory on big-screen televisions with the faithful. The papers forecast a blowout against Bangladesh, one of the lesser competitors known in the cricket world as a "minnow."

We arrived early to ensure a place, and not a moment too soon. Still several hours before the match, Tendulkar's restaurant felt (and smelled) like a morning commute on one of Mumbai's overcrowded trains. Kurt wore his jersey with pride, prompting numerous nods from the wall-to-wall cricket crazies. Mighty India would bat first.

I sensed something was wrong when the room grabbed its head en masse and the Bangladesh squad mobbed one another on television. Cricketers, unlike their baseball cousins, can take hours, days even, before they are done batting. They contemplate the ball as a painter would an empty canvas, debating when and where to stroke. Then they'll break for tea. Outs don't happen in mere minutes. Yet by the time I finished my Kingfisher beer, India had committed three.

Tendulkar will save us, the locals swore. But after he, too, registered an out, the restaurant that bore his name began to curse it. Bangladesh would score more runs during their at-bats, and, by the end of the night, the minnow had swallowed the whale.

A few days later India lost again, this time to rival Sri Lanka. Tendulkar, the Master Blaster, scored a grand total of zero runs in a game where batsmen can score in the hundreds. In cricket this is called a duck; and that's exactly what Kurt wanted to do.

India is vat-dipped in love, ever striving to sympathize and connect. Gandhi followers staked their lives on the belief that love and conviction would conquer any hostile force. Jain monks discard their clothes and pull out every follicle of hair, not wanting to harm another living thing. The nation drenches every crumbling building with flowers, incense, statues, and love.

None of this matters when India loses at cricket. The newspapers, which in the weeks prior to the World Cup printed a relentless onslaught of rosy predictions, now turned their pens against the team and its captain. "Agony," "Devastation," "The End," screamed the headlines. Gatherings of cricket hooligans (yes, there is such a thing) burned Tendulkar's effigy. Mothers and cousins of the disgraced players were forced to beg forgiveness for their relatives on national television. India wanted blood. Kurt wore the target.

The jersey he'd so painstakingly protected, the shirt he hand-washed twenty times just to remove the Holi paint stains, now became the source of a nation's derision. Is this gringo wearing the shirt to taunt us? Does he not believe that India has fangs? Has he not heard of Kashmir?

We'd initiated dozens of conversations thanks to the jersey. No more. It was as worthless as a Yankees uniform in South Boston. Kurt packed it away, and we headed for home.

World Courting: The Good, the Bad, and the Ugly

HIT. Men from the Suma tribe from southwestern Ethiopia sometimes choose a blunt and brutal approach to courtship—fights with penis-shaped sticks. After shaving their pubic hair and painting their naked bodies with intricate chalk designs, Suma men grab six-foot-long sticks with carved phallus tips for a series of free-for-all battles to determine which among them is worthy of marriage. They whack each other in a tournament series of one-on-one bouts, eliminating an opponent by knocking him down or out. Killing is considered a poor option, as the slayer and his family must then leave the tribe.

KIDNAP. *Ala kachuu* translates to "grab and run" in Kyrgyzstan, and it's the preferred courtship method for roughly a third of all wannabe grooms. With traditional "bride prices" as high as eight hundred dollars plus a cow or two, men frequently opt to abduct their chosen fiancées, usually enlisting the help of family, friends, and alcohol. Once she is detained, the poor woman's future in-laws will attempt to convince her to sport a white wedding shawl, the symbol she's agreed to the union. If they succeed in keeping her overnight, the village will suspect she's no longer a virgin and no longer marriage material to anyone but her abductor. Though illegal, *alu kachuu* is rarely prosecuted, with elders nodding their heads in agreement to the old Kyrgyz saying, "Every good marriage begins in tears."

FIGHT. On the island of New Britain in Papua New Guinea, the Sengseng men are scared to death of the women, and with good reason. According to tribal superstition, women are possessed with evil and contagious spirits, especially during menstruation and childbirth. To have any contact with them can result in sickness or death, the men aver. This can make marriage and courtship rather tricky. Women start the process, offering food or tobacco to entice potential husbands. If this fails, they resort to an ole-fashioned whuppin with fists and switches. The man can either flee, if he's able, or accept the attack, thereby agreeing to the proposal. Sengseng women are allowed almost complete choice of mate, with partners sometimes forcibly restrained to accept their fate. If the man initiates the courtship, it's viewed as rape.

POSE. Nomads in Niger take a less violent approach. Wodaabe men enter a role-reversed beauty pageant where the women determine which performers will make the best mates. The seven-day celebration, called Geerewol, starts with a dance of introduction, then a nighttime version of seduction. Personality and etiquette contests follow, with the men scoring bonus points for being able to look cross-eyed or, better yet, move each eye separately. The Geerewol itself follows, where the finalists jump and chant in a hypnotic line dance for several hours. Eligible women will choose their favorites, and the new couples will go off to dance together.

SQUAWK. Papua New Guinea myths hold that islanders are ancestors of the seemingly infinite number of exotic birds that reign over the region, magnificent and multihued species with names like the Violaceous Coucal or the Superb Pitta. To honor their heritage, and to prove to neighboring tribes that they are superb species themselves, men and women decorate their bodies in the fashion of their favored bird by adorning themselves with feathered skirts, bright-colored dyes, and intricate crowns of shell, bone, plant, and plume. They'll dance, jump, chirp, and sing, stomp, hoot, and, like their avian ancestors, try to convince their counterparts that they are the bird worth watching.

DANCE. Chileans view birds as inspiration for courtships as well, only they look to a more domestic variety—the chicken. In a national dance called the *cuenca,* men and women re-create the barnyard courtship of rooster and hen, two-stepping toward and away from each other in half circles, waving handkerchiefs in the air to mimic feather displays. Musicians squawk lyrics of love, accompanied by plucked guitars and crowing accordions. If that doesn't work, there's always the poetry of Pablo Neruda.

SHOP. Who needs roses and candlelight when you can simply deal for your bride at a desert wedding fair. That's the route of choice for Ait Hadiddou Berbers in southern Morocco. Once a year, widows, divorcees, and virgins gather for a bridal market, where men seeking a partner judge veiled women by the tone of their voice or the look of their eyes. "You have captured my liver," he'll say to his newly beloved. And if she responds that her liver is smitten too, the marriage plans are finalized. Divorcées and widows can go home with their new husbands that day, no bride fees necessary. Chosen virgins, meanwhile, must enter into a year-long engagement/dowry negotiation before being delivered on a mule to their future husbands. The expos don't offer money-back guarantees.

REVERSE ROLES. Among nomadic and matrilineal Tuareg tribes in Northern Africa, there's major role reversal. It's the men who wear veils, and the women who choose their husbands. From the time they are of age to marry, men wear a dark-colored veil and turban called a *tagelmust* that covers their head and turns their face blue with indigo dye. Women select their partners on factors other than appearance—family, wealth, status, and his ability to race a camel. If the marriage goes sour, it's the woman alone who can decide when to divorce.

TATTOO. Legend has it that the Chin people of Asia began to tattoo the faces of their single women in order to prevent them from being abducted by their enemies, the Burmans. If they were kidnapped, their markings would make them easier to find. Though on the wane, the practice has lasted for more than a thousand years, with the tattoos evolving from identity marks to beauty symbols to lure village men, full-face designs of rising suns to catch their eye, or spiderwebs to ensnare them.

AVOID. The American bar scene just might be the most bizarre courting ritual of them all. You couldn't craft a worse situation to facilitate introductions and judge compatibility. Lord knows what future anthropologists will conclude in the centuries to follow.

American bars are modeled after English pubs, as in public meeting places. Yet somehow we've let them evolve into private avoiding spaces. We demand bars that are pitch-black so we can't see anyone, with glass-rattling sound systems so we can't hear one another talk, plastered with plasma televisions so we don't have to focus on a fellow human, BlackBerrys and iPhones in hand to further isolate. We disguise ourselves in extra eyeliner and self-tanner, borrowed skirts and knockoff watches, so that if someone does look at us, they will have no idea of our normal appearance. We go in groups, huddling in corners to dissuade any nonmember of our tribe from venturing over and complaining to our friends that we "never meet anyone anymore."

What's our solution to improve the situation? Ample doses of a liquid intoxicant to slow our brains, slur our speech, and fog our memories! Emboldened, we scour the joint to find another in our dimwitted state, someone with whom to share embellishments and distortions. *Oh please, oh please, oh please. Please let me find someone in this bar whose judgment is as poor as my own.*

Thank God many couples meet elsewhere. Otherwise, I don't think our species could survive.

The Hippie

I heard from her shortly after I returned, a kind e-mail and an invite to do something. Yes, I said. I was around. Let's get together. A dinner on Friday night? Great. I'd pick her up.

"Hi," I said in her hotel lobby. "What a nice surprise."

"I changed my flight schedule. No more Rio for a while. I have Los Angeles trips for the next month."

"I didn't think I'd hear from you. I called your hotel, you know."

"I unplugged the phone," said Vivian. "My friends and I stayed out all night."

"You look great."

She did, too, in her camel stretch skirt and chiffon blouse, her dark hair pulled back tight. Vivian effused Miami, part Latina, part runway, part wow. I got acne each time I took a flight, exiting the plane with a face straight from a junior high yearbook. She flew for a living and still looked refreshed. I heard wisps of Puerto Rico in her voice.

"You hungry?"

"Sure," she said.

"I know a great Thai restaurant around here. I put our name down just in case."

She rubbed her tummy.

"It's good to see you," I said.

I meant it. I'd written my e-mail on the back of a napkin for her in Rio but felt sure she'd never get in touch. My napkin-to-contact rate hovered at around .003 percent. Vivian surprised me, but I was beginning to see she lived on surprise. Of course she danced all night. Sure she flew to Los Angeles to spend a weekend with someone she'd met just once. She seemed more Brazilian each day. No, better. She was here.

She's not here. She's in Miami or some other far-flung airport.

"You know what I mean."

Yes. Your perfect woman—attractive, engaging, absent.

"Who knows. We could make it work. Listen to India."

This isn't what they told you.

"She flies for free, remember. Can hop on a plane anytime."

If you ask her about buddy tickets I'll slap you.

"What's a buddy ticket?"

Those freebies airline employees get. Give them to their family and such.

"How many do they get?"

A slap. Hard.

At the restaurant I ordered pad Thai. She talked about moving to America as a young girl, to the Bronx, where she learned to dream and to fight to see her dreams through. I didn't notice the fighter that night. Maybe Miami smoothed it away. She'd never been married, copping only to a few long-term boyfriends. She seemed too alluring not to have been married. Anyone can get married in this country. Then I remembered my own botched attempt. *Never mind.*

I stared at the small silver cross on her neck. Down, it pointed. Come. *A cross is not a come-on.* Vivian was here for the whole weekend. My mind wandered to the infinite possibilities of the LAX Ramada. I hadn't spent a weekend in Los Angeles with anyone other than Kurt and his dogs. *Pace yourself.* I wanted her. Now.

Shoveling an overloaded spoon of noodles into my mouth, I felt a wave of something entirely different.

"Are you okay?" she asked. "You look pale."

"I'm not pale."

"Sure?"

"Just let me duck out here for a sec. Keep eating. I'll be right back."

The gastrointestinal volcano erupted sometime between the words "not" and "pale." Each step I took toward the bathroom was a mini war against the boiling cauldron inside. Was it the shrimp appetizer or the fish tacos at lunch? It didn't matter now. As I entered the door and began to relax my innards in anticipation, I froze and stared at the lone stall, locked shut and with four feet underneath, two large and two small. A young boy and his father argued over who should zip up the lad's pants. I rattled the door to let them know I was waiting.

"I can doooo it," yelled the boy.

"Okay. Go ahead," said his dad.

"Dad!"

"I can help if you need it," I said.

The bickering came to a sudden halt.

"C'mon, son."

The night would not go according to plan.

> *Franz—*
>
> *It would serve me right if you took two weeks to write me back. I'm very sorry. Honestly, I took some time off from life (the outside world) and just enjoyed being home. Pilot season was so stressful I felt like I needed a mini vacation. I hope you're well.*
>
> *I wanted to know if you'd like to go with me to a wrap party. I won't know that many people, so we could have a chance to talk. I don't usually do industry parties, but this one might be fun.*
>
> *Tracy*

A woman takes two weeks to return your e-mail, it doesn't matter what she says. The delay speaks louder than the words. Mind you, I'm not a fan of that whole waiting ritual. I can't remember what the guy said in the movie *Swingers*. Are you supposed to wait a week before you call or just a couple of days? What's the cutoff period before the wait turns rude?

The world doesn't play that game. They haven't got the time. Somebody gives you their number, you call her. She gave you her number because she wanted you to call.

I'm sure you noticed the hedges in her note. I did. She won't know many people, doesn't go to these types of things. Maybe, maybe not. Tracy didn't seem the Hollywood type. Then again, I'd seen her only once.

I bit; I went. I bit my lip as well and said nothing about the delay. "Let me check my schedule." I didn't have a schedule. My mother gave me a calendar, but I handed it off to Kurt due to the bareness of the pages. The boxes looked so lonely.

Tracy's rental home sat atop a hill on the eastern end of Los Angeles, in a neighborhood heading up but not quite there. The two-bedroom cabin had darkened wood paneling hung diagonally, worn industrial carpets that needed replacing, and built-in bookcases jammed with paperback plays. Ibsen, Williams, Shepard. Actors on television series had homes overlooking the Griffith Observatory or the skyline downtown. Hers looked at power lines and tarred rooftops and pit bulls. In the language of the real estate agent: "Entry-level dream" or "Artist's cabin in the sky."

Visitors climbed seventy-two steps to reach her front door, enough to make you want to count them and know. Sixty, sixty-one, sixty-two, I panted walking up.

At the top of the climb rested a chain-link gate, then a small yard and a patio leading to the front door. Cue dog, all eight pounds of him, a mixture of terrier and Polish kielbasa as far as I could figure, barking as loud as his lungs would allow. He'd start with a few rapid-fire bursts, then work his way to a sustained coda, only to wheeze like a smoker at the end of a belly laugh. *Rarrr-rarrr-rarrr-rarrr-rarrr-rrrrrrrrrr-rrrrrrrrrr-hhhhhhhhhhkkkkkkkk!*

"Hello," I said. "Hello!"

The mutt fled behind a hedgerow, cowered but still barking.

"Tracy?"

I looked down to a few cartoon figures etched in chalk on the pavement and decided this must be the place.

"Anyone home?" I yelled, opening the gate.

At a tepid pace I continued, eyes to the ground so as not to trip over flattened soccer balls and terra cotta pots. Maybe that's why I missed the young boy on the veranda above, clad in a green silk tunic, wooden sword in hand, staring at this gray-haired intruder.

"You're not wearing pants," I said, looking up.

The fearless dragon-slayer looked down at his midriff, then back at me.

"Have you seen my cape?"

"No. No, I haven't."

"I *really* need my cape."

"I believe you. What's your name?"

"Calvin."

He looked every inch of her, blond and aqua and sinewy and sure.

"My name's Franz."

"Grandma!" he yelled, running for the front door. "There's a strange man here."

Grandma? Martha didn't say anything about Tracy living with her mom, did she? Calvin, she mentioned. "Single" and "mom" are the first words used to describe any single mom, long before hair color or astrological signs.

Only once before had I gone out with a single mom. Yet here I was, standing alone on the porch, trying to figure out why. The trips, perhaps; they'd broadened my perspective on relationships, made me stop looking for types. Or maybe it was Tracy's silence toward the end of our first date. Or maybe I just liked her.

"Come on in," said Linda, Tracy's mom, standing in the doorway in a floral summer dress and no makeup. "Tracy will be ready soon."

The house appeared cluttered, though not quite messy enough to suggest a slob. Calvin's toy sprawl fought to overtake every corner with paper planes and Play-Doh monsters. Photos of him beamed from each wall and shelf. Calvin kissing Mom in costume for *After the Fall*. Calvin and Tracy walking hand in hand. Calvin in her large belly. Calvin doing some gardening work in the buff. He was the house.

"Don't worry," she said. "We're just in town for Calvin's fourth birthday."

"Oh, I'm not worried," I said, hearing screams in the back room. "Who's we?"

Tracy's sister, Tiffany, emerged from a cacophony of voices to introduce herself. As we shook hands, I peeked around her to see two towheaded girls wrestling on the floor in wrinkled princess dresses and Calvin, the brave knight, raising his wooden sword to protect the maidens.

"Sounds like the Crusades," I said. "How many are yours?"

"The two girls, Maddy and Sophie. The wrestlers. Don't mind the ruckus. They get like this every time they see each other. Play all day."

"Oh, I love kids."

Just usually from afar. Sure, I enjoyed babysitting my sister's two daugh-ters, Elizabeth and Eleanor. In three-hour intervals, they were flawless. In three hours, it's possible to read *Dora the Explorer* a maximum of 26 times, not 2,374,292. Their spats sounded resolvable, far from the incessant predawn bickering that could make a grown man snap before that first cup of coffee. And any pediatrician from a decent medical school will tell you an un-attended diaper can do no serious damage until at least the fifth hour. "She pottied? I didn't even notice." I viewed kids the same way I viewed boats—fun, sporty, and usually better owned by friends.

My Runaway Bride relationship didn't help. We had the names picked out. I was so sure we'd have a whole mess of kids I convinced my fiancée to go to one of those kiosks where a computer morphs your two photos into the image of your child. She frowned, and our cyber boy came out looking more hobbit than human.

As I struggled to find a proper compliment for kids giving themselves re-peated wet willies while clad in medieval wear ("What dexterous and cultur-ally sensitive children"; "What creative use of the ear canal"), Tracy emerged, sparing me from any ill-thought asides. She gave me a quick squeeze and sug-gested we get going. The ride would take forty-five minutes. Every ride in Los Angeles takes forty-five minutes. The barking began anew as we walked out-side.

"Pluto!" she said. "Relax."

"Is that their dog?" I said hopefully.

"Pluto? No. I got him for Calvin at the pound."

"He seems a tad jittery."

"I think he was beaten by his old owner. He barks whenever he sees a man. Women and kids, no problem. Anyone with testosterone, yap, yap, yap. Take it as a compliment."

"Of course."

"Welcome to the chaos."

So do your mom and sister live nearby?" I asked in the car.

"Sorry about that. No, my mom lives in North Carolina. My sister's from Snohomish. Washington. They're in town for Calvin's birthday. Did they tell you? I hired a reptile charmer."

"Just how does one charm reptiles?"

"I don't know, just that she's bringing snakes and tarantulas and such."

We'd been in the car for all of five minutes, yet I could tell something had changed since our last date a month prior.

"Sounds very Marlin Perkins."

"You're welcome to come. It's Saturday."

"I'll be in New York. Thanks, though."

"Calvin's going to explode when he sees all those animals."

"He seemed pretty deft with that sword. In case something goes wrong with the snake."

"They liked you. My sister and mom. I could tell."

"Nah. I didn't say anything. Which is usually best, by the way."

"My mother told me on the way out you had an honest face."

"Well, you tell her I liked her face, too. I mean, no. Tell her I liked meeting her."

"Sure."

She touched my arm as we turned on La Cienega Boulevard.

"Here it is," she said. "Pull up to the valet."

"Jim Henson Studios. Wow. I didn't know you played a Muppet."

"They're just having the event here. It's a wrap party for that show *The Practice.*"

Hey, my dad likes that series. Maybe I'll tell him.

"Who'd you play?"

"A prostitute."

Then again, maybe I won't.

Once inside, she surveyed the crowd and claimed not to know a soul. I looked at her, in her long linen skirt amid a room of designer dresses, and saw a working actress rather than a celebrity. She talked about the craft rather than the trappings. The television work was nowhere near as challenging or rewarding as the stage, she said. It paid the bills and allowed her to pursue theater roles. Her characters tended to be sympathetic ones—cancer victims and mothers with missing children.

Instead of working the room, we tackled the buffet and sat in a corner beneath giant plaster busts of Kermit and Miss Piggy.

"I want to apologize for something," she said. "On our date."

"Shoot," I said.

"I'd been going through a breakup."

"I see."

"I probably should have waited before going out with you. But Martha said you're going out of town again. And I already turned down that couples-only date in the Caribbean. . . ."

" 'Cause you were seeing someone. I get it."

"No, that was just because I wouldn't be caught dead at a couples-only resort. Especially on a first date."

"You're not seeing him anymore?"

"Yes. We had a long talk the other night."

"Great," I said. "About the talk."

"Why are you smiling?"

"Am I?"

"Yes."

"I'm sorry, but it's really difficult to talk with you about anything serious underneath Kermit here," I said, pointing.

She laughed and looked behind her.

"I think they make a fine couple," she said. "Opposites attract."

"Really? One of the only reasons I watched the Muppets was that I was sure Kermit would strangle Miss Piggy someday. Then they'd have all these interviews with Gonzo and Beaker and everyone, talking about how he just snapped, how he was such a normal guy. Frog."

"Everybody hates Miss Piggy, but do you know how hard it is to be a woman in show business? She's out there by herself, holding her own against all these testosterone-fueled marionettes. Think about it. Fozzie, Kermit, the Swedish Chef—all guys."

"I didn't really see the Muppets as men. More like goofy hermaphrodites."

"With deep Bronx accents."

"What about Zoe?"

"That's *Sesame Street*. Plus she's four. That's the kids' table."

I paused.

"You have a point," I said.

After a half hour, she suggested we leave. I didn't mind mingling with the gaffers and key grips but sensed she felt uncomfortable at gatherings like this. I mentioned a nearby dive bar; she countered with coffee.

We settled on her favorite coffee shop in Eagle Rock. Swork, umlaut on the *w*. They had a play area for kids, she said. Apparently, play areas make coffee taste better for single moms. We ordered our lattes and found a vacant table outside.

"So, Martha says you used to work in politics," said Tracy. "Are you a Democrat or a Republican?"

"I'm done with politics. Couldn't stand the divisions. And all the colors. Everything's about color in politics. First they tell us we're in blue states or red, then we're supposed to be green. It's hard to keep up. Travel's the opposite. It's all about commonality. You go to a foreign country and spend your time embracing all the things we share. Yeah, I'm done with politics."

"So, you're a Republican."

This prompted a man and woman to instantly look up from their iMacs to see who'd dare let a Republican in the room.

"See," I said, lowering my voice. "You can't say those kinds of things in Los Angeles."

"I've never dated a Republican before. I'm not sure what to do."

"Distrust the media, vote no on any spending initiatives, and phrase everything in terms of 'family values.'"

"What does that mean?"

"I don't know, just that it's important."

"I think this could be fun, seeing a Republican."

"Like some wacky science experiment?"

"Republicans lose all the time here. Think of all the opportunities to gloat."

Before I'd finished my latte, we shifted subjects, from politics to circumcision. Don't ask. I still can't remember the transition. Did we go from budget cuts to baby cuts? All I remember is she adamantly opposed lopping off skin and, over $4.25 coffees, she let me know it.

"You travel a lot. You must go to countries where they still circumcise young girls. You don't support that, do you?"

"Well, no," I said, glancing at my own midsection.

"Right. It's mutilation."

"But there are health benefits for guys. Much cleaner product."

"I'm going to lend you a book by Calvin's pediatrician."

"There was this kid at my junior high school who wasn't circumcised. Not that I checked him out or anything. He used to dress behind his gym locker."

"Half the kids in Los Angeles aren't circumcised. Insurance doesn't pay for it anymore. It's not a health risk."

"So I take it you only date uncircumcised men?" I said, smiling slightly. "Want to avoid the mutilations and such."

Tracy touched my hand and returned my grin. "I'm sure your parents didn't even think about it. Standard procedure back then."

I took inventory. Her latte was soy. Her skirt, natural fiber. Forget the Hollywood type; I was hanging with a hippie. How did an organic everything survive amid the cosmetically altered? I envisioned candlelit dinners with passionate discussions about cloning and Woody Harrelson. For a flash I felt envious for not matching her passion over such matters. The bigger concern was if I could see someone who did.

Brazil said be open to love. India counseled commitment. Neither told me what to do about this.

Resilience

NICARAGUA

So I decided to journey to a country where they argued about politics more than any other place on the globe. I wanted to know if love and relationships could survive. A broad-shouldered man with a gap-toothed grin convinced me to go. I met him after a speech I gave in Rancho Cordova, California.

"I loved your book," he said. "I saw you guys on the *Today* show and ran out to pick it up. I made my daughters and son read it."

I looked up from signing copies to see a large head with a fuzzy G.I. Joe haircut and tinted prescription eyeglasses.

"Thank you. Thank you very much."

"But now tonight in your speech you tell me you're going to Panama for your next book," he said, changing tone.

"Did I say something wrong?"

"Yes."

"What?"

"Panama. I might not buy this book."

"What's wrong with Panama?"

"I don't know. I've never been."

"I'm Franz," I said, extending my hand.

"Alejandro. And this is my son, Alex, my daughters, Sabrina and Kristina. You should go to Nicaragua."

"Why Nicaragua?" I said.

"Because I'm Nicaraguan. My wife is Nicaraguan. She couldn't come to-night. Sorry. My kids were born here, but they are Nicaraguan. Been here more than twenty years. I work over at Caltrans."

"I've heard good things about Nicaragua."

"They're all true. Better. We have much more interesting stuff than Panama."

"I thought you'd never been."

"I haven't. I just know that we're a lot better."

"When's the best time of year to go?"

"Anytime. Can we get a picture with you guys?"

"Sure," said Kurt, putting his arms around the teenagers. "On three, everybody smile and say, 'Panama!' "

"Nicaragua!" they yelled in chorus.

K urt phoned Alejandro several months after our event and said we'd changed our minds. Panama was out, Nicaragua was in. Did he have any suggestions? We'd go in a few weeks.

"I'll go with you," he said.

"No. Really?" asked Kurt.

"Let me call you back. I need to check with my boss."

"How much vacation time do you get at Caltrans?"

"No, my *real* boss. My wife. Without her permission, there is no trip for me."

The phone rang after twenty minutes.

"Okay, I'm going, too," he said. "I was just down there a couple weeks ago, but it's okay. I got the time off work. We can stay with my parents in Managua for as long as you want."

The flight to Augusto C. Sandino International landed midmorning, mid-chaos. *"Amigo, amigo,"* shouted the taxi drivers. Nicaraguans back from American vacations pushed mountains of cardboard boxes on their baggage carts, televisions and microwaves for relatives and friends who'd seemingly all come to greet them. We waded through the mob and felt the blast of hot air from outside, a cloak of grime and sweat and lethargy. A giant billboard of Daniel Ortega smiled from across the street. *¡El Frente, La Solución!* I translated this to mean, "Hey Yankees, I'm baaaack!"

"My brothers from another mother!" yelled Alejandro, his head sticking up above the others. "Welcome to Nicaragua."

"*Hola, amigo,*" I said. "Thanks again for this. I can't believe you're here. Us either."

"I told my wife, you cannot say no to honeymooning brothers. Are you hungry? My mother has a big breakfast waiting for you guys."

"That's so nice of them to host us," said Kurt. "What did they say when you told them about the trip?"

"My mother, she said, 'The gringos are coming. Get more soda and ice.'"

"How's my man Dan doing?" I said, pointing to the billboard.

"They think he's going to win. He's split the opposition, which isn't hard to do in Nicaragua. We split over anything."

Managua was out early that morning and every other, hustling in every quarter to earn an endurable wage. Fruit vendors hawked juice from carts. "*¡Bebidas!*" As we made our way across town, each stoplight prompted a rush of activity. Newspaper salesmen waved *La Prensa* and *El Nuevo Diario,* teenagers offered to wash windows with dirty rags, and shoeless kids peddled origami birds and grasshoppers made from palm fronds. One industrious businessman sprinted across six lanes of aggressive traffic to thrust a three-foot-long and very live iguana into my window.

Alejandro narrated as we motored on, talking about Ortega and the up-coming election. It would be the number-one topic throughout our stay, he predicted, even if we asked locals about love. After a dozen turns in what I assumed were the city outskirts, he parked the car in front of a large hill with steps to the top. We got out and hiked to the top, up to a clearing with a giant silhouette statue that bore an uncanny resemblance to the Marlboro Man.

"Augusto César Sandino," Alejandro explained, pointing to the mass of black metal. "*El General de Hombres Libres.*"

I looked out to Lago de Managua and the Momotombo volcano behind. Royal palms and *madroño* trees rimmed colonial churches and squat office buildings in the surrounding blocks.

"Where's downtown?" I asked.

"This is it."

"Is there a skyline?"

"You see that white building?" he said, nodding to the only structure more than ten stories. "That's the skyline. The earthquake destroyed everything else."

It's impossible to describe the Nicaraguan landscape or character without including Mother Nature. Old-timers talk not in decades but in intervals be-tween natural disasters. They throw around the names as if talking about re-lationships gone awry. "Mitch? Mitch was okay to me. But Joan. Joan ruined everything." The most destructive of them all, the ex from hell, the former flame who got up in the middle of the night, stole the life savings, and ran off with the neighbor—the Managua earthquake of 1972.

Arriving the eve of Christmas Eve, the 6.2 jolt and its aftershocks flatlined the Managua skyline, destroying nine out of ten buildings, including hospitals and fire stations. The subsequent blazes gutted what remained. With infra-structure crumpled, aid from foreign countries sat on ships and tarmacs, un-able to reach hundreds of thousands of displaced residents or the families of the five thousand who did not survive. The Somoza government looted what little relief money and supplies made it through.

Pittsburgh Pirates baseball star Roberto Clemente watched all this on tele-vision from his native Puerto Rico. Frustrated by the delays and incensed by the corruption, Clemente wanted to do something. If the government wouldn't act, he would. In his haste, he chartered a plane with a history of problems and a pilot with a track record of negligence. The plane doesn't look safe, warned his friends as they helped him load the supplies. Clemente ignored it all, only to perish with the plane and its contents shortly after takeoff. His body was never found.

"Such a pretty location," I said. "Water, hills, tropical green. Few cities have that combination."

"Managua will never have a proper skyline. Each time we rebuild, some-thing destroys it. There are four big fault lines right underneath us. What's worse," he continued, "is what the earthquakes have done to the sense of community. We used to be together, a real community. My parents lived not too far from here. They ran a gas station. But after the earthquake, people and money fled to the suburbs. Managua isn't as close as it used to be. And we never will be again."

"That's a shame," I said.

"Almost as damaging as the politics. Almost."

L ike the migrations after the earthquake, we continued to the new towns and communities outside Managua. Past a Parmalat factory we turned onto a paved block with a handful of new single-story homes with tiled roofs and watchmen. Alejandro stopped the car at the front of the gate and honked, prompting the guard to pull back the carport gates.

"My brother and his family live there," he said, pointing across the street. "My other brother lives next door."

"What about you?" Kurt asked.

"We want to build on that lot over there. This is my dream. Nicaragua. I can't shake it. It's in me to come back."

His parents and siblings had staked claim to the entire block. "Calle Lacayo," he said. The rains, hard and sudden, began anew, and we scrambled with our bags.

Inside, smells of homemade tamales and fried plantains filled the entryway, fueling my appetite. Ceiling fans fought a losing battle against the day's wet heat. Alejandro's mother, Olga, emerged from the kitchen wiping her hands, her dark hair up.

"Mama, these are the honeymooning brothers."

"Nice to meet you," she said, extending her hand. "I was very curious when I heard this story. We don't have this here. But Alejandro explained. Welcome."

"You're too kind to have us," said Kurt. "You're right, Alejandro. Nicaraguans are way better than Panamanians."

Ramon, Alejandro's father, chuckled at the doorway. "*Bienvenidos.* Welcome." With Olga's urging, we moved to the dining room and into a feast of papayas, plantains, *gallo pinto* (rice and beans), *nacatamales* (cornmeal, pork, and salsa wrapped in a slippery banana skin), all washed down with coffee from the northern hills and a Teletubby purple–colored juice called *pitahaya.*

"Mmmm," said Kurt. "They don't have food like this in Panama."

"You joke, but this is true, Kurt," said Alejandro. "The quickest way to insult a Nicaraguan is not the politics. It's to say they don't have the best *gallo pinto.*"

Ramon held the chair for his wife and smiled in approval of the meal, a routine they'd obviously repeated for many years. Between bites, I asked how they'd met. He was twenty-eight, he recounted as I helped myself to more coffee. Ten years her senior. He saw her on a Managua promenade after a state funeral. It was 1956.

"Her thick eyebrows, her long face, profound eyes, and calves—a body like a guitar," he said, moving his hands and prompting a chortle from his wife. "That's what I remember. I wanted to talk to her, but couldn't think of a way how."

Then, an icebreaker. Ramon fished out his new camera and angled over to ask her to pose for a picture. You're very photogenic, he said. Please. For my collection.

"Tall, *fuerte,* the way he walked, *todo,*" recalled Olga. "He looked like a military man. *¡Chachito lindo!*"

"So, after you took the picture, did you sense there'd be more?"

"No," said Olga. "I was too young for anything serious."

"Yes," said Ramon. "I wanted to know her, know her ideals, her behavior. I thought right then that she would be my wife. And over the next three months, I confirmed this. I had three girlfriends, and I told them all that I had other plans. This was difficult."

"What did your parents say?"

"My mother told me to stay away."

"Mothers can do that," I said.

"But I told her I was in love and that I wanted to marry Olga, but that I wanted to wait until I had enough money."

"So you dated," I said.

"For two years," she said. "We would go to the movies, but we didn't watch the movies."

"Back then it was considered polite to bring a little gift each time we dated," he said. "Flowers. Candy. When I didn't work, I spent all my time with her."

"How do you think dating has changed here?" I asked.

"The young Nicaraguans used to be much more submissive. If a parent said we cannot see each other, we would not," said Ramon.

"But you did," I said.

Ramon paused, then smiled.

"Chaperones," said Olga. "They don't do this anymore. Due to technology, the customs here have ended. They don't ask for permission."

Technology and permission. I hadn't thought about the correlation until she mentioned it. The technologies empowered on many different fronts—more time, more options. More leeway. With their iPods and cell phones and personal computers, young singles around the planet did seem less constrained. At least they talked in grander terms.

"Do you think the technology has been good or bad for love in Nicaragua?"

"If you have a good heart, it hasn't hurt," said Olga. "If you worry about the wrong things, this is no good."

"Morals have eroded," said Ramon. "It was not even in your dream to have sex then."

With opportunity lacking at home, Ramon and Olga moved their family to San Francisco in the eighties. He worked in a hotel, while she served in a city AIDS care office. They were educated. They had health care. They were fortunate.

"The biggest difference with the children is that in the United States, they leave the home at eighteen," said Olga. "We were lucky to have good boys. They respected the women and married good girls."

"Interesting that they all married Nicaraguan women," I said. "Even though they were all going to school and working in the United States."

"I thought they would," said Olga.

"How would you have felt if your kids married a gringo or gringa?"

"To be honest," said Olga, "I would prefer a Latina. And especially a Nica. It's easier to solve problems."

"Love is the most important," said Ramon. "Communication is very important. It would be easier to be with a Nica."

This answer didn't surprise me. Parents in many other countries swore the same. Life is arduous, they said matter-of-factly. Racism, sexism, classism, religious intolerance—they knew the struggles would continue for their children. So they counseled avoidance far more than fight. My idealist, pampered brain wished for the alternative. Ramon and Olga made me question if I would feel the same way in their position.

"The United States did give me domestic skills," said Ramon. "I learned to cook. Here, if you knew how to cook, you were considered a *maricón*."

"It also changed one other thing," said Alejandro, entering the conversation.

"What?" said his father.

"You know," he said, scraping his legs with an imaginary knife.

"*Sí, sí,*" said Ramon. "Olga wanted to start to shave the legs and cut the eyebrows. I always like the old style. Old Nica men prefer the hairy legs."

"So what happened?"

"She shaves her legs now."

After breakfast, and against the advice of the guidebooks, we decided to wade into chaos at the massive Mercado Oriental, a lattice of power lines, tin-roofed shops, bootleggers, and pickpockets. The books made it sound like crabgrass—tough, sprawling, tenacious, ugly, cropping up amid the earthquake's ruined city blocks. City leaders sought for years to stamp it out, only to see the roots grow.

"Daniel Ortega went to a meeting with the traders and old women yelled at him for hours, We won't move, you can't make us go," wrote Salman Rushdie in *The Jaguar Smile*.

Ortega relocated the wealthier merchants to the malls, but the renaissance salesmen remained, the ones who can sell anything that's a noun. The first merchant I saw at the market that morning hawked a portable gas range with one hand and a stuffed armadillo with the other. Nicaragua, along with the rest of the third world, remains infertile ground for the specialist.

As I imagined the armadillo/gas range sales pitch, a frenzied man in a soiled shirt grabbed my arm and urged me to feel the plastic implant in his head, the result of a fall from a three-story building. "See for yourself," he implored, pulling my wrist. I don't know why he didn't think I believed him. A mutt at my leg, meanwhile, mounted a fellow stray for an aggressive romp that ended poorly with the two dogs fused. Kurt poured his bottled water on the canines, and they detached and began to fight.

I loved the market for all of this. It was real, honest, and all-consuming. This wasn't commerce behind glib advertising posters and piped-in elevator music. You could touch the activity and sometimes it touched you. You could also do something nearly impossible in the expensive malls—talk to the vendors as humans and not as transactions. Each stall came with a story, a discussion about kids or politics. Or love. Everything was possible here. Including love.

"You go to the market to meet girls," said Juan, a man with frosted tips and dubious heterosexuality who approached us as we strolled. "Because they have everything here."

Sure enough. The Mercado Oriental may be a pickpocket's paradise, but it is also the most active singles scene in the country. Men and women spend their days shopping, many for relationships.

"I met my husband here at the market," said Norma, thirty-nine, the owner of a housewares booth who set down her tin pots to talk about her love life. "We were both married at the time."

"And he swept you off your feet?" I asked.

"He was attracted to me, but I wasn't attracted to him. He is not good-looking."

"So what changed your mind?"

"He was attentive. He listened to me. When we had sex for the first time, I didn't have an orgasm. But I realized he was a much better man than my husband. This was a different type of orgasm."

I never heard that at the Glendale Galleria.

"Physical appearance is irrelevant," she continued. "Though it is important to be good in bed. You need to communicate in bed. My husband is open-minded. You can talk to him about anything."

Norma and the other women who work in the market are experts at classifying the young male suitors who stop to talk. They know instantly their type. *Andando* = dating, but not serious. *Jalando* = dating exclusively. *Carreteando* = the act of chasing skirt.

A few stalls down, Scarleth smiled when she talked about her boyfriend, another Mercado Oriental romance. At twenty-four, this was her first love, and she had high hopes it would be her last.

"He's attentive," she said. "He likes to hug, kiss, talk. He lets me know how much he loves me. He says this more than most Nicaraguan men."

"Do you want to get married?"

"God willing," she said. "We are having sex. But we waited for five months."

"Who supplies the birth control in Nicaragua—the man or the woman?"

"The men. Sometimes they carry condoms. None of my friends are on the pill."

"Why not?"

"They aren't afraid of getting pregnant."

We made our way deeper into the labyrinth, nodding and smiling to the vendors and observers who made the market their daily routine. The passageways narrowed, making it impossible to walk without rubbing against strangers.

"I won't charge you to cut your hair," said a stout woman in a blue-and-white checkered bandanna.

Her makeshift salon had two chairs, a few mirrors, and a large wooden credenza cluttered with tinfoil, combs, spray bottles, and food. She wore a white cafeteria apron over her black shirt and stared straight at Kurt. A customer mid-dye-job, with orange paste and plastic on her head, rose from the chair and offered it to my brother.

"No, I'm good," said Kurt. "Thanks."

Ligia hears it all from her customers in this popular establishment, three dollars a haircut. Women prefer the layered cuts, and they like the rebel look. Waxing isn't popular, but the manicures and pedicures keep her busy. Over the past year her business brightened because she'd gained a new wave of clients, the metrosexuals.

"What kind of complaints do you hear from the women?" I asked.

"He beats me. No money. He's cheating."

"Do the women cheat as well?"

"About fifty-fifty. More. Women are trying to get even."

"Where do they cheat?"

"Here. Home. Everywhere."

"Here at the market?" I asked.

"Sí, sí," she said.

"What about the politics here in Nicaragua? Has it hurt love?"

"I don't think so. Is just the way it's been. But you should go north to ask people. That's where the fighting was."

Just then a power outage silenced the activity. The music stopped, the people paused, and the heat remained.

In Nicaragua, atrocity has many fathers. A one-minute history:
The Somozas assassinated and maimed with ease; tortured for sport, sometimes penning political prisoners with panthers and jaguars; burned newspaper headquarters that dared print the unkind word; and systematically extorted millions from business and government coffers.

Daniel Ortega and the Sandinistas used violence to counter the violence, their strength growing with each Somoza clampdown. They robbed banks and businesses to fuel their fight; assassinated and bullied, kidnapped and bombed. And when they overthrew Somoza and obtained power in 1979, the generals took their cues from the Soviet Union and Fidel Castro, directed resources to guns instead of help, and plunged the country into economic crisis the likes of which had never been seen before. They attacked Miskito Indian communities on the Atlantic Coast in the same brutal fashion the Somozas attacked them, forcing thousands of peaceful indigenous Indians to flee their homelands.

Oliver North's band of rebel rebels, the contras, bombed the airports, mined the roads and harbors, shot soldiers, and attacked civilians, all on the U.S. dime.

"I met many contra fighters during the course of the war, and was always struck by how much they resembled Sandinista fighters," wrote *New York Times* reporter Stephen Kinzer in *Blood of Brothers,* his firsthand account of the conflict. "Both armies were made up of young boys, almost exclusively from the poorest social classes. Each side had its slogans and few fighters ever questioned them."

In the end, the revolution cleaved the country more deeply than the earthquakes or hurricanes or any natural disaster.

Life was simpler before the fighting, exclaimed the older generations on all sides. Men picked bananas and tobacco, waging that never-ending battle between machete and green. Women raised children and ran households. Nicaraguans spent their free time playing *béisbol* and cheering Major League pitcher Dennis Martinez on black-and-white television sets; asking for second helpings of *ropa vieja* ("old clothes," or shredded beef on rice) and of course *gallo pinto*; shuffling to church and sometimes believing.

You married young, and safe. You married a village friend, a schoolmate of a sibling, a woman or a man with family ties to yours. Many married cousins, and many still do. There were problems—corruption, infidelities, inequalities. There always were. But there were also roles and customs. When in doubt, Nicas returned to the tried and traditional. The revolution forced the country to re-examine all aspects of its society. Including love.

"What you need to understand is the Sandinista movement grew and got strong during the women's worldwide movement," said Gioconda, a bestselling author and former Sandinista revolutionary now living in Los Angeles. "Morality was no longer about the ways of our parents. We invented a new morality code, one with more of an equal footing.

"Nicaragua likes to think of itself as traditional, but more than they are," she said. "The Catholic Church has never been strong enough to change the ways Nicaraguan men and women interact. Free love has existed here forever, especially in the poorer regions. The middle and upper classes had their affairs, too, but they were more discreet."

Empower yourself, the revolutionaries preached. Join. Fight inequality. Fight to live your life as you wish. Scores of Nicaraguan men and women took this to mean a sexual revolution as well.

"The revolution professed women's equality," said Gioconda. "Sexual freedoms were the subtext, though never part of the official platform. The result was the same—more affairs, more free love, but more divorce and split families as well."

The strength of the Sandinista revolution took root in northern hills, amid the rain forests and coffee plantations, among the peasants and disenfranchised, away from the Somoza grip. The setting proved more than a battlefield.

"In many ways, the revolution was romantic," said Gioconda. "You were in a beautiful setting in the mountains, fighting for the poor, fighting alongside people who would die for their cause. The bond you forged with *compañeros* was intense, beautiful. Your life depended on each other. We were young. We had great music, poetry. It was all very appealing on that level. But for all the love, there was no future. You could fall in love with someone, then they'd be gone the next day. Plus the conditions were very rough."

When Ortega and his forces took control of the country, they ushered in a new era in love and dating as well. Families loyal to Somoza or antsy about the future of their bank accounts moved to the United States or Europe. The Catholic Church quieted its concerns. Locals fed a diet of liberty and liberation extended those words to the bedroom. Divorce rates climbed. The impact on families remains a hotly debated topic.

"The Sandinistas changed everything," said Rhina, a physician we encountered in Granada. "Morals were swept out. Free love was swept in. They didn't care. They sometimes had marriages just by crossing guns. We lost all formality. We lost morality. It's been difficult to regain."

"All the politics has changed love," added Dora Maria, a Sandinista politician. "It would be good if the country relaxed."

Ortega and his generals talked much about equality for women, about making Nicaragua less machismo, more progressive. They canceled the beauty pageants and outlawed the use of a woman's body in advertising. They urged the schools and health centers to offer women more. The results never matched the rhetoric. They could manage an army but were incapable of running a government.

"After the Sandinistas took over, there was more separation, more di-vorce," said Manuel, a Managuan who makes his living parodying Nicaragua in political cartoons. "That is mostly because they were not true believers in women's rights. It was enough for them just to be a revolutionary. They sepa-rated from their church . . . and their wives."

Disenchanted with the unfulfilled promises and constant refrains of *"mañana, mañana,"* Nicaraguans ousted Ortega with votes rather than guns in 1990. They elected Violeta Chamorro, the wife of an assassinated dissident and the country's first female president. Families opposed to the Sandinistas moved back to Nicaragua. The Catholic Church raised its voice. And most Nicaraguans found themselves in unfamiliar territory, caught in a mishmash of nostalgic norms, am-plified evangelism, lingering revolutionary ideals, crippling poverty, twenty-first-century economies, and new international influences. All of this made for a puzzling society, let alone relationship scene, the locals said.

"We are copying a relationship model we are not accustomed to," said Manuel. "Modernism has caused a lot of problems. Twenty-five years ago we were a simple agricultural country. Globalization hit us hard. We are not pre-pared for a modern society. We don't have enough education."

In the villages and the countryside, young Nicaraguans wear Che Guevara T-shirts and text-message their girlfriends. On their MySpace pages, they post hip-hop lyrics to honor slain relatives. They've seen curfews and clampdowns and freedoms ebb and flow with each administration. They talk of travel and education with glints of optimism, then retreat to the paths of their parents. Their role models are guerillas and Fortune 500 businessmen, rappers and family members who've made small fortunes abroad. They've seen free love and the increased divorce and AIDS rates that followed. They are like the American baby boomers who embraced selected ideals of their parents, then formulated a new way. Like all generations, they want to improve the model.

L ook at this," said Alejandro, pointing to the store window as we walked the streets of Matagalpa. "This is typical of here."

He paused in front of a photo shop that offered one-hour processing on modern Fuji equipment. In the display window, where other stores of this kind would advertise wedding photos and family portraits, the Matagalpa owner hung old color photographs of the Sandinistas training in the nearby jungles. The Sandinistas found strength and recruits here in the city. Its citizens died in disproportionate numbers.

We continued on past a group of children playing soccer under the glare of a large mural of Carlos Fonseca. Native son and Sandinista movement founder, he stared down at them with blue-tinted sunglasses and an overgrown goatee. Red and black Sandinista banners hung from windows and car antennae all around.

Alejandro noticed a group of men clustered on a stairwell, five tough-looking guys in their early twenties clad in Billabong T-shirts and baseball hats cocked backward, the largest of the group in baggy camouflage shorts with a long chain draping from his front pocket. They pointed and stared, bored with their prospects on the Wednesday afternoon. A generation ago, they'd have been prime Sandinista recruits. To Alejandro's surprise, I summoned up my courage and high school Spanish, and headed toward them.

"*Perdon me,*" I said. "*Estoy escritando una libra de amor en Nicaragua. Quiro hablar contigo.*"

Puta. That word I recognized. I think I heard a *gringo* and a *madre* in there too. Alejandro stepped in, explaining in rapid-fire Spanish what I meant to say.

"They think you are writing a pornography or something," he explained.

Avener, Jasser, Pablo, Mario, and Carlo ranged in age from twenty-two to twenty-four. Three attended school; one trained to play soccer; the other drove a taxi. They were the sons of the revolution.

"Okay, they will talk with you," said Alejandro.

"*Gracias. Gracias.* First question. Very important. Do you prefer women to have their legs shaved or hairy?" I asked with a straight face.

For a few seconds, a few too many, they paused and stared, prompting me to eye the easiest escape route should they choose to attack. Then Mario started to chuckle, and the others followed suit. Alejandro, too. Shaved legs, they said, though Pablo confessed a preference for the old style, triggering a torrent of ridicule from his friends.

Of the five, three were married, each with a child and a preference for one more. *The planet is really embracing the whole two kids, one boy, one girl, thing.*

All had cheated, save one, and his friends weren't so sure. One got caught in the tryst. His wife left with their baby for a month, then returned. Angry, but back. All five stated *claro que sí* for support for women's rights, yet the three fathers expected their wives to raise their kids and handle the domestic chores. They would support the family, they said from the street corner. This was how their parents divided responsibilities. Did the wives and girlfriends get together for afternoons like this? Yes, they answered, then added, "With the kids."

"What's love to you?" I asked.

"An incomparable feeling," said Jasser. "When you're not in love, you can feel the difference."

"A really strong feeling," added Mario. "So strong you will give up your friends."

Kurt told them he was hungry, and we shifted the conversation to a restaurant a few blocks away. A television in the corner broadcast a New York Yankees game, and the gang watched with one eye. They asked questions about rent costs in America and Visa requirements, Kanye West and iPods, and women. Were things much different there? A "yes" crept to the tip of my tongue before I yanked it back in.

"No," I said. "Not really."

"Ortega," "Fonseca," "Sandinista," "revolution"—the words never found their way into our conversation without my prompting. When I did bring them up, the guys nodded their heads in silent assent, the way American schoolkids acknowledge the roles of Abraham Lincoln or Martin Luther King. Their clothes looked straight from Urban Outfitters, their attitudes from any U.S. street corner. It wasn't until the end of the evening that I learned Jasser had lost his father in the fighting.

"But I was too young to remember," he said. "You should come to my house for breakfast tomorrow and talk to my mother."

Like many small businesses in Nicaragua, the dimly lit store doubled as a home, with a commerce area in front and living quarters behind. Sonia ran both all day. Ample-figured mannequins modeled simple dresses and shirts, dust gathering on their shoulders. I didn't see a sign with the hours of operation. In the third world, stores are always open for a sale.

"Come in, come in," she said warmly as Jasser led us through the showroom to the adjoining dining area.

We plopped down at the table and helped ourselves to the mounds of eggs with cheese and stacks of homemade tortillas.

"She makes breakfast for all my friends," said Jasser.

"A world of thanks," said Kurt between bites.

Sonia, a widow twice, dreamed of marriage once more.

"Just somebody with nice feelings. Respectful. And affectionate."

Cariñoso. You heard that a lot. She didn't mention physical attributes until asked. You heard that, too.

"I like the eyes with the dark eyebrows. And tall, with a muscular build."

"Tell me about the men here," I said.

"The majority are hardworking. But they are also hard drinkers. And I'd say eighty percent cheat. The politics makes things worse. The men cheat more in an election year. They say they have to go to a political meeting."

"How about the women?" I asked.

"Now that women work, they feel they deserve the right to cheat. As the women gain equality, they cheat more, too. Equality means good and bad things."

Sonia reads American and Nicaraguan fashion magazines, though she doesn't think she's changed her tastes. Most of the time she prefers to read the Bible. She watches television during a rare free moment but hasn't yet learned how to navigate the computer in Jasser's room.

"They seem more liberal in America," she said, referring to TV shows and magazines. "But it is almost the same here now."

"Would you ever ask a man out?" I asked.

"Perhaps," she said, straightening up in her seat.

"Would you have done that twenty years ago?"

"No. And if I do it now, the man still has to pay."

"Even if you asked him out?"

"That's the way it is."

I heard the crack of thunder and looked outside to a storm moving in, always a storm moving in.

The roads around and out of Matagalpa were drenched in reminders of the upcoming presidential election. Daniel Ortega's campaign opted for billboards featuring his picture and multiple exclamation marks. *¡La Solución! ¡Nicaragua Triunfa!* Supporters of Eduardo Montealegre painted curbs and telephone poles with the red and white stripes of their party. The other candidates hustled to cover whatever space remained with their sym-

bols and slogans. The election cloaked the country in promises and divisions.

Yet when we talked to people about their love lives, rarely did they raise
the issue, even in political hotbeds like Matagalpa or León, even people who
fought in the wars. I realized that Sonia and her countrymen had done something amazing. They'd lifted love from the fray. Love not only survives in
Nicaragua, it is the most powerful force.

After talking with numerous Nicaraguans, I scolded myself for allowing
trivial matters like never-ending political debates to seep into my love life as
much as they had in the past. How silly I was to allow political labels to influence whom I dated. "Well, the politicians reflect my values," I rationalized in
the past. "And I want to be with someone who shares my values."

"Really?" I said now. "Lines drawn by politicians I'd never met, for no
other reason than to curry favor and win votes, somehow reflected a deep-
seated part of my psyche? People whose job it was to divide could somehow
help me unite? Free trade, fair trade, shade-grown, American-made, no nuke,
no Nike, pro-life, three strikes, yes drill but don't cut, smart growth, safe
streets, keep our (fill in the blank) clean. *¡Mierda de vaca!* If Nicaragua didn't
allow politicians to have any say in their love lives, why should I?"

I thought back to India, which has a history of tossing politicians from office and maintaining low divorce rates. Kurt and I were there after the ruling
party lost in a landslide. So India keeps its marriages and dumps its leaders,
while we dump our spouses and reelect our politicians. We've got the formula
backwards.

I may not have been able to define love, but I now knew it was the opposite of politics. Just ask Nicaragua.

We left the Sandinista home ground and drove to the beach, San Juan
del Sur, a Pacific Ocean fishing enclave near the Costa Rica border,
now home to a growing number of surfers and real estate developers. We'd
wandered all morning, watching kids play soccer on the sands of the shell-
shaped bay, pausing to help their fathers and tourists carry hauls of bonita
and yellowtail from the boats. Families operated *tiendas* and Internet cafés in
one- and two-story colonial buildings of dulled pink, washed-out green, and
rusted red iron roofs. Zapped from the walk and the sun, we rested for a few
minutes on a bench in the town square in the shade of the old church.

Perla sat on the adjoining bench, staring ahead and contemplating the day. When I nodded, she smiled the third world smile, covering her teeth with her lips so as not to show her metal fillings or gaps where incisors should be, the way a teenager with braces smiles. She wore flared white pants and an orange tank top that might have fit before but not now.

I asked if I could ask a few questions, and, like most Nicaraguans, she was happy to tell her love story, warts and all. Perla's former husband drank heavily, she confessed. He beat her when he had work. He struck her harder when he did not. The slaps and the shoves, she could stand those blows. It wasn't until he tried to molest her oldest daughter that Perla decided to fight back.

He's now in Costa Rica, and Perla raises the four girls on her own, cobbling rent and food money from the wages she earns in a dry goods store. If anyone has the right to repudiate the false hope of love, it's Perla. There are millions with her story.

But Perla still believes in love, she said. *¡Claro que sí!* As her bruises fade, she searches San Juan for passion and lasting partnership. That's why she sat on the bench alone today. Perhaps, she said. Her friend met a good man here in the square and suggested Perla do the same. Sure, Nicaraguan men are "irresponsible," and they "just get the woman pregnant, then they go to drinking." She waved off such thoughts, telling me, with a gesture toward the town, that there's a decent man out there. She knows it.

"I just want a responsible man who will work hard, be affectionate," she said, brightening at the thought of finding one. *Cariñoso.* "Looks are not as important as good feelings. Love means for a man to understand me. And no more of the bad things—drinking, cheating. Just love."

Perla excused herself to go back to her small shop.

"You'll find it, love," I said.

"I know. I just don't want to sit here too long. It's too hot."

The sun had now robbed our bench of afternoon shade, so we looked to move. That's when I heard the soft giggles behind. A clean-shaven young father kissed the belly of his infant baby boy, a roly-poly child with deep creases around his wrists and ankles. "Snap-ons," Kurt called them. Carlo was happy to share the bench and talk. He'd been married eleven years, and when his wife worked selling lottery tickets, he brought Randy to the park.

"I have taken care of both our kids," he said with pride. "And I like it. I cook and clean, too. We have good communication."

"That's pretty rare for here."

"*Sí,*" he said, going in for another kiss.

"How have the kids changed you?" I asked.

"Before I had children, I wasn't responsible. When you are by yourself, you don't care."

"Do your buddies tease you for being Mr. Mom?"

"They call me a *mantenido,* a kept man. I just smile. I want to have a girl now."

"Sounds like a great relationship."

"When I met my wife, I had never felt this way. I feel so happy next to her. I feel the change in my heart. This is where the feelings are," he said, pointing to his chest. "Love is for real. I believe it."

The sun continued its assault, and I decided to part with Kurt and Alejandro to enjoy an ocean swim on my own. Kurt took my backpack, and I headed toward shore. There was something about this country, that day, those two conversations, that resonated, and I wanted to savor them alone.

That's when it hit me. The conversation with Perla opened my eyes.

Love is the only belief on which the world agrees. Meters or feet, coffee or tea, Buddha or Allah, *fútbol* or football, cars on the left or right—our planet cannot come to a consensus on anything. Except love.

The world believes in love. Deeply. Ardently. With a shy smile and an instant nod, people around the globe say it exists in all of us. It can thrive. Sure, they have a hard time describing it, let alone capturing it, but it's there. They know it. From closed societies or Western worlds, in bodies wrinkled or smooth, with preferences for the opposite sex or the same, with pockets well stocked or barren, the world sings the same love song. The practices vary, but the passions remain identical.

Perla proved that. If anyone had a right to discount love, she did. She could have easily given up. The last time she opened her heart to a man, he attacked it with physical and emotional blows. Instead she gathered her strength and redoubled her faith.

I never expected to feel this inspired in Nicaragua. The name alone sparked images of guerrillas, torched villages, the Clash's *Sandinista,* Ollie North and "I am not a potted plant." Love? Never. Yet here I was, a teary-eyed believer walking out of a church after an unexpected Sunday sermon. If Brazil showed me love's openness, and India its ability to grow, Nicaragua proved love's resilience.

At the water, I peeled off my shirt. I was in.

Our new friend left us in San Juan del Sur. I was sad to see him go. Alejandro took two weeks off work, the remainder of his vacation time at Caltrans, shelled out for a last-minute plane ticket, kissed his wife and children good-bye, and convinced his parents to open up their house, all so he could show two American strangers his country. He typified the goodwill and kind hearts of his country, dropping everything just to make us feel welcome. If given the resources, most Nicaraguans would do the same.

In fact, most of the third world would follow suit. The best hosts on this planet are the ones with the least. The world is proud of their piece of land. They are eager to show you. More than anything, they are dying to connect, to feel relevant in the world of unilateral decisions and Western-dominated culture. As in any relationship, they want to be heard.

"All this talk about love has me fantasizing about my wife," said Alejandro.

"That poor woman," said Kurt.

"You should be president of this place, Alejandro," I said. "You have the country's biggest heart."

He drove back to Managua, while Kurt and I boarded the bus for Granada.

The two cities sit like old prizefighters in the boxing ring of Nicaragua— León in the west, Granada in the east. They are centers of power and pride, each with an avid fan base and a history of violence. León, the intellectual, has been the seat of liberalism since long before the Sandinistas. The yin to León's yang, Granada, on the northwest shore of Lake Nicaragua, is the conservative cosmopolitan, often adopting a personality of whatever León is not. In the middle, ringside, watches Managua, the clumsy and scarred giant. Managua is the compromise and, like all compromises, appears far from fulfilling. Forget Managua, urges half the populace. Go to León. Forget Managua, argues the other half. Go to Granada.

Though they are loath to admit it, Granada and León are more similar than not. They share the country's riches and opportunity, writers and idealists, cobblestone streets and colonial buildings, ex-pat dollars and Condé Nast mentions. They are the past strongholds and the future boomtowns. León brags about its progressiveness, then acts conservative, often following the lead of the church. Granada proclaims itself conservative, then embraces liberalities.

Kurt and I discovered this as we entered Asia Latina, a corner restaurant in one of Granada's many refurbished colonial buildings. The white walls and blue trim around the arched windows and front doorway give the establishment the feel of the national flag from the outside. It was another flag that caught our attention, a rainbow one shooting out from the entrance, a rifle cocked and pointed at the town.

The owner, Rafael, a wrinkle-free forty in a pressed linen shirt yet to sag in the humidity, stood in the doorway, encouraging tourists and countrymen to come in, give it a try.

"Do the locals know what it symbolizes?" I asked.

"Some do," he said, lighting a cigarette. "They talk about it in code. 'There's a place for you on Calle Libertad.' Women here are more hip to things like rainbow flags."

A taxi slowed in front long enough for the driver to yell, "Hello, sweetie!" As if he'd done so many a time before, Rafael blew him a kiss and invited us to join him at a window table for a mojito. He'd decorated the bar like a United Nations display case, with Indian tapestries and African wooden masks. A young Arab waiter in a maroon caftan took our order.

Rafael lived in New York during the Sandinista revolution, then moved back to Nicaragua in 1998 to be near his family in Masaya. "They weren't ready for me then." The government took a schizophrenic approach to homosexuality, criminalizing Nicas who "induced, promoted, propagandized or practiced sodomy in a scandalous way." Don't ask, don't tell. Rafael returned in 2004, choosing Granada as his entry point.

"I could have opened a restaurant in Masaya, but it would have been more difficult. I'd have to do something more for the locals. That's a problem here, too. I have a hard time attracting locals.

"I get gay and straight couples who come in here and kiss. It's the only place. If people aren't comfortable with it, then good-bye," he said, flicking his hand away.

"Is Nicaragua ready to come out?"

"It depends on the social class . . . and the personality. If you're poor, and you are feminine, you can see that everyone in the neighborhood accepts them. They may joke, but they tolerate them. They'll defend the gay person as their own. Problems come when the gay man moves to a new neighborhood."

Nicaragua is gay-curious, he said, claiming men frequently interrupt his days to ask about his lifestyle. Some touch him. Some want to experiment. With peeks and whispers, Nicaragua today stares in fascination at the gay lifestyle. Rafael doesn't complain about options.

"If you are a gay man here, you can have sex with anyone. Men flirt with me all the time. Guys here have a girlfriend or a wife and they meet someone who wants to have oral sex. It's okay. The *machistas* see it as no big deal. They don't consider it cheating. You don't have to go to a 'gay bar' to have gay sex."

"What's the best pickup?" I asked.

"You ask directions," he said. "To an obvious place everyone knows. If they want to have sex with you, they'll take you there. You buy them one drink and the rest is history."

"What if their friends caught on? This is a small place."

"If someone found out that a *machista* had sex with a gay guy, they wouldn't do much because they've all done it themselves. At the end of the evening, if you have sex with a young guy, the gay guy will pay the straight guy 'taxi money.' It ranges between fifty and a hundred *córdobas* [three to six U.S. dollars]. When they do it for real, two to three hundred *córdobas*.

"They talk about the money before. They say, 'Can you give me money for a taxi?' But then they all walk home. It's easier to pick up men here in Nicaragua than it is in the U.S."

"How about AIDS?" I asked.

"It's more and more talked about. They are getting better about awareness. The gays are better about using condoms. The *machistas* have kids. The problems are the older gringos who come here to look for young boys. We are becoming a little Thailand."

He rose from his chair when he saw the young man enter the bar. They embraced quickly, with Rafael giving him a peck on the cheek but receiving none in return. If Rafael had the nonchalant attitude of someone who'd been openly gay for a long time, his friend fidgeted like someone with a secret to hide. Kurt invited him to join us.

After a nod from Rafael, Umberto opened up about his situation. He didn't find the environment in Granada quite as friendly as Rafael did. He had to keep his homosexuality hidden from his parents, his work, and all but his closest friends. Asia Latina was an oasis of autonomy for him, but when he left its doors he was forced to put his true nature back in the closet.

"It is really hard here," he explained. "There's a lot of discrimination. They don't accept the tide of homosexuality. No famous Nicaraguan has ever come out. There are many famous gay politicians and famous people, but it's don't ask, don't tell. I had to break up with my last boyfriend because he thought he would be fired."

Umberto longs for the day when Nicaragua legalizes gay marriage and gay adoption. Until then he has an "arrangement" with a friend. She'll allow Umberto to impregnate her twice, and he'll get one of the children. "Preferably a daughter. But first I want a dream man, somebody nice, funny, charming. I like someone who has attention to detail. Looks don't matter, but I would prefer somebody tall with dark hair, and lots of it."

"Have you ever dated an American man?" I asked.

"*Sí,*" he said, smiling for the first time. "American men are so simple. The sex is different. Nicas are hot. They want to kiss and hug and more. My American was nice, an exception. But I prefer the Cubans."

"Are the men faithful here?"

"There is more cheating in gay relationships here. *Machista* doesn't stop with straight relationships."

From the air they looked like two splotches of green cookie dough on a baking pan of Caribbean blue. The plane ride lasted just twenty minutes from Bluefields, though the landing took us to a world far from the Nicaraguan mainland. The Corn Islands—Big Corn and Little Corn—a mix of creole and country music, idled lobstermen hoping for the crustaceans to return, Latino and mulatto and gringo, backpackers, and children, children, children.

It's also the most promiscuous place in the world.

The Corn Islands are the sexual equivalent of the perfect storm. Start with its original inhabitants, the Kukras Indians. They succumbed frequently to the power of the flesh. They were cannibals. Add randy French pirates in the seventeenth century, the kind featured on the Pirates of the Caribbean ride at Disneyland chasing maids and wenches around and around. Substitute the Kukras for the maids and wenches. British pirates commandeered the party a century later, bringing African slaves with them to spice up the mix. The British unshackled slaves in 1841, though they'd freed them for bedroom trysts the moment they landed on shore. Latino Nicaraguans crashed the gates late in the nineteenth century after realizing the festivities raged in their backyard. The Americans joined the festivities as fun-loving chaperones for the decades that followed.

Named for the shape of the land, not a product from it, the Corn Islands used to make their living on coconut and copra, lobster, and fish. Hurricane Joan came in 1988, killing island incomes overnight. Most hurricanes move north when they reach the Caribbean. Joan rumbled west, straight for the Corn Islands. She took her time, gaining strength and spreading fear as she advanced at a walking pace. Her first punches included 150-mile-an-hour winds that flattened every tree and structure on the islands. The residents somehow survived thanks to island caves and prayer. Her rains washed what remained out to sea, including a way of life.

What's left today are hastily reconstructed cinder block homes and one-star bungalow hotels, beach shack bartenders and snorkel boat captains, and bored schoolkids with dreams of finding cocaine shipments dumped overboard by Colombian drug runners who use the islands as a safe house. "White lobster," the locals call the catch. A bag will buy a plane ticket away. Anywhere away.

Undisturbed in Joan's wake is the island's most marked trait—sex. Sex survived. Sex thrived. Sex has always thrived in places like this.

The Corn Islands never had rules or role models. It's the pool hall where all the bad kids prefer to talk dirty and smoke cigarettes away from guardians. It's minuscule. You can walk around Big Corn in a couple of hours. Residents know the land so well they give directions using trees as landmarks. It's tropical and beautiful, with bowed coconut trees and arched beaches.

With no jobs and limited prospects, it's also bleak for locals. You're not going to go to college or score that internship at the local business. You're not going to marry your high school sweetheart and live happily ever after. You're going to live your life like your parents, whoever they are. You're going to do whatever you want to kill time and mark your turf. You're going to have sex. And lots of it.

I decided to brave the heat and walk the island for myself, stopping first at a small *tienda* for a bottle of water. The septuagenarian owner, with his weighted eyes and a stack of bills on his desk, looked like he'd never left the shop. A metal fan whirred at full speed, making no difference. As we talked, villagers sauntered in for smokes and batteries. They all knew Edward. An AIDS prevention billboard towered over the building. I asked him about his kids.

"Only twelve. Not too active. My brother has forty-two."

"As in four-two?"

"Forty-two!"

"Can he name them?"

"I think so. But he's getting old."

"And you?"

"Of course."

"How about the grandkids?"

Edward laughed from deep within. His heavyset young girlfriend, with feathered earrings and penciled eyebrows, emerged from a back room. She put her arm on his shoulder and asked who I was. Edward guessed her age as twenty-three, but he couldn't say for sure.

"No. But I help any that ask."

"Do you plan on having any more?"

"She can't," he said. "She wants to but cannot. I don't mind. I've never used a condom. No, never. I don't like. I have no inconvenience if I have a kid."

He told me he had children with five different girlfriends. "Four before my marriage and eight after."

"How about kids in wedlock?"

"Nope. We tried, but none ever appeared."

"That sounds hard to do."

"Marriage here don't stop having someone on the side. But they don't last long. We switch common."

That's an understatement. Spend a day on Corn Island talking to villagers and you quickly discover an intricate and overlapping network of bed partners and flings, half brothers and stepdaughters, shared mistresses, dirty old men. Kids who grew up in the sexual anarchy know not to speak of a friend's parent's dalliances for fear their parents may be involved as well. They watch and carry on the same. They hone the model, having sex at younger ages and with more partners.

Farther along my walk, I met Yorda as she stacked coconuts in her yard. A grandmother to several score, she had a short gray-and-white afro and sun-speckled cheeks. She birthed twelve children on Corn Island, nine with her husband, three prior to marriage. One died at birth and another didn't survive Hurricane Joan, she said, adjusting her thick glasses. Her remaining children all still live on the islands; as proof, several grandkids poked their heads out the door while we talked.

"They're here all the time," she said with a shrug. "Some just show up."

I asked her about love on the island, and she waved her hand. Sure, all men cheat. She didn't want to know. The problem with young Corn Island women today, she said, shaking a finger, is that they do.

"I always let mine go," she said. "But they don't want them to talk to anyone, to go anywhere. A man is a man."

"Did you worry about AIDS?" I asked. "Did you use protection?"

"I don't believe in condoms. I believe they create cancer. The way they use it, and when they are drunk they do anything. Having a condom makes a man do bad things."

Heading back to our hotel, I noticed the large block letters spray-painted on the side of an idled fishing boat. BIG BELLY. NO HUSBAND. SHAME ON YOU. The islanders all knew the story, a familiar one involving a father who refused to take responsibility for a newborn. The irate mother voiced her displeasure on several other vacant walls farther down the road.

Clobbered by the sun, I limped back to Casa Canada, a newer hotel constructed by a group of Canadian tradesmen. The partnership consisted of electricians, drywallers, accountants, and plumbers who flew to the island for several months to ply their trades on the new property. With the infinity pool filled and the bungalows furnished, they decided to throw a party at the complex's small patio restaurant to celebrate. Who better to honor than Mom.

"We had at least seventy-five people here for our Mother's Day brunch," said the manager. "The place was packed. You couldn't get a seat. Moms and kids everywhere. It was such a success we decided to do the same for Father's Day. We ordered all this food and waited for the crowds. They never came. We didn't sell one plate of food."

Baffled, the Canadians asked a few locals for an explanation.

"You've got to understand," opined a resident. "Father's Day on Corn Island is the most confusing day of the year."

The World's Top Five Relationship Gripes

(and five I had about Tracy after a date to a sushi restaurant and a return to Sẅork)

1. **COMMUNICATIONS**
2. **MONEY**
3. **INFIDELITY**
4. **LETHARGY**
5. **SOCCER**

Nicaragua convinced me that politics don't matter in a relationship, but these did:

1. **SHE DIDN'T FINISH HER DRINKS.** Tracy obviously didn't grow up Amish or in the household of Bob Wisner. At dinner, she ordered a beer, a large beer, and polished off the first three-quarters before we received our food. Then that poor Asahi remnant had to sit there through the edamame, miso soup, spicy tuna rolls, and green tea ice cream, begging to be rescued. As a not-too-subtle hint, I nudged the glass toward her when she turned to the waiter. Instead she ordered "a beer; large, please."

> "You sure you don't want to finish that one?"
> "Why? It's warm."

Note to self: Single mothers adopt the eating patterns of their children. Use smaller glasses with her, though nothing with cartoon characters or sippy cup tops to suggest you're on to her shtick.

2.   SHE CARRIED HER MONEY, ID, AND CREDIT CARD IN HER BACK POCKET. I mean, c'mon. That's just irresponsible. How could I ever take her to the Oriental Market in Managua or anywhere with pickpockets?

> "But you do the same," she said.
> "That's different. Mine's in a wallet."
> "Oh."

3.   PEOPLE RECOGNIZED HER. For a star, this is an inescapable annoyance. For a working actress, it's worse. For the significant other, it's hell. Invariably someone would approach our table and begin a conversation that went something like this:

> STRANGER: You look so familiar to me.
> TRACY: I live nearby.
> STRANGER: No, no. That's not it.
> TRACY: Maybe here?
> STRANGER: Your face.
> ME: She's an actress.
> STRANGER: Yes! Though I don't really watch too much television.

Note: Everybody in Los Angeles says they don't watch television. They watch television. The stranger lingers, trying to figure this one out. Tracy and I freeze, lattes in hand, not wanting to be rude by drinking in front of her. As a compromise, I blow on the foam.

> TRACY: *After the Fall,* at the Fountain?
> STRANGER: (*smiling, searching*) No.
> TRACY: *24?*
> STRANGER: No.
> TRACY: *Lost.*
> STRANGER: I don't watch *Lost.*

How could we be so stupid.

> TRACY: *Six Feet Under?*
> STRANGER: No.
> ME: *Ally McBeal, House, Shark, Cold Case,* or any of the 723 variations of *CSI?*
> STRANGER: I don't think it was one of . . . *Beverly Hills 90210!*

I may now proceed with my latte.

> STRANGER: Laura Kingman! You played Steve Sanders's girlfriend!
> TRACY: Yes.
> STRANGER: You accused him of date rape and organized a Take Back the
> Night rally.
> TRACY: He had it coming.

More latte.

> STRANGER: Wow. Laura Kingman. But he didn't touch you.

At this point I pick up my newspaper and turn to the sports pages while the woman chastises Tracy for wronging Steve Sanders.

4. HER USE OF COMMAS AND EXCLAMATION POINTS WHILE TALKING. Tracy paused during her sentences as if to gather her thoughts for the final push. She waited a beat before her answers. This left me believing she was both (a) ingenious and (b) stockpiling every inane utterance from my lips to be used against me at a future date and time. I concluded it must be some acting trick.

The exclamation points came fast and unexpected, usually around *Utne* issues or anything to do with kids.

"So I heard they're doing another *Mission: Impossible* movie," I'd say. "You know they shot the first one in Prague."

"Tom Cruise might be off on other things, but he's a hundred percent right about children being overmedicated," she'd respond. "They give kids vaccinations for chicken pox these days! Chicken pox!"

Wow. Where did that come from? I thought we were talking about Ethan Hunt.

5. THE BLOND HAIR. This made me a walking cliché. Until Tracy, I'd never dated a blonde, probably the only Californian since Hiram Johnson was governor who hadn't. Then I realized it was the blondes who had avoided me, and the whole thing didn't seem as unusual.

The Split

I can't do it," I told the restaurant bathroom mirror.

The veal?

"A relationship. Not now. It just wouldn't work. I'm going to the Czech Republic in a few days for the rest of the summer. How's a girlfriend going to fit into my backpack? She's not part of the plan."

Your honeymoon was all about discarding plans, about living by passion and feel. You've done that with all other parts of your life, yet here you're reverting back to your old self.

"I'm going to Prague. Why would I want to see someone when I can't even see her?"

Don't yell at me.

"Nothing against her. I just think a relationship is way too much for me right now. Especially a single mom."

Ah, the kid. So basically you're scared.

"If that's what you want to call it. Fine."

You're afraid of a mom and a four-year-old.

"Mortified."

You're scared they'll change your lifestyle. Or worse, they might change you.

"Don't be daft."

Show me how you're going to tell her.

"Tracy, I need to talk with you about something."

That sounds too much like an agenda.

"Tracy, I'm glad we're getting a chance to talk tonight."

Better. Are you going to sleep with her before you leave?

"No. That would complicate everything."

You want to. I want to.

"No, really I don't."

C'mon. A little?

"Why would I lie to you?"

You have before.

"Well, I've changed. The world has made me more honest. I'm rethinking this whole love thing."

So am I.

"Great. Maybe we'll agree someday."

We don't have a choice.

This was a prudent decision, I told myself as I sat back down for dinner at my favorite neighborhood restaurant in Los Angeles, Il Capriccio, with its mood-altering pastas and living room bonhomie, all accompanied with hugs from Mama and the waitstaff. Tracy had filled our wineglasses with pinot while I lingered in the bathroom. Even if I wanted to make the relationship work, it would be impossible to do so from afar. Why attach strings right now?

"The sole here is great," I said. "And the lamb rigatoni."

"I don't eat lamb."

"Right."

"You seem distracted tonight. Everything all right?"

"It's just this trip to Prague. I've been thinking . . ."

"I had an idea about that. I'm going to get a computer. Then I thought we could send each other a question of the day. Whatever you want."

"A quiz?"

"No, a conversation. A nice long chat on a deck at sunset with a big glass of wine. I have a list of things I want to ask. Cheers," she said, raising her glass.

"Like what?"

"I can't ask you now. That would ruin the surprise."

"C'mon. Just one."

"Okay. If your wife was pregnant, would you want to know the sex of the baby prior to birth?"

"Of course."

"Interesting. Why?"

"You'd want to know what color to paint the room. Or things like clothes and such."

"Babies kind of wear the same stuff that first year."

"Did you know Calvin's sex?"

"No. There are so few real surprises in life. This is the best one."

Why did she say "is" instead of "was"?

I looked at her and saw a smile, that smile, a well from deep within, making its way to every crease and corner of the face, a look felt more than seen. That smile ruined everything.

Is she smiling at you or the thought of Calvin in her arms for the first time?

"Let's have more wine," she said.

Which we did, the details of my breakup spiel becoming hazier with each glass. Was it the "timing's not right" angle or the "not right for each other" approach? By the end of the meal I couldn't remember. *Just as well. Why ruin a good dinner. You can mention something on the way home.*

Playful, suggestive, she kissed me on the lower lip when I dropped her off, letting her mouth linger for an extra few seconds. "Wow," I whispered without realizing it. Pulling her close, I devoured everything she offered. She grabbed the back of my head in return, lightly scratching my scalp as if to wake up the contents inside. She tasted like apricots, sweet soft apricots at that exact moment when they're at their summer best. If she hadn't said anything, I would have kissed her all night and never noticed the time.

"Come inside," she said. "Calvin's going to sleep with Libby in the bedroom downstairs."

"How about Pluto?"

"He's down there, too."

We didn't bother with the lights. She strode backward as I kissed her more, never allowing our lips to part, both of us fumbling to remove clothing while trying not to crash into the furniture. I kissed her again on the couch, and looked down at the most sensual body I'd ever seen, ivory and warm. I set aside "the talk" for another day.

You are the wrong woman at the wrong time on the wrong side of the world.

I slept deeply, content and inveigled. At one point I rolled over, wrapped her body in mine, and drifted back into slumber, smiling at the realization I'd never been able to do that before. Tracy felt comfortable, and right. I'd never known that sleep. Down, lovely, further down.

"Mom!" came the blast at first light. *"Mom!"*

The smash of the bedroom door triggered an immediate spasm that sent me diving under her comforter, a soldier in the wee hours ducking for cover in an air strike. Tracy grabbed her bathrobe in equally quick fashion.

"Calvin," she said. "You're up early. Where's Libby?"

"She didn't want to get up."

"Great. May I make you some breakfast?" she said, turning his small shoulders away from the large mound in the middle of her bed.

Too scared to come out, I stretched out under the covers and somehow returned to sleep. It felt like an extra few hours, but apparently not.

"What time is it?" I said, ambling into her kitchen.

"Seven. I let you sleep in."

"Seven is sleeping in, huh?"

"In our house it is," she said, nodding to Calvin at the breakfast table.

He played with a muscled action figure that looked like he'd just finished a Tae Bo workout at a Hollywood Hills gym. I poured a cup of coffee and sat down beside him.

"What's your guy's name?"

"Chad."

"He's pretty buffed."

"You wanna make a fort?"

"Sure. Just let me finish this cup of coffee and wake up."

"Chad's got a lot of friends."

"All the bodybuilders do."

"Calvin, finish your waffle. You want one?"

"Thanks. I didn't finish my dinner last night for some reason."

She smiled. That same smile. That smile is even better in the morning. Calvin positioned Chad on the windowsill and ignored his breakfast.

"Here, you can play with this guy," he said, handing me a Jesus doll.

"Jesus!"

"I know."

"Do you believe in Jesus?"

"Yes."

"That's pretty advanced for a . . ."

"I believe in all my action figures—Spider-Man, Hulk, SpongeBob."

Tracy handed me the waffle—buttered, syruped, cut into dozens of dime-sized pieces. Calvin ran off to the living room. I paused and stared at the plate.

"Oh, sorry," she said. "Habit."

"Hey," I said, leaning in and lowering my voice. "Out of curiosity, what did you tell him about last night? I mean, not about last night. About what I'm doing here."

"I told him I was having a sleepover."

"Oh. Of course."

"With kids, the simplest approach is usually the most effective."

"Men, too."

"Do you mind if I take a shower?"

"Go ahead."

She sauntered off, leaving the Tipton Way fort engineering project to a man who had a hard time rearranging the four pillows on her bed that morning in their preset order. My initial attempt, a pyramid of sofa pillows, flopped like a first-time soufflé. Calvin suggested a structure with the kitchen table and his bunk bed as the base, but I thought his mom might not approve. I countered with a sure-fire solution, the teepee. He cheered the idea, pushing for multiple blankets and enough sheets to cover half the room. The end result looked like a yurt after a tornado. Calvin skipped around the structure while I poured more coffee and sat on the sofa to admire the effort.

"Great job," said Tracy, emerging from the bathroom.

With that, he started to sob hysterically.

"It's okay, Calvin. What's the matter?"

"This guy ruined my fort," he said, pointing at me.

"No, no. You did a great job on this."

His cries doubled. Tracy knelt beside him.

"Sweetheart, what's the matter?"

"That!" he said, pointing to the sofa cushion upon which I rested my bom-bom.

"You wanted to use that pillow to make this fort?" she said sweetly.

"Yes! He ruined it!"

"I'm sure he didn't mean it, Calvin."

"I, uh, think I'm going to take a shower now that you're done," I said.

I turned on the water to drown the commotion from the other room.

Remember, he's four. And a Christian.

Dexterity

In theory, the stack of books on the plane ride to Prague was supposed to help take my mind off Tracy. Midway through the first one, I found the opposite to be true. Milan Kundera's bowler-topped sex scenes in *The Unbearable Lightness of Being* made me question what I'd done, especially as I perused the exploits of Franz, a weak-minded academic who left his lover to travel and died in Cambodia. "A return after long wanderings," read his gravestone. Philip Roth's *Prague Orgy* wasn't much better.

This was my fourth trip to the Czech Republic, and each time I stayed with my former Little League teammate Jonathan Terra (Bears, 1974), a steadfast and lovable friend, Eastern European scholar, and world-class procrastinator. Over the years, we'd bonded over pinball, discus, the English Beat and the San Francisco 49ers, turkey steaks, International Relations 101, foreign girlfriends, and debates over minutiae until 1 A.M. He'd cropped his gray-specked hair recently and shifted to dark-framed Italian eyewear. Jonathan had the biggest calves I'd ever seen.

Armed with a few degrees and dollars, he came to Prague as a student in the mid-1990s and, like so many others, stayed. You could rent a two-bedroom apartment in a cubist building back then for one hundred dollars a month. Sure, the food was bland and fried. You didn't come for the food. The government fixed the price of the luscious pilsner at five cents a bottle, fearful of uprisings should they be a smidgen more. Prague was a never-ending stroll through history and nature, art and religion, architectural highs and undiluted Central European flavor. Never did you say, "Imagine what it used to be like." In Prague, it was.

Its denizens, more than the buildings, made it special. They embraced like no other. They opened their doors and welcomed the world to come and explore. Stay. Revel. We ain't seen nothing like this, said the initial guests. So pure, so laden, so rare. This was mainlining for the traveler, a true and unique experience in a world with all too few. "May I practice my English?" still meant "May I practice my English?"

Between trips back to the Czech Republic, the party's atmosphere changed. I noticed little things at first. They sold Corona in the bars and knockoff Nike T-shirts on the streets. ATMs cropped up, and the blue jeans traders faded away. Then the Western hotels began to open their doors, and the chain restaurants edged their way in, denting the landscape. Even the faces began to change. Women plastered on makeup advertised in the Western fashion magazines, and Czechs headed to the tanning salons, changing their shades from Central European gray-pink to rusty orange. Don't worry, the hosts said. We've done some redecorating, but the celebration is still going strong.

On my last visit, a few years earlier, I felt something larger had changed. Attitudes. Both traveler and tenant. They'd lost their innocence and gained an edge. Czechs tired of the endless stream of exploitive ex-pats and British bachelor parties that marched around Prague with their plastic cups and ribald T-shirts. I'M ONLY TWO GIRLS SHORT OF A THREESOME. Bars and restaurants now hung placards that read NO STAG PARTIES. Foreigners griped that Czechs became steely and cliquish, more than they already were, smiling only when they wanted a favor. Morning came and the party ended. The ex-pats and the locals rolled over in bed, took a look at each other, and both complained of being used. It's your fault, they said. Prague now seemed like so many others.

I recognized the familiar voice above the din at the airport exit and turned to see my friend.

"Wiz bud to extreme," sang Jonathan, taking license with the lyrics to the song "Whisper to a Scream." "Wiz bud to extreeeeeme!"

He lifted me in the air with an exaggerated bear hug.

"Hey, man," I said. "How you doing? More important, how are the calves?"

"Looking good. Check this out," he said, setting me down and pulling his pant legs up to his knees with difficulty.

An Asian family stopped to stare.

"Impressive."

When I'd told him about my world love mission idea months earlier, Jonathan urged me to include the Czech Republic in my journeys, offering to help translate interviews and rent me a room in his flat for six weeks. He hadn't changed a sliver since the last time I'd seen him. Catching my breath from his embrace, I picked up my backpack and threw it in the back of his girlfriend's rental car. I was excited to tell him about Tracy.

"So how are you and Iveta doing?" I asked as we sped through traffic.

"We're breaking up."

"No. I'm sorry. What happened?"

"Long story, Wiz. I'll tell you later."

"Anything serious?"

"No. We'll still be friends."

"Are you still living together?"

"She's going to buy a flat here soon. Her dad's going to help her with a fixer."

"Dude, maybe I should make other arrangements."

"It's fine. You'll help things. Give us something else to talk about."

Jonathan and Iveta met at a university reception five years prior. She worked at DHL and spent weekends with her parents in the countryside. I liked her accent and demure smile and had thought since I met her that they'd marry. Jonathan assured me they still cared for each other, that everything was civil.

Iveta greeted me with a large hug at the door, more American than Czech. She'd cut her copper-tinged hair above her shoulders and seemed her serene and affable self. Missing from past visits were Jonathan and Iveta's hallway cuddles and taps on the derriere when one of them reached into the refrigerator. At a minimum, my presence stifled conversations that should have been taking place. "It's fine, Wiz. Really." The only thing worse than walking in on a couple having sex, I concluded, is walking in on a couple that no longer does.

"You mind if I check my e-mail?" I asked.

"Go ahead. My laptop's in your room."

Franz—

Okay, here's the first one. Would you rather have a long life with very few friends and lovers? Life rather predictable without much excitement. No great sadness but no great happiness. Or a short life adored by many? Shot down in your prime but having a blast.

For bonus points you can tell me what you think happens to our souls (if you believe we have one) after we die.

Love,
Tracy

Love? Okay, yes, the term is overused, especially in Los Angeles. "Oh, I love their cranberry martinis." But her four letters seemed calculated ones, not a throwaway line. She saw my "yours" and upped the ante. I couldn't care less about the questions and the souls and stuff. I mean, I cared, but I didn't focus on it then.

Love, Tracy? She didn't mean it, did she?

I took a class in college where the professor argued that movies had hidden messages about the era in which they were made. So if you were watching Dustin Hoffman rebuff the charms of Anne Bancroft in *The Graduate,* you were also witnessing a Vietnam War protest. Did relationships act the same? What did her words really mean? He didn't cover that in class.

Bonjour—

Dating, huh? OK. Do I get a title or something?

Now, you went easy on me with the first question. Thanks. You know I'd take the firecracker approach rather than a Prozac existence. The big guy gave us a powerful sports car. Let's take it for a drive! And give rides to as many people as possible.

Here's one for you. Name me three things in life you think are overrated. They can be simple or deep. Up to you.

As for the soul question, I think I need more wine.

Besos grandes,
Franz

Bonjour? "Easy" questions? Could I have been more pompous? Jonathan's computer didn't have an instant retrieve function; otherwise I would have withdrawn that one immediately. I did like the question exchange, though, and was curious what we'd learn.

Wiz, you want to walk around town a bit?" asked Jonathan.

"Sure. I'd like to get a cell phone. With a card so I can call America."

He kissed Iveta on the cheek and told her we'd be back late. I made a mental note to spend as much time as possible out of the apartment. Jonathan handed me a batch of tickets, and we rumbled down from his neighborhood on the hill, across the Vltava, and to the historical pulse point of town, Wenceslas Square. The good king looked ever so regal that afternoon, cast in bronze, astride his steed, flag in hand.

"Just what did Wenceslas do to be known as the Good King?" I asked.

"He got killed by his brother, Boleslav the Cruel. Then again, when your name's 'the Cruel,' you tend to do stuff like that. But Boleslav had a bit of slayer's remorse, and he ordered his brother be buried at St. Vitus Church. Bad move. This encouraged mourners to come to church and reflect on Wenceslas's goodness and Boleslav's cruelty. He goes from martyr to saint overnight. Centuries later, a British clergyman paired the story to a traditional Scandinavian carol and voilà, Good King Wenceslas."

Jonathan was great for these historical tidbits, though you had to be careful or they'd tumble into tangents and consume the entire day.

"You know it used to be a horse market," he continued.

"Cell phone?" I asked.

He steered me to a company called Oskar, with happy red keypad character mascots and long lines. Jonathan negotiated the terms before the saleswoman interrupted.

"Do you want a sixty-nine?" she said, straight-faced.

"Excuse me?"

"For your phone number. Do you want a six and a nine?"

"No thanks," I said. "How much would that cost?"

"A hundred and twenty dollars. Extra."

"Is that a popular thing to do these days?"

"Most of the young people insist on the sixty-nine."

                                    *   *   *

Still one of the planet's premier walking cities, Prague stretched out that afternoon in the patchwork Middle European sun. We ambled down cobblestoned streets stained dark with history, from the march of the Good King to the Prague Spring and the fall of the Iron Curtain, all giving way to the current victor of history, commerce. Over a footbridge to Slav Island, we found an outdoor café and ordered a few pilsners. A young couple, each with greasy hair and a cell phone, sat nearby, holding hands with one and texting with the other.

"Sorry about Iveta," I said.

"It's okay."

"Your decision or hers?"

"Both. We just kinda ran our course. The environment here is brutal on relationships."

"How so?"

"Czechs have been raised to be secretive, stoic, to keep their emotions and everything else hidden. Open your mouth in the Communist era and you could find yourself in jail. The Wall's down, but the mentalities are in full force. The result is chaos, all these affairs and double lives, and Czechs are taught to keep quiet and deal with it."

"That seemed like a constant in the books I browsed on the way over—chaos."

"Very true. Kafka, Havel, Hašek, Kundera—they all write about characters who overcome the insanity."

"You think it's the same with love here?"

"Absolutely. If you want a relationship to survive here, you better be pretty damn creative."

The text messagers set down their phones long enough to kiss.

"Speaking of insanity," continued Jonathan, "how's your love life?"

"Good, actually. Or I think. Bit chaotic. I started seeing a single-mom-slash-hippie-actress."

"Wow. That's a change from your past. No more Stepford women, huh? Can you handle that?"

"I don't know."

"She sounds polar opposite from anyone you've ever dated."

"Oh, yeah. I'm discovering that more and more. We're going to do an e-mail exchange, ask questions each day while I'm over here."

"You ever hear from Annie or find out if she minded having a book written about your nonwedding?"

"No. Not since Kurt and I ran into her during the honeymoon. We still have one mutual friend who says she's fine with everything, just doesn't want anything to do with it."

"She did you a huge favor."

"I think so."

Jonathan's cell phone buzzed in his pocket. He fished it out and rambled in fluent Czech.

"Good news," he said when he hung up. "I made arrangements for us to go talk to an expert on women. We're going to meet him at a club."

The nightclub pulsed on the ground floor of a five-story Renaissance building spared ruin from the Nazi air bombers and destruction from the Soviet architects. By the time we arrived, the central focus had evolved from freedom rallies to a belching contest. That evening I discovered women's equality in the former Iron Curtain nation has taken a giant leap forward, at least when it comes to chugging beer and forcing gas up from your diaphragm. They put the men to shame.

Americans spent billions of dollars in a crazy cold war arms race while Czechs sacrificed their liberties and their lives fighting the devastating forces of Soviet control just for the right to stage a belching contest?

"There's Robert," said Jonathan, waving to a clean-cut man in a light blue polo shirt, collar turned up. "You recognize him?"

"No. Should I?"

"He's one of the Czech Republic's biggest porn stars. So to speak."

"How do you know this guy?"

"I met him at a porn convention last year."

"Porn convention?"

"I was doing a story for *Czech Esquire.*"

Robert motioned for us to join him at his corner table, pointing to the chairs as he chatted on the phone.

"He's had sex with more than three thousand women," said Jonathan.

"Wilt Chamberlain can rest assured. His record's still intact."

What do you say to a man who's had sex with a village?

"Hello," I said, shaking his hand and hoping he'd washed it. "Did you come from work?"

Did you come from work?

"Yes. This was a busy day. We are shooting all day."

Robert slipped his phone back into his pocket and didn't hesitate when I asked about his line of work.

"So where'd you get your first big break?"

"McDonald's," he said. "I was the best employee there two times."

I didn't remember seeing his specialty on the menu last time I purchased a Big Mac.

"But then I was at this club, Radost."

"I know Radost. Been around forever."

"This is the one. A photographer he sees me there go-go dancing and he says he would like me for a gay porno movie. I told him that I do not like the man's body. If this is the women, then I am fine. I do it. I bring my girlfriend to the audition. She helps me get the job."

The rest is XXX history. Today Robert's face and nether regions are plastered across the Internet and on movies produced on the cheap. Thanks to low labor costs, a plethora of talent, and the country's permissiveness, the Czech Republic has thrust itself onto the world pornography stage. The business of booming is booming.

Robert rubbed a kink out of his neck and told me he had sex several times a day, "except Sunday. And no Viagra. Czech women know how to have sex better than any other women on the planet," he said. "They are more open than women from other cultures."

When you're a porn star, every comment is a double entendre.

Affable, athletic, almost preppy except for the sweet cologne, and without a shred of hesitation to talk about sex and his business, Robert used his real name onstage and shook his head at porn stars who paraded as if they worked in another line of business. Bar patrons waved and nodded as he reclined on the couch.

"Czechs like to joke, love to flirt. Heavy flirting is part of the game. Very little is off-limits. And sexual harassment is not an issue.

"All countries have beautiful women, but Czech women have the minds for sex. Slovakians aren't as good because they are more conservative. The

Germans are too rigid. Good sex has more to do with attitudes than fig-ures."

"What about the Americans?" I asked.

"Americans are okay. Very professional and talented."

So we have that going for us.

"See that lady over there, she wants to be in my movies," he said, pointing to a goth-looking woman on the other side of the bar. "Those guys there, too."

"Do you do job interviews?" I asked.

"Audition parties. Every Sunday. You should come and give it a try."

"Thanks, but I've just started seeing someone. I don't think she'd go for the porn star thing."

It's difficult to chitchat with anyone who buys condoms by the crate. Your stories tend to pale in comparison. Despite his line of work, I liked Robert. Above all, he was honest. He voiced his opinions to all who would listen. Sex is what we live for, opined the porn star. According to Robert, people shuffled off to crummy jobs, then spent their earnings on overpriced drinks and over-styled clothes just to have a shot at sex. They should reverse the order. Make sex the basis of their relationship rather than the offshoot.

As we talked, Robert repeatedly touched a whey-haired Slovakian girl sit-ting at the next table over, pinching her thighs and at one point even grabbing her foot and attempting to suck her toe. He blew out her matches as she tried to light a cigarette, then lit it for her.

"I love women," he said with a smile as she jerked her foot away.

Bibiana, the pinchee, shrugged off the whole affair as "typical of Czech men. They behave this way all the time."

Months later I heard Robert lost the country club look by shaving his hair and adding a Maori face tattoo to his ensemble. The makeover didn't scare the Czech Health Ministry away from questioning him about a syphilis outbreak in the local porn industry. Robert swore the tests were false positives and started posting his own results on his Web site.

Not to be stopped, he ignited an imbroglio by attempting to shoot a XXX film at the site of a former concentration camp.

"I don't know why the people of Terezin are so mad about it," he said in an interview with the Associated Press. "We went to Auschwitz, too, and the people there seemed much more helpful."

Franz—

I've thought about your question and this is what came to mind—your twenties. A time to live it up, be carefree, and just have fun. It's never like that for anyone. At least none of the women I know. You have no career, no home, no family (except the one you desperately want to disassociate from) and you drink too much, trying to find your way, and floundering at every step. I'm much happier in my thirties, although I would like my twenty-year-old body back.

Also, designer clothes. Somehow designers and magazines have convinced people (mainly women) to buy ugly clothes for far too much money.

This I say blushing . . . a really big penis. All men seem to want one. Most women find them inconvenient. I'm still blushing. I've got an easy one for you.

What do you find most appealing—a sexy body, intellect, a good sense of humor, goodness, optimism? Be very careful, your answer says a lot.

My best,
Tracy

P.S. Calvin just sprayed the dog with water and laughed. Should I be worried?

First of all, no, I didn't take the penis stuff as a slight. She wasn't talking about me. Really, she wasn't. That part of the e-mail had me laughing. But "My best?" I didn't mind the penis comments. I just didn't see how you could write them and sign off like that. This is exactly what I wanted to avoid.

Tracy—

I'll place intelligence in the overrated category. Important, but overrated. The decisions for New Coke, Esperanto, and Ishtar were "intelligent" ones. Ample data and much study said none could fail—except they all did.

So my vote is for goodness, for goodness sake, because from a pure heart the others will follow. A kind and decent soul makes the spirit more optimistic, the wit well honed, the body much more sexy. And, by the way, if your wish is granted, and you do end up exchanging for your twenty-year-old figure, please forward the current version to me.

Here's an easy one for you—what's your favorite ice cream and why?

Cheers,
Franz

In the morning, I told Jonathan I'd like to speak to the older, non-porn-star generation. I was curious about love before and after the Wall. He arranged for me to meet Jitka, a magazine editor who arrived with oversized sunglasses and a large handbag packed with papers. We drank orange juice in front of an old hotel.

"You know the number-one reason why people got married back then?" she asked, meaning under Communism.

"Love?"

"For the apartment. In the seventies and eighties, it was impossible to live alone. Any singles who wanted an apartment were told by the government they needed to get married. This was a big reason why people got married—they wanted their own space."

Indeed, marriage rates outpaced housing starts for much of the Communist era. Many singles didn't bother placing their names on waiting lists for apartments, knowing the government wouldn't even consider their application. Migration to the cities exacerbated the problem. Rural Czechs who owned land had a difficult time rustling up labor, materials, and machinery to build dwellings themselves. Each time the housing market tightened, the push to wed grew.

During the Communist era, Czechs applied for the best schools, looked for jobs with the least amount of government interference, pursued passion on the side, and, most important, looked to get married as soon as possible, she explained.

Now, choosing a partner for marriage was a balancing act. Money was less of an issue then, with the government confiscating assets and opportunity. Physical attraction and sexual compatibility were important, though many Czech men and women planned to continue their third-party trysts unimpeded by something as trivial as a marriage license.

Plus, "during Communism, you had to be careful with whom you con-versed," continued Jitka. "Some students were narcs, government spies. In a class of thirty, one to three would be narcs. They were easy to spot. Their par-ents were usually Party officials. Nobody dated the narcs. They dated them-selves. They didn't get a lot of action. After the revolution, they changed their overcoats, as we say."

So you married someone from your hometown or village, a person you could trust to the degree you wished. You married Czechs most likely to be good parents or well-received in-laws. You married safe.

Then you cheated.

"That seems like a big theme here," I said.

"There are too many possibilities," said Jitka. "And a lack of traditional values. The church is weak here. Cheating is a habit ingrained. People had two faces during Communism. Children were confused by this. They saw their parents complain at home and smile outside."

Then the Wall came down.

"At first everyone went to Spain to pick oranges," she said. "Then they came back and looked for jobs here.

"Women began to form a lot of loose alliances. And we got picky. Before, the plan was simple—you married someone from your town. Now you had a whole smorgasbord from which to choose."

When they returned home from the Spanish orchards, the Czechs found a force as threatening and omnipresent as Soviet tanks—the American bohemi-ans. All hail the YAPs, the Young Americans in Prague.

I put them in several subcategories. There were the firecrackers, the ones who rushed over, consumed every cheap drug available, dated nineteen-year-old girls until they realized it wasn't a lot of fun to spend every waking mo-ment with someone who spoke a different language, gave up on their novel or Internet start-up, flamed out within a year, and went back to Greenwich and grad school. The Presto Logs did what they could to blend in, learning the language, finding a job, moving in with their Czech girlfriends or boyfriends and sometimes marrying them. Still they stood out, burning in false oranges and blues amid Czech flames of amber and hazel. Then there were the pilot lights, the transplant bohemians who lowered their grandiose plans with each pilsner, abandoned careers in favor of teaching gigs to cover rent and the weekend trips to Karlovy Vary, and crafted a long-term existence with the least possible exertion.

Of course, this sounded idyllic to me when I first ventured to Prague at the age of twenty-five. I'd see these YAPs strolling around town with their six-foot-tall Czech girlfriends, *Prague Posts* under their arms, walking hurriedly to meet fellow ex-pats. But each time I returned, the appeal waned. I'd see the same YAPs with younger girlfriends, hanging out at the Globe Café amid the racks of American fashion magazines and paperbacks. The party dimmed steadily as Czech ties with the rest of the world grew. Once the Czechs learned English, they realized the YAP conversations weren't any more interesting than their own.

Two paradigm shifts shook the love and dating scene in the 1990s, according to Glen, an American friend of Jonathan's from the first wave who opened a favored ex-pat hangout, Jo's Bar. We met him for dinner later that evening.

"One, the emergence of women's magazines in the mid-nineties," he said. "This filled the heads of innocent Czech women with all the garbage of the West. The other is the emergence of leasing, mortgages, loans. This made people overextended, more addicted to spending. It also made people show up in ties and suits. The Czech Republic had to get serious overnight."

Not so fast, said dozens of Czech women I interviewed during the rest of the trip. We were sheltered by Communism but never as innocent as the ex-pats believed. The foreigners were a welcome break from the gruffness of old-school Czech men. They opened doors. They paid for dinners. It was as easy as saying, "I want to show you a romantic restaurant." They listened, or at least faked it better than the Czech men. Relationships with Westerners went hand in hand with the collapse of the Berlin Wall and the explosion of individual freedoms. We dated them because we could. We flirted. We used them more than they used us. In the end we went back to our own.

> *Franz—*
> *I guess I must now fess up my feelings about ice cream. I have to say it's my favorite dessert. That and dark chocolate. I like it so much I'm not sure I can express love for just one flavor. So, if I may, I'll list three tried and true. The ones I ate when I was ten. First is rocky road. I loved the*

*marshmallows and nuts. Second is mint chocolate chip. I loved the color.
And third is pralines and cream. I felt very grown-up ordering that.
Always in a cup like an adult.*

*Now I have a pretty easy one for you. It can be answered with a yes or
no. But please elaborate if you can.*

*Do you like to dance? Not alone (white man–overbite style), but with
a partner. If not, would you consider learning? Swing, tango, waltz, or just
hugging tightly and swaying to sappy music? I guess that last one you
really wouldn't have to learn. But we can practice anyway.*

Write back soon. I love getting your e-mails.

Tracy

She "loved" getting my e-mails. She "loved" rocky road. She must have loved
messing with my mind as well.

Tracy—

*I was in Buenos Aires a couple of years ago. Late one night, I went to
this locals' bar in San Telmo. I sat next to an elderly couple; he wore a suit
and fedora, she was dressed to the nines. The band started up again, and
the couple hit the floor with this slow but elegant tango, a dance they'd
obviously performed for decades. Beautiful. So loving. The guy came back
and sat by me. I bought him a drink and asked him his secret. Without
pause, he told me: "Choose wisely. Because in tango, you should only have
one partner for life."*

*I guess I'm in the dancing DMZ, a middle ground. I like it, but I don't
do it much. If it's a loud disco, my preference is to pass. Around the world,
the discos all look the same, sound the same, smell the same. With a
forgiving/willing/strong-toed partner, I'm in. So if you see Richard
Simmons around town, please let him know I'll be back soon.*

*Okay, now one for you. What's a common moment in life you dread?
Nothing heartbreaking or extraordinary, just something in everyday life
you don't like to do or experience.*

Su perro vagabundo,
Franz

I had no idea what love was, but if it required sacrifice and an open mind, dancing must have been my lamb to the volcano.

I read another e-mail later in the day, this one from Vivian. She had a week-long break and wanted to join me in Prague. But she sent the note to an old e-mail account, one I didn't access regularly. By the time I saw it, she'd made other plans.

Jitka talked about women, but what about the guys? Where were they during this massive transformation? Every aspect of Czech society went through radical changes in the final decade of the twentieth century—new borders and clothes and freedoms, technology centers on old farmland, haute cuisine alongside the dumplings and pork. For every physical change, the ones in attitude stacked higher. Václav Havel ushered in a new era of openness and humanity; writers and filmmakers voiced expressions long repressed; women stepped out from the shadows.

The only glaring exception seemed to be the common man. It's as if he and his friends watched the entire Velvet Revolution from a perch close enough to see all and far away enough to avoid it. Ask a woman from any part of the country if she and her friends have changed since the fall of the Wall and you'll hear a litany of proof. Ask a guy if he's changed much over the last decade and he'll tell you he was fine to begin with.

Jonathan made arrangements for me to meet a man who'd experienced the changes from a different perspective. Karol invited us up to his third-floor apartment and served tea in his grandparents' china. His excitable bichon frise yipped each time I tried to sip my Earl Grey, causing me to rattle my glass and think about Pluto. Jonathan translated after Karol apologized for his poor English.

"Guess my age," he said while adjusting the crease of his dark blue linen pants.

"Forty."

"Fifty-two!"

Dancing and now choreographing kept him young, he boasted. That, and being gay.

"Why do gay men look younger than us straight guys?"

"We take more care. We don't sit around."

"This must have been tough, in the old Czechoslovakia, being gay."

"Not as much as you'd think. There were secret meeting places, like the Hotel Europa. You felt comforted, empowered, as you sipped coffee with other gay men."

"How could you tell?"

"Everybody knew. They knew more back then. Except the women. The police knew. The narcs, too. They kept records. They tracked the community like a mafia, compiling secrets to be used later. I had a policeman come up to me at a wedding, someone I'd never met. 'Hello, Karol,' he said."

"So if you couldn't be with men in public, what did you do?"

"We got married. Just like everyone else. We married young. Then had affairs."

"What happened if you got caught?"

"Czechs are good at this." He meant cheating. "But sometimes they sent us to hospitals or asylums. Mostly they held the secret over your head and waited until they needed something."

"You must have been pretty ecstatic when the Wall fell," I said.

"Of course. But for all the talk of openness, there's still not enough. Czechs still don't understand homosexuality. They still talk about it as a disease that can be cured with a pill. The discrimination now is more subtle. Just a comment or two. Things like 'Look at Karol.' "

So Karol and his comrades advance gay rights at a different pace and style. They don't hold as many gay pride parades or public civil union celebrations. They don't organize as many protest rallies for additional AIDS funding, or, as the Communists called it, the "American disease." The focus here is more basic—education, understanding, existence.

"On the plus side, you don't get a lot of gay bashing or hate crimes or anti-gay ordinances," added Jonathan. Karol nodded his head to agree. "The Czechs are far less judgmental . . . unless you're a Gypsy." Again Karol nodded.

The clubs—that's where the homosexual community can meet and relax. A handful of gay discos in Prague offer shelter to regulars and lure gay men and women from the countryside.

"Join us tonight if you wish," he said before interrupting our conversation to take a call from his mother.

She and his three brothers live nearby. None of them know he's gay.

Franz—

*If we are talking about common everyday details in life, I'd have to
say fixing dinner. I don't seem to balance my life in such a way that I
have the energy to fix dinner. By the time six o'clock comes around,
I usually want to collapse. The last thing I want to do is plan dinner.
I blame my parents for that one. They both owned restaurants in which
we ate every night.*

*The other problem is I can't accept this flaw in myself, because I
believe a home-cooked meal is very important. I want Calvin to grow up
with healthy meals and everyone sitting at the table together to eat them.
It's something I'm working on. I must admit, if I were very rich, I'd have a
cook before I'd have a housekeeper.*

Your fellow lonely sleeper,
Tracy

Okay, so she wasn't a homemaker. If a man or a woman tells you they "usually" don't cook dinner, it means they never cook. "I'm working on it" means
they'll always be working on it. Tendencies worsen in relationships, not improve. That much I'd learned. A person who's a bit untidy in the initial stages
will be a FEMA disaster before the first anniversary.

If she confessed to being lax on dinners, you could assume she was AWOL
on the other domestic arts as well. Add housekeeping, gardening, sock darn-
ing, canning, and macramé to the list. Then again, I didn't do them, either.
Did anybody do them anymore?

Franz—

*I haven't heard from you in a while. Is the honeymoon over? I'm sure
Prague is a great distraction. Especially compared to Los Angeles. The
thing is I can't keep writing if you're not going to write back. What
would people think? I might look lonely and desperate. Which I'm not,
I'm not, I swear I'm not!! Okay, maybe just a little lonely. But never
desperate.*

Love,
Tracy

I swear to you I wasn't playing games (even if it did work). I promise I wasn't put off by the antihomemaker stuff. It's just I was busy. With the book, for sure. The interviews kept me occupied for the most part of each day. At night I wrote.

What silenced me for a couple of days was, well, fear. Through Tracy's typed thoughts and bon mots, I began to see where the relationship could go, snags and all. And it scared the vagabond out of me.

Here I'd teed up numerous gallivants around the globe, prying into foreign love lives, getting paid to do so. Now after a night together and a dozen notes shared, I knew I'd have to change plans. I didn't even have a warm body to coax me into a partnership. I had Yahoo!

> *Tracy—*
>
> *You went easy on me this time. No questions. So I'll pick my own. Name a few random things you enjoy.*
>
> *Okay, I will. Warm tortilla chips and fresh salsa, safaris,* Catch-22, *Spinal Tap, Pac Bell Park, my nieces (of course), Los Roques, late night writing sessions and early morning coffee, new gym socks, Ryan Adams (the drippingly sad songs), Spanish moss, Richard Diebenkorn (figurative more than the geometric works), the* NY Times *Sunday crossword puzzle or the one in* The Wall Street Journal *on Friday. My question is for you to do the same.*
>
> *Here's another something I enjoyed. Remember when you and I were having morning coffee on your couch? We started to talk about plans for the day; I needed to go to Orange County. You asked what time I planned to be back in L.A. and, before I could answer, asked if you could come by my house. I loved that moment. You apologized for being forward, but needn't have. When you said it, I thought for the first time, "Ahhh, she likes me."*
>
> *Best,*
> *Franz*

Oops. That was a dumb one, I thought immediately after I sent it. You just told her the first time you thought she liked you was a moment *after* you slept with her. You basically called her a hussy while explaining you're more than happy to jump into bed with people regardless of whether they like you or not.

And yet it was true. The feeling she needed to see me, that is. Not the hussy part. After Tracy put her hand on my knee, everything felt different.

Jonathan and I decided to hear more views outside Prague, so we rented a car and headed to Moravia. His friend Šárka offered to show us around Nový Jičín, a countryside town with muted boasts of a postcard-perfect central square and a history of making fedoras. The ride away from Prague mirrored the country's evolution over the past couple of decades, with long stretches of forest, cattle farms, and felled fields of grain, punctured without warning by high-tech office parks and Costco-sized "hypermarkets."

After a decade in the country, Jonathan now practiced fluent Czech driving, racing our Škoda to the rear bumper of any car that dared occupy the fast lane, then flicking the headlights repeatedly to signal it to move over. There seemed to be a causal relationship between the antagonism of Jonathan's motor skills and the aggressiveness of the music. I popped Green Day out of the CD player, inserted Chopin, prayed, and closed my eyes.

Šárka met us in the square, in the shadow of buildings pushed together like desserts in a bakery window, each colored as if to taste, custard, caramel, lemon meringue. She looked like a tennis player with her athletic build, bobbed hair, and black culottes, every stride with a bounce. She split her time between Moravia and California.

"I'm actually feeling better about the dating scene," she said after Jonathan explained the premise of my trip. "I show you."

We followed her to an office building nearby, walking up several flights of stairs and into a large room with dozens of computer stations and camouflage netting on the walls. Gen-Xers answered e-mails while the Y's battled online dragons and ninja fighters.

"I've just started," she explained, logging on, "but I've already had a few good dates with guys in nearby villages. This Internet dating has really changed things in rural places like this. Look at these people. We are all on the same dating Web site."

I glanced around, trying not to seem too nosy, and saw the same banner on the handful of screens within view: www.rande.cz for randy CZ. Šárka explained that the Czech version of Internet dating varied slightly from the

American variety, with many traditional Czech customs still in place. For instance, she surfed online each day but waited for the men to make the first contact. Her friends did the same. The chat room registration numbers at the time: 1,252 men, 799 women, 36 gay men, 31 lesbians.

"Seems so funny to me that all these people here in the room are looking for dates on the same Web site. Why don't you just go talk to one of these guys?"

"Oh, no," she said. "Czech women just don't do this. The man must take the lead. We don't ask them out. This is so ingrained."

"Then why don't they approach you here?"

"They are too shy. The Internet is good for countries with shy men."

"So you could be e-mailing with someone on the other side of the room."

"Maybe. That's why I try to spread the dates out over different places. I don't want to run into the same people again."

"Wiz, you should try it," Jonathan said. "I'll translate something for you."

"Here," said Šárka, offering Jonathan her seat.

Scanning the www.rande.cz lineup for people currently online, we settled on a woman named Tulipana. Great name. Sounded like a fancy new iced tea. Jonathan typed a few words of introduction, and she wrote back within minutes.

"Doing research for a project," he typed. "May I interview you?"

"Your Czech is very impressive," she responded. "Tell me about this project."

"I'm interested in love, dating, romance, around the world. How people meet and fall in love. Check out my Web site, at www.honeymoon withmybrother.com."

With that, her name disappeared from the list of participants logged on.

"C'mon," said Šárka. "I want you to meet my mom and her friends."

The women gathered regularly to devour tea and sandwiches and the staple food of all such gatherings in the Czech Republic—men. We joined them at a country restaurant idling between the lunch and dinner shifts. Šárka kissed her mother and introduced us to the group of five, all mothers, all in their fifties and sixties. They were more than happy to have us enter the conversation, bubbling and laughing until I asked about the Czech men.

"They don't see women as equals," and they're definitely "not gentlemen." "They haven't progressed as much as women in recent years." "They expect women to be housewives and mothers," and then when they are, "the men cheat." They "demand *smažény sýr* and *svíčková*." Grilled cheese and beef. They "like to give orders, but this is more in the villages." They "drink too much and burp."

"What would you change?" I asked.

"Communication," they said in chorus and without pause.

The words could have come from any corner of the planet. Lack of attention—the number-one complaint from the better half, and also the cheapest to change.

"They should take more responsibility," said Jiřina. "And stop giving orders."

Of the five, only one had a husband who helped clean or cook. Future generations of Czech men would be more supportive, they agreed, though those with sons pled guilty to spoiling them by "doing everything they asked." A woman at the end of the table boasted about her daughter, who demanded her boyfriend prepare dinner a few days each week. The others nodded in approval, then paused as a ruddy-faced man strolled over from the front door, having no clue as to the atmosphere he entered.

"My angel!" one of them announced.

"Do you know him?" I asked.

"Sometimes. He is my husband."

"Please ask him to join us. Tell him I'll buy him a beer."

This widened the grin already in place.

"Would you change anything about Czech women?" I asked the man.

"No, they're fine," he said.

"Nothing?"

"Well, maybe more sex."

He started to laugh to himself, then turned to the soccer match on the television over the bar.

"When it is on, nothing else matters," he said.

"See. They watch too much football," said Jarmila. "But it's better than other vices. If it wasn't football, it would be something else."

"What do you like about Czech men?" I asked. "What do they do well?"

The group: "They have goals, and want to achieve something." "They can provide and take care of a family." Šárka's mom added Czech men were "loyal," prompting the others to shake their heads in disagreement.

"What I like about the Czech women is that they are good-looking," blurted the man.

"We were at an Internet café earlier in the day. Would any of you ever consider Internet dating if you were single?"

"No," they responded in chorus, though their sons and daughters all did it.

"Would you ever ask a man out on a date?"

Again, no, they said, adding that they had no problem with their children reversing that trend.

"Describe your dream man," I said.

"George Clooney," said Vera.

"Richard Gere," said Zdenka.

"Dolly Buster," said the man, referring to a famous porn actress.

They threw napkins at him and returned to their tea.

Yet despite the gripes, and across all ages, most Czech women, after the comparisons have been exhausted, confess a preference to be with a Czech man. An improved one, mind you, but Czech still. Foreign men are enjoyable, they say, but they lack shared history and psyche. They may try to understand Czech women, but they can't. Czech men can but don't.

"I want someone who knows the same fairy tales," said Leona, a flight attendant for Czech Airlines I met during a trip to South America. She lived a few blocks from Jonathan in Letná. "I just wish they treated us with more respect.

"Czech men can solve problems. They have gold hands, we say. The environment here required them to be creative.

"I had a watch with a band too big. It needed altering. I took it to an Italian man I'd dated. He took a look at it and told me to go see a jeweler.

"So I gave it to a Czech guy, who examined the watch, pulled it apart, removed a couple metal slats in the band, snapped it back together, and handed it to me. The whole process took a minute."

> *Franz—*
> *Tonight I told Calvin that he could fall asleep in the car and that I'd*
> *put him in his bunk bed when we got home. He said he wanted to sleep in*
> *my bed. I said that I liked it when he woke up in the morning and came*
> *into my room to wake me up. I asked, "Don't you like that? Isn't that*

fun?" He said he liked it on the outside (he pointed to his head), but not
on the inside (pointing to his chest). I got it and told him I'd put him in
my bed to sleep tonight.

Okay, now on to some of the things I enjoy: the smell of a baby, down
comforters, oysters and champagne, Joni Mitchell, Philadelphia Story *and*
any movie with Jimmy Stewart, fall leaves, sweatpants, cold watermelon,
Calvin's laugh, Tennessee Williams, John Fante, Kurt Vonnegut, Eudora
Welty, steak, an empty theater just before the house opens, the smell after
a thunderstorm, all holidays, my bed (with you in it again please), Edward
Hopper, hot chocolate after shoveling snow, swimming naked, van Gogh's
black crows flying, toasting at sunset, Tom Waits, fishing, old photos,
Vanessa Redgrave onstage, watching the ocean, and sleeping.

How about your not-so-favorite things?

Yours,
Tracy

Hippie. Definitely hippie. I mean, c'mon, Joni Mitchell? She'd probably
have me composting and playing Hacky Sack within a year. Plus that "smell
of a baby" reference was a not-so-subtle warning she's not using the pill. The
smell of a baby is diaper.

But steak and sunset toasts balance out sweatpants and Vanessa Redgrave.
Foreign women chuckle at sweatpants, especially in the third world. They
can't imagine wearing cheap clothes if you can afford better ones.

I'll admit it, though. Tracy's crunchy qualities were starting to wear well.
Her notes felt easy, comfortable. Like sweatpants.

Tracy—
Questions. Glad to see them back in action. Excluding the obvious
(mad cow disease, etc.), here are a few annoyances that come to mind:
driftwood sculptures, all-you-can-eat, modern jazz, Vegas after more than
thirty-six hours, sake (sorry), nonfat foods, gated communities, Wieland
paintings of seascapes, excuses, karaoke, Doonesbury, golf, gin, cell
phones, self-help books, rhythmic gymnastics, lotteries, boob jobs, the L.A.
Dodgers, relish, fundraising, couples who wear the same clothes.

Is this an appropriate place in the e-mail to tell you I slept and woke
with the image of you in my head? I don't care if it isn't. Them's the facts.

Franz

Her e-mails were like an Advent calendar, a little gift at the beginning
of each day. They forced us to do something new couples often avoid—
communicate. Gone were the competing forces that steal time in every budding relationship, the girls' nights out, golf outings, gyms, TiVo, work. I had
Tracy all to myself (except for the fact I didn't have her at all). Even though
she was half a world away, the contact felt more intimate than any I'd
known.

Maybe the best thing a potential new couple can do is to run away from
each other.

Jonathan and I woke late at our hotel near the square. We'd been up well
past midnight, as one tends to do with Jonathan, arguing over non se-
quiturs. He'd embraced the Socratic method in school, you see, and brought
it to every discussion since, ramping up chitchat sessions to Oxford debates.
The best way to combat this, I'd learned over the years, was never to let him
settle into an issue. As a result, our conversations would ricochet from Robert
Mugabe to absinthe to Thai massage. At 2 A.M. he unleashed his tongue on
fiction, all of it. I rolled over and went to bed, which prompted his continua-
tion of the crusade at noon.

"I feel I've been swindled by fiction," Jonathan said as we ordered lunch
on the restaurant patio. "No one's got anything interesting to say. The real
world's more interesting than some pretentious person's imagination."

"You can argue about anything," I said. "How can anyone take on an entire category in the Dewey Decimal System?"

A young couple straight from the "after" shot of a Clearasil commercial—
cute, conservative, with blemish-free skin—sat beside us. Not wanting to
spend the next hour defending the honor of fiction, I turned and asked if I
could buy them a drink. With relief—mine—they accepted.

Pavel's attire looked more Maui than Moravia: beige linen pants, black
sandals, orange aloha shirt, puka shells, and short hair spiked as if fresh from

a morning set of waves. He'd opened his Hewlett-Packard laptop and answered e-mails while she smoked and stared. Two years his junior, Simona, nineteen, hesitated with her English, allowing him to do more of the talking. She played with her long black hair and rolled her deep-sea blue eyes in faux exaggeration when he mentioned her by name. They'd met only a week before, although the pauses and opened computer suggested longer. He saw her at a small disco and left his friends to begin a conversation.

"About what?"

"Michael Jackson."

Okay, so not all changes are for the better in the Czech Republic.

Later that night, they took a necessary step for all new Czech relationships these days among people under forty—they texted. As it is throughout the world, text messaging is as central a part of dating in the Czech Republic as the participants themselves. It's an equal partner at every stage in the relationship, including sex. Several young Czechs raved to me about the joys of text-sex when the real thing was afar. "And you don't need to worry about a condom." Locals who hadn't gotten their fill talked about "textual frustration." I even saw texters messaging at a wedding. Half of me expected the groom to reach into his tuxedo, grab his phone, and reply. Carpal tunnel doctors, prepare. The entire Czech population will soon be in for an exam.

Pavel texted Simona that night. "Nothing serious. Just 'I enjoyed our chat. I want to see you again.' " She thought he was handsome. Their relationship "just evolved" the way most do among the younger generations these days, informally, amorphously, gradually. Like their American counterparts, Czechs don't talk about dating. They "hook up," "get together," "meet up," "text." They end their relationships just as casually.

"We don't have talks," explained Pavel. "It's how we were raised. In school you are taught to be quiet. So it's harder for us to initiate things."

Pavel excused himself to go to the men's room in the hotel lobby.

"So what do you want in a relationship?" I asked Simona.

"Something that is not possible. I don't dream."

"But you guys seem like a nice couple."

"I've had bad experiences."

She talked about marriage ("twenty-seven is a good age") and children

("two—a boy and a girl"), but she reined in each thought with a hardened reality check. "Probably not." "I don't know." "This is not likely."

Pavel exuded practicality as well, but a different kind.

"I don't want to be married," he said flatly. "I see divorce everywhere, and
I don't want that."

Instead he talked of travel. A quarter century before, Pavel and Simona
would have discussed marriage by now, if for no other reason than the apartment. Today he's part of a growing demographic: single by choice. She is, too:
jaded by choices.

> *Franz—*
>
> *Let's see how wrong we are for each other. Although I did strongly
> agree with many of yours, I disagreed with a few, quite emphatically. We
> can discuss later.*
>
> *Junk mail, microwavable food, books based on movies, Celine Dion
> (well, her music), malls, Happy Meals, commercials, power lines, short-
> short skirts and tight-tight pants, plastic flowers, Bible thumpers, beige
> lipstick, genetically altered vegetables, rebel flags, Hallmark cards, self-
> tanners, warm beer, ideologues, fake nails, Hummers, Hooters, anyone
> under twenty with a cell phone, a Brazilian bikini wax (I'm sure you
> know about those), modular homes, Speedos, air guitar, and reality shows.*

Of course she disagreed with a few. And of course she differed quite emphatically. She did everything quite emphatically. I was beginning to like that
cheekiness. From afar, that is.

But air guitar? Did she really have something against air guitar?

Vivian e-mailed again, saying she hoped I was safe and nothing about air
guitar. If I was safe, she said she would be mad, since she hadn't heard from
me in weeks. Was I lost? she asked. Or maybe in love?

> *Franz—*
>
> *Now, I didn't know you were such a big football fan. You didn't
> include that on your favorites list. Funny how you snuck that one in. Do
> you yell at the TV, too? I'll forgive you that one, but you have to watch*
> Antiques Roadshow *with me.*

Love,
Tracy

P.S. Calvin wants to know your favorite cartoon character.

If you were a gambler, would you confess to a condo in Las Vegas straight-away? If you loved shoes, would you cop to an account with Manolo Blahnik right off? I rest my case.

Plus I'd gladly trade a three-hour football game for an hour watching garage-sale junkies share that one item they'd purchased in thirty years that wasn't trash. I kind of like *Antiques Roadshow.*

Back in Prague, the afternoon tram to the Letná district burst with bodies and body odor, a mix of mildew, jockstrap, and a college library during finals week. By some stroke of luck, I secured a window seat, allowing me to gaze at the Vltava River. *So striking, this city. Even with the smell of underarm as backdrop.* A group of women pushed aboard at a stop near the Charles Bridge. I turned and found myself eye-to-midriff with a young woman in a polka-dot dress. Nodding and standing, I offered her my seat.

This, for some reason, caused a ripple of laughter among her friends. Probably an inside joke, I rationalized. They mumbled a few words in clipped Czech, and she continued to pout. Still smiling, I pointed to the chair.

"All yours," I said.

"No, no, no," she said, now with a look of horror.

"I mean it. I'm getting out soon anyway."

"No."

"I mean it."

"No!" she said, turning her back to me in disgust.

I mentioned the incident to Jonathan as soon as I reached his apartment.

"You didn't," he said.

"I did."

"And she was with her friends?"

"Yup."

"In the Czech Republic you only give up your seat to a woman if she's old or pregnant. Was she overweight?"

"Shit. She must have thought I thought she was pregnant."

"Smooth, Wiz."

"Any tips to lessen the chances of being slapped?"

"Men usually enter restaurants, bars, and elevators before women to make sure the areas are safe."

"Safe from what?"

"A naive gringo."

"Thanks."

"Men also tend to go before women on down escalators and behind them going up so they can catch them if they fall. You see a lot more Czech men doing the behind part, especially if the woman's young."

"Note to self."

"Other than that, it's tough to go wrong here. The men tend to be pigs."

I opened the refrigerator in search of a snack. Jonathan liked strong coffee and yogurt in glass jars. Iveta, whom I hadn't seen in days, trended toward the sweets. Somehow seeing their food preferences in the icebox made me sad, as if the jars and wrappers would never be combined again.

> Tracy—
>
> Tell Calvin Bugs. Definitely Bugs. He proved it's okay to be erudite and whacked-out at the same time. And educated us along the way. "Kill the wabbit, kill the WABBIT!"
>
> I'm beginning to see where you and I will disagree, but that's another discussion. Why spoil a honeymoon. Things are getting interesting. Plus it's not that big of a gap. Later, later.
>
> That's all, folks,
> Franz

I don't know why I wrote it. Nervousness, perhaps. The last time I committed to a relationship like this, I ended up with wedding cake for one. I panicked. I scoured her words for differences. Of course, this was defeatist and self-fulfilling. And stupid.

I wanted to embrace her. I just didn't know if I could away from the safety of a computer and an ocean.

My inbox remained empty for forty-two hours, thirty-four minutes. But who was counting.

* * *

The next morning I took a crowded morning train to a feminist center. A woman in her mid-fifties set a bag of groceries at my feet. *Oh, no. I'm not going to fall for that again.*

The Prague Gender Studies Center ran an information clearinghouse and hosted lectures. They conducted studies on women's issues and offered counseling to Czech women in need. Lada, married and pregnant with her first child, oversaw the small library. Her colleague, Alena, with her dark, spiky, tangerine-tipped hair, ran the education programs. She dated a Norwegian man long-distance. Like most men when they enter an organization fighting to reverse sexism, I felt like a motorist with a highway patrolman behind, skittish, perhaps guilty, perhaps not.

"Do you want some coffee?" Lada asked.

"Yes, please."

"Cream?"

"And sugar, please."

"I'll get it."

"Oh, no. Maybe I should get it. Don't want you waiting on me."

"It's no problem."

"No, I insist. Just point me in the right direction."

"The room at the end of the hall."

"Would you like one?"

"Um, sure. Black, please."

Coffee served, we sat in a conference room and talked about love in the Czech Republic.

"I'm interested in the feminist perspective on such things," I said.

"We don't use that word," said Alena.

"But you are feminists, no?"

"You'd never say you are a feminist, even though you behave like one."

"Czech women are afraid of the word 'feminist,'" added Lada.

"Why?"

Because of the connotations, they said. Feminists are bra burners and megaphone holders. They raise ruckuses. They're loud. They're American. Czech supporters of women's rights have taken a different approach. Persistence. At times it paid off.

The Czech Republic has a maternity leave program that gives mothers six months at 80 percent of pay. Women can take an additional two and a half years' paid leave at three to four thousand crowns a month, enough to meet basic expenses, though little more. The program isn't as progressive as those in Scandinavia, but it bests the most generous government programs in the United States. Czech men can take six months, too, though very few do.

"I'd say about one percent of the men decide to do it," said Lada. "Culturally, it's not acceptable for them to take time off work."

Abortion is legal. The cost is about the same as a month's maternity leave payment. Surprise. They don't bomb abortion clinics here, and they don't make every election, from city council on up, a referendum on choice. The number of abortions is declining.

Before the fall of the Wall, women seeking an abortion needed the approval of a medical board. They asked nosy questions, prompting fathers to stay away. This was a problem in that the law required two applicants. So women were forced to bring male friends and concoct twisted tales about why ending their pregnancy would serve the state. *My fetus is a nascent capitalist. I can feel it in the way he kicks.* Pragmatic Party chiefs usually obliged. For them, abortions were a twofer. The tribunals saved the state money and they stockpiled chits to be cashed later. Stamp: approved.

The Czech government faces the opposite problem today. The country's fertility rate is the second lowest in the world, lagging behind only the flaccid Ukraine. Demographers predict the population will shrink by 10 percent or one million people over the next fifty years. You don't see a lot of government-sponsored condom ads.

Lada and Alena spend their days fighting pay gaps and glass ceilings, pushing for more female representation in government. They battle when they can, though the money from the European Union hasn't flowed as promised. Sister programs in the United States treat them with condescension, they complained. "They don't appreciate the differences in culture."

"Have either of you asked a man out on a date?" I asked.

"No," they said at the same moment without pause.

L ater in the day, I posed similar questions to Mirka, a professor of Czech and English who'd taught at Stanford while Jonathan attended graduate classes there.

"Relations between Czech men and women are better than those in other countries," she said.

"Really?" I asked, having spent weeks listening to endless complaints. "Why?"

"Because people here are better than people in the United States. Less superficial. There is a better integration here from a young age. There's Sokol." That's a Scout-type program for kids. "Boys and girls compete, they learn together. Therefore they relate better.

"Under Communism, even though rights were suppressed, there was an equality between men and women unlike the Western world. The Czech Republic was one of the first countries to have a legal guardian law. It passed in 1949. Women had the right to vote in 1919, a year before the United States.

"The country has hugely generous maternity and parental leave programs. And then they can't be fired for three years after the child's birth."

"How about rising divorce rates and declining births?"

"But there is also a growing class of citizens who choose to be single. This is a big trend. People didn't do that during the Communist era. It wasn't fashionable or easy. The family structure was much stronger during the Communist era."

"What about ex-pats?"

"The Czech women who chase foreign men today are mostly parasites," said Mirka. "They are only chasing money. Most Czech women aren't parasites. They are socialized to earn their own money."

I took the tram back to Jonathan's apartment, standing the entire ride.

Tracy—
Attaching a poem I stumbled on, so to speak.

Best,
Franz

A Non Poem

I'd like to craft you a poem
But I'm having a really hard time

Shifting the words in alignment
Making them sing, dance, and rhyme

Traipsing through the verses
Reading every line
At least an A for effort
'Cause you knew the words were mine

You'd consume it thrice over
Deciphering as if in a game
Like the way a few first letters
Just spelled out your name

No, no, no, no, no, no
This task is far too hard
I've given up the foolishness
In search of a greeting card

I heard from her within the hour:

Franz—

You've definitely got my number, boy. I want more than anything to curl up with your poem (a piece of you) and sleep. Write me a poem like that and I'm putty in your hands.

I'm over this Prague research trip. I want you here (I'm stomping my foot as I say this)! Did you know this spoiled brat side of me? Probably not. I hide her pretty well.

So, where would you like to escape? I've always had this fantasy about Tuscany. I saw the movie Enchanted April *and it looked like heaven. An ancient house tucked in the hills, surrounded by trees and flowers. Wonderful food, lots of wine, and nothing to do.*

I'm now very curious about what you think we will disagree on. You won't blindside me, will you? Oh, I bet I know what it is. You're a polygamist, aren't you? You have ten other women you e-mail the same letter to.

I hope we still like each other in person.

Love,
Tracy

For the location scout on any Prague-based movie, it's tough to beat the Charles Bridge. If it's a romance, make sure the cameras are rolling at sunset. Lovers stake out their positions alongside the statues of saints Augustine, Ludmilla, and John Nepomuk, stretching out for their nightly embraces in the gaslit glow. And as I walked across the structure for a final time, alone, dodging happy couples as they cooed and whispered, the stone saints frozen in their blessings, all the while thinking of a woman a very long distance away, I concluded this to be the bridge straight to hell. Curse these happy couples. I wanted to go home.

That evening, I'd decided to walk back to Jonathan's apartment on the other side of the Vltava to soak up a few last images of Prague. The scene couldn't have been more idyllic, the Prague Castle on high, a last rowboat on the river, not a puppet salesman or British bachelor party in sight. Prague was a living gallery, the guidebooks said, and for that moment I believed them.

Yet despite the picture-book setting, handsome buildings Renaissance, cubist, and art nouveau, old towns and islands and the river between, all stage-lit and perfect as the sun left for the day, something about this place felt chaotic, insane even. The interviews and events over the last six weeks confirmed it—all the affairs and double lives, resentment and repression.

For nearly as long as it has been inhabited, governments and outside leaders tormented the land and its denizens—the Catholic Church's burning Jan Hus at the stake, Hitler's unchecked annexations, Brezhnev's tanks. The result has been a culture of secrecy and survival that washes over into all aspects of Czech life, even love. Love in Bohemia has always been shaped by the madness that surrounds.

Though as I crossed the bridge and made my way through Malá Strana, the Little Quarter, I thought about the flip side of the chaos. Deep within the Czech psyche is an uncanny ability to adapt, and even to thrive under any conditions. For every leader who's foisted his evil on the Bohemians, there are countless millions who've obtained their revenge in brilliant and clever fashion. Hus and Wenceslas became martyrs; Neruda wrote poems and Havel wrote plays; victims of the Second Defenestration of Prague, sentenced to death and thrown from the high windows of the Bohemian Chancellery, survived by landing in a pile of manure.

What do you do when your society spins in folly? You embrace what you can control. You adapt to what is unchangeable and make the rest as comfortable as possible. The Czech Republic is indeed a nation of Golden Hands. They will get by.

And more. One commonality of everyone I met during my stays in the country was an appreciation of the small pleasures in life. They effused about theater, literature, nature, family, sex. Is it any wonder a disproportionate number of brilliant artists and thinkers has risen from these grounds? Imagine the importance of a Rolling Stones record if your government banned rock and roll. Feel the depth of those first few power chords of "Satisfaction." Dunt-dunt-duh-da-da-da-da-da-duh-duh.

So, too, in love. Love adapts here, and often thrives amid harum-scarum circumstances. Successful couples fashion relationships that can survive amid the affairs and restrictions. Czechs are far less judgmental, less apt to criticize what works for another. They'd have a much more open mind to beginning a relationship with, say, a single mom who likes to speak her mind.

I wondered if things with Tracy would pick up from where they had left off. The e-mails felt encouraging, but six weeks is a long time, and trips are always easier for the departed than the ones who stay at home. I reached Jonathan's flat and flipped open his computer.

> *Vivian—*
>
> *I apologize for being incommunicado as of late. Being abroad is no excuse. I've wanted to talk with you about something. The reason for my distance recently is that I've started seeing someone in Los Angeles. I've decided to see her exclusively.*
>
> *Best,*
> *Franz*

A World of "Issues"

Franz—

I want to ask you about something immediate. Not one of our courtship questions. Or maybe it is.

You said you've never dated someone with a child before. Well, there is a lot that goes with that. First there is the issue of how overwhelming it can be. It takes a lot of energy being around a four-year-old all day. I am used to it and can cope (mostly), but you're a virgin. I want you to really consider what that is like. I love my child, and this has nothing to do with him, but more with us having time to get to know each other. Plus you'd be seeing me in all my motherhood glory, which is not always pretty. I'm not sure how I feel about you seeing the real me just yet. Shouldn't we still be in the "you're wonderful, you're marvelous" stage?

I guess what I'm trying to say is that my life is really complicated in the fact that I have a child. And if it was just you and me it wouldn't be a problem. We could spend time traveling together and getting to know each other. It gets harder with a child involved. I just ask that you think about that, ask yourself if it's something you're comfortable with. I don't know a lot of the answers to my own questions. These things never came up in my last relationship, because it was always kept separate. Calvin wasn't involved. Which is part of the reason it didn't work out.

I guess I don't know how to be clear about this because it's unknown territory. I want you to be comfortable and not to be taken by surprise. I

want Calvin to be comfortable and to feel safe. And then at some point,
hopefully, I'd like to feel comfortable, too. This may all be a nonissue and
we might just have a wonderful time. But I feel it's important to talk
about.

    Your fellow lonely sleeper,
    Tracy

The world shows little compassion for the single mother. Each day is a battle for acceptance and opportunity. The difference between countries is the difference of degree. All societies are stacked against them; in every land they fight.

Western nations do a better job of hiding the biases. The rest of the world doesn't bother as much with pretense. Some would say they're more honest. Oh, you're a single mom? I'm sorry. Maybe if you lowered your standards, you could find yourself a nice man to help bail you out of your predicament.

I saw how India viewed single mothers every time I opened the *Sunday Times*. Each week and for decades, Indian parents parade their single sons and eligible daughters in front of the newspaper-reading public via thoroughly entertaining classified advertisements. Capitol Hill spin doctors have nothing on the good folks who take out these ads.

A quick glossary: "Stunning" means "attractive." "Attractive" means "homely." "Homely" in the Indian context means "domestic." "Fair" or "wheatish" means any shade of skin lighter than black.

"Status family" means Mom and Dad aren't interested in freeloading in-laws. "NRI" means "nonresident Indian" or "green card holder, so please overlook the unibrow." "Caste No Barrier" means caste definitely is a barrier but we've added these words because the *Times* gives us a 25 percent discount on the ad if we do so. Matrimonials that omit any mention of dowry mean it is important to the family and it's gonna be high.

"Issue" means child.

The classifieds are categorized like the country itself, by caste, religion, geography, profession, and language. Brahmins go first. Brahmins go first a lot in India.

An example from the *Sunday Times,* March 4, 2007: "By Gods [*sic*] infinite

mercy, 34 year old smart, fair, NRI batchelor [sic] doctor from Highly educated [though not educated enough to spell "bachelor"] UK based family
looking for God fearing homely girl having interest in charitable develop-
ment programs for global community in UK and India. Girls merit main con-
sideration" (with boys as a backup plan, I guess).

Kshatriya and the other lower castes come after the Brahmins. Then the
Sikhs, Muslims, and Christians. "Disabled/Handicapped" follow. Their entries make you pull with every emotion you can muster for those without priority. "Slight palsy." "Rt leg polio." "Blind though independent." "Rt eye
artificial but looks original." They tend to be the most honest advertisements
in the paper.

At the end of the matrimony sections, after the untouchables and infirm,
come the pleas from India's least valued: the divorcées, single parents, and
those who would have them.

From the same edition of the *Times*: "Match for smart unmarried 26yrs old
PB girl, Teacher in a reputed School. Have minor problem in conceiving, otherwise fit. Willing to accept Unmarried/Divorcee/Widower up to 35yrs of
age with an issue up to 5yrs."

Poor woman. Her parents are so rattled they'll entertain offers from men
with children! Oh, the panic that set in once they discovered their daughter
had a "minor problem in conceiving." There is no such thing as a minor
problem in conceiving. That's the equivalent to being a little bit pregnant.
More important to the readers of this ad: How would the family know? Did
their daughter try before? Is she a, gulp, nonvirgin? In India, that's almost as
bad as having a child out of wedlock.

You can *feel* the desperation in the ads from single moms. "Innocent divorce," they write, as if they were kidnapped into the marriage. "Qualified
legally divorced, 8 year issue male but no liability." You won't have to pay for
anything, they plead. As any stepfather will tell you, "no liability" exists in
court documents, not life. "Willing to accept the same," they offer. Parents of
single moms and dads drop all pretense and standards. Fifty-year-old men
with no jobs and a fondness for the bottle are suddenly fine matches for twenty-
five-year-old women with an infant, provided the astrological charts match,
that is.

Some single mothers go along with this new reality. Others look for fellow
single parents or foreigners who don't see children as a major liability. Some

fight, some concede. All agree that when you have a child and not a spouse, India shuttles you to the back sections.

Karla's journey to single parenthood began at a cemetery in Managua. Don't laugh. It's a common romantic rendezvous in this poor ole world of ours. They're private, locals say, with plenty of open space and flowers. They're free. We met her in Granada at Asia Latina.

"He was a fireman," said Karla, now twenty-five and studying to be a psychologist. "I was an admirer. And one night in Managua there was no condom."

His family worked in government. They "didn't want this kind of situation made public," hinting at abortion but never offering to arrange one in a country where they remain illegal. Karla had had one a few years before. Never again, she swore.

"It's a ghost that never disappears."

Her partner refused to see the infant, let alone pay for the boy's upkeep. Nicaraguan law lets him stay detached. The baby is hers.

"There is a big stigma with single mothers," she said. "The guys are curious at first. They ask about the baby, but they don't care. They leave. They are more direct with you. They talk about sex. Or they think you're an easy girl."

"Umm, but you were easy," I said.

"I know. I've learned. No more easy girl. Before, I believed in the innocence of the love, but no more."

"So what's your plan?"

"I know girls who look for a foreigner because they think the men will not care about one or two or three kids. Especially from Spain. Spanish guys don't care."

"Do you tell them about your child right away?"

"I always talk about my baby. But not because I want him to take care of my baby, but because he is part of my life."

"How about your taste in men? Has that changed?"

"Before my baby, I only want someone who I will enjoy. But now I look for intelligence. Someone who will not like a bar or a disco or a party. Someone not jealous. Not machista. Someone who loves kids—that is the most important part."

"Do you think that's possible in Nicaragua?"

"Maybe with a man from another country, but probably not someone from here. Nica men think love is an empty space you need to fill. For me, love is if I am happy and you are happy, we can share. But if you are not happy, you can share nothing.

"When I had sex with the fireman, it was not love. Just I needed a hug. But love doesn't leave in the morning."

The problem in Egypt and the Arab world is not so much the single mother part as how she got there.

Egyptians are smart when it comes to divorce settlements. They require the groom to agree to a level of support prior to the wedding. I've never understood why we don't do the same. Who invented the system of deciding such things during a divorce? Could the logic have been more flawed?

I've got it. Let's take two parents who now despise each other, who can't agree on the time of day, let alone anything to do with money, doing everything possible to hide their resources, adults who are more than happy to use a child as a bargaining chip for their preferred lifestyle, and *then* we'll sort everything out. Oh, yeah, throw in a couple of attorneys at five hundred dollars an hour to ease the process and enhance the result.

In theory, Arab divorce is simple. A man just needs to say "I divorce you, I divorce you, I divorce you" with a few friends to witness the act and nod in agreement. That's where the snags begin.

Before the wedding can take place, Arab Egyptian couples must sign a marriage contract that outlines financial commitments to any children. The document can include everything from required alimony payments to furniture color.

One of the biggest issues with the document isn't the contract itself but who holds the original copy after the marriage, the groom's family or the bride's. Apparently, White-Out is available in the desert. Tightfisted or hyperopinionated clans have been known to take the occasional liberty to protect their son or daughter. Another sticking point occurs when the money or goods are delivered.

"Egyptian women feel unease," explained Raafat, a woman we met in Cairo. "They think their husband can leave them or take another. That's why they demand the money up front."

Makes sense to me. If I knew my marital partnership could turn into a matrimonial quintet at any moment, I'd demand cash on delivery as well. Just ask Ivana Trump or Bianca Jagger.

Catholics in Egypt don't have these issues. They have others. They're not allowed to get a divorce. Protestants can if their partner cheats on them. But then if you get one, you can't get married in the church again. And if Christians get really mad, they switch to Islam.

No, the Arab Egyptians don't have a problem with the concept of the single mom. It's that whole getting-there process that gives Arab men such distaste. You see, a woman who has a child isn't a virgin. Arabs are big on virgins. The Koran urges all good Muslims to find a virgin for their bride. Find four, for that matter. After that, you've overvirgined. Too much of a good thing. No more unless you become a martyr for Islam, according to some scholars. Then you can enjoy your "seventy-two black-eyed virgins." If you can remember their names, that is.

"We see them as bitch," said Ahmed, an unemployed resident of Luxor, when I asked about single moms.

"Don't hesitate to speak freely," I said.

"You know, bitch. Easy for sex. The other women don't want this woman to come to their home. They think their husbands will sleep with them."

"What if someone falls in love with her?"

"Too much. This will be difficult for the woman to marry. We prefer virgins. This is not preference, this is normal."

The Babysitter

LOS ANGELES

I took a long run to the Prague Castle before I answered her e-mail. Couldn't she have waited until I came home to start this discussion? What happened to all those flirtatious notes about ice cream and swimming naked? It's so much easier to talk about pralines and cream.

No. These thoughts must have been bottled up inside her for a long time, I supposed. We needed to have this talk at some point. Maybe it's easier to begin over the Internet? If only I knew what to say. I still didn't have any answers when I returned to the flat and turned on the computer.

Tracy—

Remember how they pitched the movie version of Honeymoon with My Brother? *"Jerry McGuire* meets Planes, Trains and Automobiles.*" I laughed when I heard that but, after chewing on it some more, thought the two flicks are a decent summary of my twisted tale. I decided tonight you are either Renée Zellweger or John Candy.*

If you are Renée, the story has a happy ending—guy gets dumped, demoted, changes course, falls for a single mom who makes him see himself, and the world, a bit differently. On the other hand, if you're John C., then we end up in a cheesy motel and you start selling shower curtain rings.

I appreciate your words about the impact of kids on a relationship. I have been thinking about it. Since I've never done it before, I don't have any immediate answers, either.

Calvin is a great kid. He makes you more attractive, not less. In fact, if you tire of me, I may borrow him for an afternoon or two to round up some dates. He's a magnet, you see. He'd help my rap.

Funny how we see ourselves. We all have commitments. Especially at our age. Yet we think of ourselves as burdened and others as tabula rasa. For instance, we're dealing with one of my commitments right now— distance. I felt guilty for taking off so suddenly. In the future, I think the trips will be shorter. But that doesn't change the fact Kurt and I will be on the road for a decent chunk of the coming year.

So I could put the same types of questions right back to you. Are you sure you want to see someone who spends this much time living out of a backpack? I'm the Webster's definition of "geographically undesirable."

Franz

Of course the e-mail was about as forthright as a GOING OUT OF BUSINESS sign at a carpet shop. I had no idea if I could be in a long-term relationship with a single mom. The only child-related issue we settled in the overseas e-mails involved circumcision. That's because I caved to her argument there was no medical urgency for it. The caveat was she would no longer refer to my appendage as "mutilated," "shortened," or "lopped off." I thought it was a pretty good deal. Everything else remained up in the air.

I wanted to be with Tracy. And Calvin. I just didn't know if I could.

In Prague my brain played host to a daily WWE bout with flying body slams and no clear victor. The voice in the white singlet roared: *Of course you can date a woman with a child.*

His opponent in black and with an ugly case of cauliflower ear howled for immediate cessation. *You can't even look after Kurt's dogs for the weekend without panicking, let alone be with a child who can actually talk back and point out your every wrong move.*

Are you really that inflexible? Think of the Czechs. Use your golden hands.

Right. Talk to me after a weekend of Goldfish crackers and stomach flu.

And there they were, standing outside LAX, Calvin on her hip holding a single white rose in one hand, a severed stem in the other, and several splotches of ivory on the ground. Zuzu's petals. I hoisted my backpack and quickened my pace toward them both, ready to unleash a he-man hug. Tracy, Tracy. She looked as pretty as I remembered, more. I'd thought about this moment throughout the multiple plane legs west. The kiss would let me know immediately, just as the Brazilians counseled. In five seconds I'd see if the passion remained.

Or not. Whoops. I forgot to factor in Calvin. Can you kiss a mom in front of a four-year-old? Two, three, perhaps. But don't memories begin at four? What if we kissed and felt nothing toward each other, prompting us both to go our separate ways in the days to come? Would that make Calvin a man-hater for the rest of his life?

No, no. I couldn't kiss her. Not here. Yet if I didn't, she'd assume I'd soured on the whole long-distance affair. Shit. Was this what it's like with a single mom? I hadn't made up my mind by the time I reached them.

"Here," said Calvin. "We got you a flower. It broke."

"Thanks, buddy," I said while giving them both an embrace. "What a nice surprise. Hi."

"Hey," she said.

Without negotiation, we settled on a compromise, a formal, quiet peck, on the lips and lingering for a beat. Thank God for that extra second. That meant the world.

"Yuck," said Calvin.

"Oh, I'm sorry, Calvin," I said, kissing his face and head with amplified sound effects like in his favorite cartoons.

He giggled and told Tracy he needed to go to the bathroom. Now. Ten thousand questions about kids flashed before me. Welcome home.

We decided to get a pizza for dinner and to put Calvin to bed early. Tracy ran a bath for him; I volunteered to make the pickup at Casa Bianca nearby. Immediately outside the house I called my friend Andy, a kindly New Englander who married a single mom from Tallahassee. There he remained, bound by love and a court-ordered parenting agreement.

"Help!" I said.

"What's going on?"

"I've started seeing a woman with a kid."

"Great."

"I've been out of the country for the last couple of months, and I just realized I have no idea what the hell I'm doing."

"Like what?"

"Like can I kiss her? In front of him?"

"Sure. What's wrong with showing affection?"

"How about the more intimate side of things?"

"I hope you don't need my help on that."

"Not how. Where. And when."

"I'd get your groove back tonight, Stella. Sex in the morning is out. Kids get up much earlier than you'd imagine."

"I learned that one already."

"Make sure you're under the sheets."

"I'm going to lock the door from now on."

"She won't let you lock the door. They don't want their kids to feel shut out."

"She says she lets Calvin sleep with her."

"Hmm. Attachment parent. You'll need to plan and get creative. Cartoons and nap times and such."

"I don't know."

"Relax. Those cartoons are longer now."

"Like what, twenty minutes?"

"Just be careful of anything on television. Go with the DVDs. All you need is one commercial for Barbie and bam, he's in the room."

"Got it."

"You can't take anything they say personally. Especially if he's four."

"I already do," I mumbled to myself. "How long until you felt completely comfortable in the whole thing?"

"Not too long. About two years."

"Two years? Really?"

"Maybe longer. It just takes a while to grow into these things."

Damn. So much for the instant solutions. Andy explained his four-year-old stepdaughter lived with them, then spent alternating weekends at her father's house. Stepdaughter. Stepdad. Stepford. Stepladder. I suddenly hated any word with "step." What did it mean, "step"? A step to what? Are "stepfathers" a step away from being "real fathers"? By definition, would they ever get there?

Stepfathers. Claudius in *Hamlet*. Humbert Humbert in *Lolita*. Robert De Niro as that son of a bitch who beat up cute little Leonardo DiCaprio in *This Boy's Life*. Yuck. Thank God for Mike Brady, even the permed-hair version.

Yet, as bracing as his words were, Andy's tone gave me encouragement. He seemed happy, griping only once about being so far away from Fenway Park. Plus he and his wife were expecting a child of their own, another girl.

If he can do it, I can too.

Maybe. Perhaps.

I don't know.

I planned to be subtle with Tracy when I returned with the pepperoni-mushroom pie. Savor the easy parts first, I self-counseled. See if her voice felt as comfortable as her e-mails. Calvin ate half a slice and retreated to his bedroom to resume construction of the Great LEGO Wall of Eagle Rock. A wave of jet lag hit me as we lounged on Tracy's veranda.

"So, explain to me exactly what this whole attachment parenting thing is. I mean, physically attached?"

"Sometimes," she said. "It means when you shower a child with love, and you make him feel more secure, he'll be more independent and confident."

"Like, what, he sleeps with you once a month?"

"Whenever he wants."

"Doesn't he prefer bedding down with Jesus and Chad?"

"Sometimes."

"Or don't you worry that he'll still crash there when he's a teenager? Guys get comfortable in their routines."

"You're afraid of spending a night with Calvin."

"No, no. Of course not."

"You get used to it, although he thrashes around a lot."

Just then, something rare started to take place. Maybe it was jet lag, or my conversations in the Czech Republic, but for some reason I began to open my mind. The more Tracy talked about attachment parenting, the more it made sense. Meet children's needs and they'll be less needy. Give them constant love so they will love constantly. Share and they will share. From here on the veranda it made sense.

After all, I thought to myself, this is how most of the world parents. Whole families share single rooms and single beds. They spend their days farming or selling with young children slung around their backs or running between their legs.

I remembered the small faces in Africa and Southeast Asia, the looks of those children who spent all day on their mothers' hips and backs. I saw their content eyes and serene stares, and I remembered how infrequently they cried. The third world has no choice but to smother its children with affection and love. Outsourced attention through nannies and day care and after-school programs is rarely an option. Parents shoulder the load alone. Their children reflect the results.

"Bring him on," I announced.

"Thanks."

"Tomorrow."

She looked at me.

"Okay."

"Speaking of which, what are our plans?"

"Remember from my e-mail? My best friend, Adelaide, just had twins? I told her I'd watch her other kids for an afternoon so her husband can visit her in the hospital. She had a C-section."

"How many others?"

"Just two, a boy and a girl. You'll do fine."

"You, me, we'll do fine."

Adelaide's husband, Ned, gave us a quick list of instructions before hurrying off to the hospital to be with his wife and new twin boys. Juice boxes in the refrigerator, diapers in the drawer. "Good luck."

"He looked familiar," I said to Tracy. "The red hair."

"Ned does a lot of movies and TV. *Apollo 13*?"

"That's it. Mission Control."

I heard the first scream while thinking about astronauts and scouring the refrigerator for a soda behind the walls of Frogurt and mini carrots. Tracy jumped on it. No worries, she reported. Just an argument between three-year-old Miller and five-year-old Hannah over oversized LEGOs. Tracy separated the two blocks and gave each child one. The simplest solution is usually the best, I reminded myself.

"I'm going to help straighten this place up," she said as the three kids played contentedly in the family room. "Do you want me to put on a movie to keep them occupied?"

"You don't trust me, do you?"

"No, I just wanted to give you some peace. You're probably still exhausted from the flight."

"I can handle it."

"Sure?"

"Go."

Miller grabbed a Wiffle Ball and fired it into the back of my head. Impressive arm for a three-year-old, I thought as I rubbed my scalp. Decent aim as well. He bolted out the backyard door. Did this mean I should follow him? Was he allowed back there on his own? I saw him heading for a large tree. Damn if this kid was going to hurt himself on my watch. I left Calvin and Hannah positioning livestock in a playhouse living room and sprinted outside to catch Miller's daredevil show.

"Miller. Miller. Let's come down now. Miller."

But no worries, I thought as Miller continued his assault on the backyard ecosystem, scaling a large tree and staring me down. I'd wait him out. Surely the law of gravity would kick in soon. After fifteen minutes, I thought back to my college history classes and realized that battles were usually won by forces on higher ground.

As Miller continued his sit-in, I poked my head in the family room to check on the others. Hannah put her thumbs in her ears and waved at me. Grade-school reflexes came roaring back as I pulled my lower eyelids down à la Lon Cheney and stuck out my tongue, a real crowd-pleaser with Hannah. She laughed. She jumped. She copied the contortion and sent it back my way. I returned the sentiments with animated emphasis before having to resume my pleas to Miller. *Should I put in a movie? Ha!*

I'd like to say I heard Calvin's crying from outside and rushed in to help. I didn't. Tracy did. She stood by him when Miller and I came back to the room.

"Hannah stuck her tongue out at me," he sobbed.

"He did it to me first!" Hannah said, pointing to me. "That man there."

"She definitely started it," I pleaded. "With the elephant ears thing."

"I'm going to put in a cartoon."

*   *   *

That was a bit much," I told Tracy as we sat in the car in front of her house.

Calvin ran inside to play with Libby and Pluto, who remained at DEF-CON 4 each time I stepped within a ten-mile radius.

"I'm sorry," she said. "It was bad timing, but she needed the help."

"I don't know if I can handle one, let alone three."

Tracy shifted toward me. "What do you mean?"

"I'm joking."

"No, what do you mean?"

"The noise, the crying, the tantrums. Not being able to figure out the potty safety latch thing."

"That's pretty much my life. I have a kid. It's not always fun."

"I noticed."

"Thanks."

"I'm sorry. I didn't mean it like that. Jet lag."

"Do you think you can do this?"

"Do what?"

"Have a relationship with a woman who has a child."

"Whoa. Where'd that come from?"

"I just assumed since you're seeing me you've decided you can."

"Why are we having this discussion now? I've been home for all of a day."

"Do you?"

"I have no idea. I've never done this before. You gotta give me some time."

"I just don't want us to get serious, then have you wake up one morning and say, 'Hey, she has a kid. I'm out.'"

"I need some time."

"Okay."

She opened the door and left. I didn't know for how long.

Love on a Leash

n the car I idled.

Impressive. It usually takes you at least forty-eight hours to blow up a relationship. You did this one in twenty-four.

"What the fuck was that? I need a bath and bed, not the hammer."

Even if you were joking, you picked the touchiest subject imaginable for a single mom. Chris Rock wouldn't have gone near that.

"I don't need this shit."

Yeah. You've got the road. And Kurt's dogs.

"How the hell can you decide something like that anyway? In a day? Impossible."

Stop cursing.

"Screw you."

i," I said on the cell phone.

"Hi," said Tracy.

"I miss you."

"I'm sorry I pressured you. I'm tired."

"I've decided it's Renée Zellweger."

"Who?"

"The movie. Of *Honeymoon with My Brother*. It's *Jerry McGuire* over *Planes, Trains and Automobiles*."

"I didn't mean to pressure you. It's just . . ."

"There's that scene where Tom Cruise is walking with Cuba Gooding after

sleeping with Renée Zellweger. 'Single mothers don't date!' Cuba says.
'They've been to the circus. They've been to the puppet show. They've seen
the strings.' "

"You shoplifted the pooty."

"I shoplifted the pooty."

"I wanted you to shoplift the pooty."

"I respect you for that."

"It's a good pooty."

"For putting Calvin before everyone, everything else. You're a good mom."

"Thanks," she said. "Where are you?"

"I'm still outside in the car."

"Get your ass on up. Calvin's asleep . . . in his own bed."

I felt comfortable yet distant at Tracy's place, like visiting the summer cabin
of a longtime friend. Tracy tried to make me feel welcome by pasting my
e-mailed photos from Prague on the front of the refrigerator and adding a six-
pack of Coronas inside. Pluto did not share the house diplomacy. The second
I unlatched the gate to the front patio, he launched into one of his histrionic
wails.

"Shhh. Shhhh. Good doggy. Scram!"

She met me at the front door, dog leash in hand.

"Truce?" she said.

"Depends on what you're planning to do with the leash."

"Stay."

Within a few minutes she returned, carrying a frozen Pluto, tail curled between his legs.

"We're going to put Pluto on a leash and clip the other end to your belt,"
she said. "It's supposed to show him you're in command."

"But I'm not in command."

"He doesn't know that. Here, try it."

I don't know who seemed less enthusiastic about the arrangement. Pluto
stiffened his legs so much I thought he'd get rigor mortis, carving little bob-
sled ruts into the carpet each time I walked from room to room for the rest of
the evening. When I sat, he ducked under the couch, pretending his entire existence wasn't tethered to a stranger. I heard Calvin cough a few times from
his room. On *Antiques Roadshow,* a bifocaled grandmother yelped when a

man in an ascot told her the umbrella holder was actually valuable arts and crafts pottery, suggesting with condescension she should move it inside. Tracy came as a package deal.

L et's make love," she said, turning to me on the couch.

"Is that a trick question?"

"I want you to make love to me."

"Maybe we can use this?" I said, holding up the leash.

Tracy unclipped Pluto and placed him in his crate for the night. Andy said it took two years to feel comfortable with a child. I wondered if that included a dog. And did the "I want you to make love to me" comment mean I was supposed to do most of the work tonight? I stripped down to my boxers and planned my route of attack. These relationship things took a lot more thought than traveling. Tracy kissed me on the forehead and hopped in the shower. *You might want to stretch out. You're a bit out of practice. Don't want to pull anything.* I was in the process of peeling off the rest of my clothing and joining her under the water when I heard a small voice from the other room.

"Mom. Mom."

"Tracy?"

"Mom!"

"Tracy? Calvin's calling for you. Can you hear me?"

"Mom!"

I pulled on my shirt and walked to his bedroom.

"Hey, buddy," I said, stroking his head. "How ya doing?"

"I can't breathe!"

"That's impossible. You need to breathe to say 'I can't breathe.' "

"Mom!"

His voice sounded like Darth Vader's, the forty-pound blond version.

"Okay, okay. Lemme get you some water."

I dashed to the bathroom and filled the Spider-Man cup from the tap.

"Here you go, Calvin. Drink away."

"I still can't breathe."

This time, wheezing and panicking, he sounded more convincing.

"It's gonna be okay. Just try to relax. Breathe deep. Your mom will be here any second."

He looked so helpless and scared, his little body tensing each time he tried to inhale. And for the first time I felt responsible for him. I pulled him onto my lap and ran my fingers through his sweaty hair.

"Relax. Breathe."

Then something happened, like in those sci-fi movies where the robots instantly download languages. I can't explain it, only that suddenly I knew stuff about Calvin. Lifting him off the bed, I knew what to do.

"Leave the water running," I said as we entered Tracy's bathroom.

She jumped out of the shower, and I sat with him on the toilet seat.

"Mom, I can't breathe."

"Just try to relax," she said. "The steam helps, remember?"

Tracy closed the door and turned off the cold.

"Croup, right?"

"Yeah. It usually doesn't last more than ten minutes."

"I remember my sister talking about it."

"I'll go get him some water."

"I already did."

The room soon refilled with warm mist and white noise. In the stillness, we waited without saying much more. I lifted his exhausted body to her bed and the space between us.

Ten Global Threats to Love

1. **TEXTING.** In theory, technology should enhance a couple's communication. But let me just respond to my friend's urgent message about her cheating boyfriend, or check the score of this cricket match. Now, what was I saying?

2. **MISS UNIVERSE.** How about a pageant that showcases a true sampling of world beauty? Add one for the men while you're at it. Instead, the world watches (and mimics) a bizarre display in which the contestants look eerily similar: straight hair and thin noses, unnaturally slender bodies, tanned but not too dark skin. Cut that afro and cover those tattoos. Don't want to be too ethnic.

3. **CARS.** Brazilians flirt on the buses. Africans share rides in vans. Europeans comingle on subways and trains. Cars, though, separate us from the masses. Instead of interacting, we listen to talk show hosts lecture about interacting. Around the world, we're becoming that man who knows a thousand ways to make love to woman, yet doesn't know any women.

4. **DOWRIES.** Throw in bride prices, trousseaus, and gift registries as well. They're about as helpful as a drunken wedding guest who loudly toasts to his old trysts with the bride.

5. **WEDDINGS, TOO.** In many wealthier nations, weddings have evolved from simple ceremonies to grand multiday affairs. The events require so much time and planning that couples spend their days talking more about golf tournaments and lobster crostini and less about their upcoming commitment. Once couples set a date, their weddings, and their relationships, go on autopilot. They should take a lesson

from the third world, where such celebrations are handled by families and communities, leaving couples with more time to focus on each other.

6. MUSIC FROM THE UNITED STATES. I know I sound like my father. I don't care. I still cringe every time I hear kids in rural Asia or Africa spout off about "pimps" or "hoochie mamas." Ah, yeah. That's how we roll here in Zambia. Keeping it real.

7. BANANA DICTATORS. Hugo Chávez pits rich against poor. Robert Mugabe turns blacks against whites. Mahmoud Ahmadinejad divides Arabs and Jews. They widen societal schisms and make it harder for couples to bridge the gaps. The United Nations should begin sanctioning leaders who squash love.

8. SOCCER AND SOAP OPERAS. I've yet to visit a country where romantic dates aren't contingent upon the viewing times of soap operas or the final whistles of soccer matches. With the emergence of twenty-four-hour soap opera networks and nonstop soccer channels, it's a miracle couples even date at all.

9. THE WORD "LOVE" ITSELF. Maybe that's because, in America, the word is so overly broad and overused it has become nearly meaningless. Other nations do a slightly better job, with a handful of words to describe the variations and degrees of love. But, c'mon, people. We have hundreds of ways to describe our hairstyles and coffee preferences. It's about time we threw a little love to "love."

10. THE LACK OF ROLE MODELS. UNICEF estimates there are more than 140 million orphans on the planet. Countless more grow up with single moms, cheating fathers, or couples who can't get along. They copy the sins of their parents, and pass them on to their children, beginning the cycle anew. The most serious threat to love is not being able to see love.

Faith

I thought you guys would be a lot older," said Magued as he met us at the Cairo airport.

"This gray hair doesn't count?" I said.

"They told me you guys were professional writers. You mind if I take off my tie?"

"Don't," said Kurt. "We're very important."

"Of course," he said, taking off his tie.

The Arab world is all about delegation, even when there's no responsibility to delegate. Residents spend each day readjusting pecking orders more often than a professional football coach during training camp. New York told Cairo we'd be in the country. Cairo told Golden Tours, who told the Isis Agency, who informed Ramses Tourism, who called Magued. Before we'd set one foot in Egypt our tourism dollars had already been split a dozen ways, with Magued assigned to do all the work and receive the smallest share.

Egypt is one of those countries that does everything possible to keep you from exploring on your own. Just try. We received countless calls in the months before our trip urging us to sign up for the twenty-one-day Egyptian Extravaganza or the Wonders of the Nile. No, no thank you, we said. We just want to go talk to people. Impossible, they replied. Only if you go on the tour. You can talk to the guides at the pyramids. They speak perfect English and twenty-seven other languages.

Most people assume this relentless tourism shuffling is the result of a heavy-handed government that doesn't want foreigners to see their less-than-picturesque side, the slums and cinder-block villages, hometown turf for fervent anti-West sentiment. View the Sphinx, cruise the Nile, ride a camel. Oh, and tip heavily. *Baksheesh! Baksheesh!* Now go home.

I don't agree. This gives the Egyptian government too much credit. They have a hard enough time clothing their officers, let alone getting them to act in a coordinated fashion. No, I peg the push for package deals to a much more powerful force: Egyptian businessmen. They'll know your full itinerary, wife's ring size, spaces in your house that could use a "handmade carpet," and preference for dromedary or Bactrian camels before the government agent even stamps your passport. In the worldwide tourism game, the fewer the dollars, the quicker the knives to divide them. Egypt is Freddy Krueger.

So are you writing for a magazine?" Magued asked as we motored toward the city in a rickety white van.

"No," I said.

"Who do you work for?"

"Ourselves."

"That's nice. It's not possible in Egypt. Welcome to the land of a million bosses."

"Thanks," I said. "We're jazzed to be here."

"What can I take you to see? The pyramids? Egyptian Museum?"

"Love."

"Love?"

"We want to talk to Egyptians about love."

"This is a first for me. It's usually the pyramids."

Magued apprenticed for a few tour operators before joining his current company. The business afforded him the chance to travel as well, an unfathomable rarity for most of his countrymen. He giggled as he talked, slouching and turning in his seat while barking the occasional instruction to our silent driver. His forehead looked like it came straight from a hieroglyph, and his five o'clock shadow appeared daily by noon. Behind his dark-rimmed glasses his eyes darkened on the corners. Doonesbury eyes. I guessed he was twenty-five, though I was usually far off on that sort of thing in the third world.

"We want to find out how Egyptians make love," said Kurt.

"Your brother, he is the joker," he said.

"Yes," I said. "But I am curious about that. Sex. Dating. Anything"

"Okay. I know where I can take you. We'll go to your hotel now, then take a walk around. You can ask me anything you want. I'm an expert on love."

"Are you married?"

"No. But all Egyptian men are experts in this subject."

Bags unloaded, we strode through the bubblegum-in-your-hair snarl that is the Cairo street system. Past the aged deco and art nouveau apartment buildings kept together with plaster and promise. Down Talaat Harb Street, in front of the bakeries packed with Arabs and *asabeeh* pastries; beyond the storefronts with the planet's least sexy mannequins (no bare midriffs or thrusting pelvises here). Over cracked sidewalks and past the outstretched arms of the unrich.

"The money has gone to the suburbs," said Magued. "The big malls are on the edge of town."

"Where are you taking us?" asked Kurt.

"Here," said Magued after crossing over a pedestrian bridge and descending into a crush of shops and overcaffeinated salesmen that made the floor of the New York Stock Exchange seem tranquil by comparison.

The pleas were frantic, but the goods were divided neatly by subject. This street housed the hardware hawkers, that one the furniture dealers, and everywhere the souvenir. "Meester, you look. No charge." Carts and browsers blocked every inch of sidewalk and street, making it impossible to drive, though don't tell that to the trucks that attempted to do so.

"Love it," Kurt said. "Complete chaos. Here, get a picture of me with the crowd in the background."

"I don't really need to shop," I said.

"You said you wanted to see love, right?" said Magued.

"Yes."

"Here is love."

"Here is Target. On steroids."

"Stand here. Watch. I'll take a photo of your brother."

I stepped back to the stoop of a butcher shop and waited, between the skinned goat heads and a wheelbarrow of plastic sunglasses, for whatever Magued had in mind. A weary fruit vendor rested his arm against his cart and listened without expression to customers as they haggled over oranges. His scale looked to be from another century, with hand-cut weights of dubious measurements. Kurt and Magued emerged from the crowd.

"Am I right?" asked Magued.

"Yes. About what?"

"The love. Do you see it?"

"I see a bored shopkeeper and a lot of finicky shoppers."

"My friend. Look at this. Watch this man over there. He is not buying fruit."

A balding Egyptian in a dark wool suit fondled oranges without looking at them. Beside him stood a portly woman half his age in a long maroon skirt and bejeweled *hijab* headdress, a laden bag of market groceries by her side. In a brusque and sudden fashion, the man's arm grazed against hers while reaching for another piece of fruit. I would have missed it had Magued not pointed it out.

"He's hitting on her?" I asked.

"More like a small collision to see what happens."

In this case, the young woman picked up her bag and moved along without comment or pause.

"That's it? That's his pickup?"

"It's not so much the action as the reaction. Does she protest? Does she look back at him? The man, he is trying to test things. The Egyptian man, he likes to test."

We saw it time and again in the land of the Nile. Behind the veils and social codes, there's a crab dance in Egypt between men and women as intricate and omnipresent as those on the world's other courtship floors. It's just more subtle. Soft shoe instead of tango. The more conservative the region, the more delicate the ritual.

Arabs are masters of the stolen glance. They see all from the far corners of their eyes, with heads fixed and expressions stoic. A woman caught gazing at a man would be considered a harlot and likely be castigated by the masses nearby. Men have no problem berating female strangers for what they view as lapses from the Islamic social code, the loudest to condemn often the most likely to violate.

The results can be equally ominous for men who overstep in their advances, especially if the woman is married. Few Egyptians would stop a man from being beaten by an outraged husband. Few Arab courts would convict a husband who killed his wife's paramour. Best to keep your eyes trained ahead and your hands to yourself.

"So, Magued," I said. "I've always wondered about this. How do Arab men spot the woman of their dreams if she's covered in cloth?"

"Very carefully," he said. "Egyptian men will tell you they can decipher a woman's beauty even when she's wearing a black *abeyya,* fully covered. The wrists and ankles, they say, speak of hidden curves. And the eyes, the *eyes,* give everything away."

Magued's countrymen told us the same.

"You can tell from the face if she prays five times a day."

"Most Egyptians check out the back of the ankle. If it is round, it's a good body. If it sticks out, she is too thin."

Yes, you heard them right. Many men and women in Egypt see slenderness as an indication of poverty or infertility. Women encourage each other to pad garments and take second helpings to bolster figures. They alter even the most conservative dress to emphasize curves.

The women keep their preferences in men hidden among all but their closest of friends and relatives. Sure, they have strong opinions about physical appearance and conduct. Of course they notice. All Egyptian women notice. They just can't do anything about it in public. This would be detrimental to the one route Muslim society affords them, a goal to which they aspire without pause. Marriage.

After a few days in Cairo, Magued signed us up for a Nile cruise. I am now certain the cruise booking is genetically encoded in all Egyptians who work in the tourism industry. Kurt protested, but Magued assured. This package would be different. We flew south to Aswan to board a boat heading north. All hail our new ruler, the *Crown Princess.* The activities board at the check-in desk read: BELLY DANCING, ARABIAN FEAST. Similar boats lined the shore, all sounding like entries at the Westminster Kennel Club: *Domina Prestige, Alexander the Great, Nefertari.*

"I've got to get off this boat," I told Kurt.

"Let's call Magued and see if we can get our money back."

"It's Egypt. Nobody gets their money back."

"Then at least give him grief."

The cruise ships stacked against each other like cattle in semis. After an hour on one, I felt the same. To reach land, and freedom, we shuffled through the lobbies and metal detectors of the five liners between our boat and Aswan. *Sun Princess, Luxor, Sun II.* Land. We quickened our pace away, anywhere away.

Kurt spotted a call center off the main road. A block off the tourist zones, the streets and buildings atrophied and crumbled. They are the dried arteries where foreign dollars don't flow. He disappeared into the phone booth while I paid for the call.

"Congratulations," I said to the young Nubian attendant.

She lifted her head from a stack of papers.

"Your engagement," I said, pointing at her thin golden ring.

"This is just a ring."

"Ooops. My bad."

"No problems. I am engaged."

"Whew. Congrats again."

"Thank you."

Her headscarf sat back on her hair, exposing her arched eyebrows and shiny forehead. I looked around the room to make sure no one else had entered.

"My name is Franz."

"Marwa."

"My brother and I are over here on a mission."

"What about?"

"Love."

She looked over my shoulder to scan the room as well.

"Do you mind me asking how long you've been engaged?"

"Five months."

"And you met him in town?"

"Right here. He needed to make a call."

"Big wedding? I hear Egyptians love big weddings."

"About a thousand."

"When you met, what did he say? Did he compliment you?"

"No."

"Did he smile?"

"No."

"Did he say or do anything to lead you to believe he was interested in you?"

"No."

He did what most men do in Egypt when they decide they are ready to take a wife: He went to her family; introduced himself; gave them his age, education, job prospects, and family history; then told them he wanted to marry her. This is a delicate process, a high-stakes job interview more than anything, one that varies from region to region.

Relationships get serious quickly here. Forget skipping steps. Forget awkward first dates at Applebee's or that moment of panic when you fret about kissing your partner good night. Egyptians fly past the whole courtship thing altogether. In this land of Islam, and especially in the rural villages of Lower Egypt and the western desert, you don't date. You marry. The Koran says if you date as a couple there will be three of you—you, her, and the devil.

In some parts of Egypt, the groom-to-be sends his parents to plead his case. If he does it himself, he can never praise their daughter too much for fear they'll view him as a letch. Comments about her beauty are considered vulgar. A line like "I see where she gets her good looks" would land the Romeo on his derriere outside. He must maintain an amiable poker face throughout, focusing on the aspects most important to her family: his faith, his income, his family, his prospects.

Marwa sat in a corner for the entire engagement pitch.

"Were you surprised? Elated? Terrified?"

"I cannot say too much because my family will suspect I am too forward. This is the way that it is done."

"But did you want to marry him?"

"Yes. He is respectable, kindly. You can depend on him. The relationship suddenly happened."

I'll say. Egyptians, by and large, are comfortable with this scenario. Including the women. Love, as they see it, is something that grows through commitment and marriage. It's a product of a healthy union rather than a prerequisite to one. If the woman longs for another, she sees it in those terms, longing, not as a once-in-a-lifetime bond that will never be re-created. Why would you risk a decision as important as marriage on something as trivial and fleeting as crushes or butterflies? Far more important in that foundation are the I beams of family and monetary support. Marriage is a decision of the left brain more than the heart. Only a fool would tell you otherwise.

After her suitor left the house, Marwa's family began to ask about him. Not to ask Marwa, mind you. Her opinion wasn't as important as the thoughts of those who knew him and grew up with him. They took two weeks to cast about for character references, a standard amount of time according to the Egyptian social code. If the quest lasts a few days, it wouldn't be due diligence; longer than two weeks, and the groom-to-be can assume the answer is no. Many families consider this to be a polite way of declining his proposal. Exceptions occur when the suitor's family lives far away.

This is all well and good from the man's perspective. He'll have completed his research, too, asking around, in a tactful way, about the woman he contemplates marrying.

"Please come to my wedding," said Marwa in a soft tone so Kurt wouldn't hear.

"That's very kind of you."

Another customer opened the front door.

"Just please bring a woman with you," she whispered. "I don't want people to suspect anything."

B rother," said Kurt, putting his arm around me as we walked out to the street. "How do you like belly dancing?"

"You didn't get the money back."

"Franz, a Nile cruise is a must here in Egypt. A once-in-a-lifetime experience."

"Hey, my friend," yelled a shopkeeper on Saad Zaghloul Street.

We stopped.

"I've never had as many friends as I do in Egypt," said Kurt.

"How's business?" I asked.

Never ask an Arab businessman "How's business?"

"I haven't made a sale all week! Come. Sit down. Looking for free."

The shelves spilled with brass candleholders, inlaid boxes, and all things Tut.

"Okay," I said. "Let's talk about love."

"Okay. Hamid!"

An assistant appeared with a tray of tea. Ahmed instructed him to set it on the floor, then looked to us before lighting a cigarette. Do you mind? Go ahead. He inhaled deeply and stroked his goatee. His clothes and cockiness seemed American. Las Vegas, even. No, Laughlin. He was twenty-eight, ancient according to his mother, who nagged him at each meal to get married.

"Mohammed says we must have many kids to make more Muslims," he said. "So the country can stay big, strong, prepare to fight Israel."

Without moving his head, Ahmed gave the once-over to every female tourist and Egyptian woman who strolled past his shop.

"How about those two?" I said, pointing to two young Egyptian teenagers in jeans.

"This is very bad. These girls don't marry. After her religion, she should have good manners, good family, be respectable, polite. We like the ones who have beauty, but it is not a necessity."

Ahmed echoed the opinions of most Egyptian men we met. They professed to place beauty at the bottom of the bridal wish list. Piousness, "as prescribed by Mohammed, peace and blessings upon him," was the clear number one, with "good family" second, the translation here and around the world being "rich family." Motherhood potential and industriousness usually followed on the desirability chart. Egyptian men boasted they weren't as obsessed with physical appearances, though they were equally quick to give their opinions.

"First is the face," said Ahmed. "And her breasts. And shape. We prefer the skin to be between black and white. Like Jennifer Lopez!"

"Sounds like there's a worldwide crush on Jennifer Lopez," I said.

"Oh, man."

"But how can you gauge a relationship's potential after such a short time? What do you do after the family has given their blessing?"

"Test!" he said.

Tests, said his countrymen. Egyptian men are consumed with challenging every stage of the relationship, prodding and poking so often it's a wonder any last at all. So far, all Ahmed's potential brides had failed.

"We meet again in the cafeteria," he said. "I say things like 'I forgot my wallet.' This is because I am rich. I want to see if they love me or my money."

"I thought you hadn't made a sale all week?"

"This is before."

One woman aced the first round. After Ahmed told her he needed to pay some money to the bank, she took the bracelets off her wrists and offered the gold to him.

"She passed this test, but she failed another. She told me she had slept with a man. I need to marry a virgin."

Yup. Muslim men in Egypt waver not on this point, though most confess the sex on their wedding night was not their initial encounter. As one groom-to-be told me, "When you go to buy some fruit, do you want what has been out on the street or a piece that is from the box inside? I don't want a piece of fruit everyone has seen. I want from a box."

"In America, you cannot compare a woman to a piece of fruit," I replied. "You can only compare *parts* of a woman to a piece of fruit. Lips like cherries and such."

Divorcées are an exception to the Arab virgins-only rule.

"No problem," said Ahmed, while a fellow shopkeeper nodded in approval. "We see them as easy. The other women don't want this woman to come to their home. They think their husbands will sleep with them."

Tourists get a pass as well.

"For a foreigner, it is not a problem if she shows flesh or is not a virgin," he said. "This is my dream, to marry an American woman. If I live in America, I will clean the plates. She can be a Christian or even a Jew."

"Wow, that's love," I said.

"The Jews, you know, told their people about the September eleven the day before. This is why no Jews died."

I shook my head, depressed more than angry, and told him he was wrong.

In the early morning light, as the French tourists slept and the boat stewards swept the Astroturf deck, I sat with my coffee on the top deck of the ship and looked for the Egypt of old. Across sand banks and date palm clusters, birds I'd known only from the crossword puzzles, ibises and egrets, waded through flotsam. A distant minaret stirred men to prayer. Patchwork feluccas shuttled goats and boxes, and the nascent sun stretched out for its daily attack.

After an hour, the deck chairs began to fill with leathery Europeans, and with their arrival went my romantic image. We docked midday in Edfu, and I wandered off the boat thinking about Egypt's relationship tests. I waded past the knickknack carts and deeper into town, past the horse-drawn carriage drivers with their talking-point English and well-worn dirty jokes. Tests. No wonder the Egyptian women we'd met seemed a little jaded.

We do the same.

Truth is, I'd come to find out, most Egyptian women knew the games their suitors played, as well as the proper answers to satisfy their mates. Their tears were often as theatrical as the ruses played by their men. *Again, just like America.* It wasn't the most honest way to begin a relationship, but both the men and women swore by the importance of challenging the bond before it is consummated.

I paused behind a group of schoolchildren watching SpongeBob Square-Pants on a grainy television outside. A young girl turned her head from the program and stared my way. I waved, and for a second she waved back. *At what age does that stop here?* A man in his twenties approached.

"Do you know this show?" he asked.

"Yes, though I still can't figure it out. Something about a hyperactive loofah with a bad tailor."

"The kids like it."

Mohamed wore Levi's knockoffs and a Nike windbreaker. He talked about visiting the United States one day. "My dream!" From where we stood, he embraced large swaths of American culture, blending style and tastes with ancient Arab norms. Mohamed gushed about Hollywood love stories, though he stopped short when it came to his own life. A movie is fantasy, he said, a relationship serious business.

"Egyptian men and women are not friends," he said. "We have custom. We cannot do this friendship. If I live like a Westerner, then I can never trust my life."

Mohamed explained he'd recently accepted a two-year job in Saudi Arabia. From his wallet he produced a computer-enhanced wedding photo, his bride seated and stern, Mohamed with his hand on her shoulder, airbrushed purple skies and streaking stars all around, their silhouette superimposed in the corner in case you forgot. HAPPY WEDDING, read the caption. He planned to bring his wife and young daughter to Riyadh as soon as he earned enough money to support them. For now, they lived with her mother.

"When I decided to get married, I made a list of girls and I ask questions," said Mohamed. "Who are their families? Who will be the grandfathers and grandmothers of my children? Family is first."

"That sounds very practical," I said.

"The prophet says you marry a woman for four things—her internal beauty, her money, her family, and her religion. He said, I recommend you to choose the woman to marry for her religion. You will never regret it. He also said the most important thing, after being religious, is a good woman. When you look at her, she pleases you. When you are away from the house, she will not betray you.

"I try to test her manners after I decide to marry her. I ask her colleagues questions about her manners. Does she go around with any of them? Is she polite? I follow up with this criteria, and I was convinced."

But he hadn't convinced her family. That's because there loomed another prospective groom, one who had asked to marry before Mohamed stated his intentions. This is a no-no in the Arab world. Don't buy what your brother buys, the saying goes. Better to let the family make their decision separately. Mohamed didn't know there was another. Worse than the competition was the fact his rival had a job. He did not.

After a worrisome couple of weeks, fortune smiled on Mohamed. His prospective father-in-law had studied abroad and viewed himself as progressive. The young woman's opinion swayed the decision, a rarity in Egypt and a lottery win for Mohamed.

"Her father's point of view was to decline me because I had graduated but hadn't had a good job. The other man was employed as a teacher. So he wanted this man."

"But you did it, man. Congrats."

"I was very happy, but sad somehow. I felt for the other one. He asked first, and I had no right. As soon as I got engaged, I looked for work immediately. I got a job two weeks later."

Women we interviewed, usually in private homes or areas away from public scrutiny, talked of good jobs, good families, good manners. And religion above everything else. Frequently they'd quote the Prophet. "If a man comes to you with good religion, good manners, marry him to your daughter." They acknowledged that denying too many men their hand in marriage would ultimately lead to bad reputations for them and their families. "The shadow of a man is better than the shadow of a wall," advises an Egyptian proverb. Don't be too picky.

Egyptian women, especially the single ones, prize marriage as prerequisite to a happy life. You need a husband to have children and children to have contentment, they said. Simple. This is prescribed in the Koran. Pray, marry, pray, multiply, pray.

The goal is so etched in the hopes of young women they avoid actions that could be counted against them in the march to wed—casual conversations with male strangers, overly Western clothing and tastes, a raised voice, public affection, sex. Premarital urges are squashed despite high divorce rates, frequent cheating, and a drone of criticism from every village and large city about how badly men behave. "Trusting a man is like trusting the water in a colander," goes another Egyptian saying. To most women, their future, their prospects, remain with a man and a marriage. They play the endgame rather than the dating game.

"Egyptian women can't give up their ideals of a marriage and family," said a married women hesitant to give us her name. "American women don't think as much about consequences. They focus on what they want. Egyptian women think only about the consequences. They want to advance, but they don't want to risk losing their wishes. They will wait here, wait for the opportunity. Egyptian women are patient, calculating."

But c'mon. Even with this deliberate concept of love and marriage, with all the extensive background checks and personal references, with supportive families and strengthened beliefs, aren't there ample cases of buyer's remorse? What happens when a couple discovers they have nothing in common?

No problem, said Egypt. That's what the engagement is for. To many Egyptians, this is Plan B. The engagement portion of the relationship is a formalized dating period with the cover of marriage to lessen the chances a woman or her family will be dishonored. Kurt and I met several men who'd been engaged two, three, or four times. Still, there are limits.

"You can't get engaged too many times," said Magued. "You will be broke."

What about sex? Well, the good news for anyone thinking about sex in the Muslim world is that the Koran is filled with explicit instructions and encouragements. The bad news is that the Koran is filled with explicit instructions and encouragements. No coded messages here. In fact, Muslims historically have been much more open than people of other religions about sex and the role it should play in society. They even have their own how-to manual, the Perfumed Garden, a fifteenth-century text that matches the Kama Sutra stroke for stroke.

Today's imams and clerics are seen not only as teachers of the Koran but as sex and relationship counselors. They are Dr. Phil/Pat Robertson combos, and their advice on both fronts is usually intertwined. As part of their job descriptions, they're expected to marry early and produce as many offspring as they can afford. An imam without children would be like a professor without a degree. Clerics are more than happy to talk about sex to anyone who will listen. That's where the disagreements begin.

The Koran is PG-13 clear on a set number of sex-related issues. Have sex for reproduction or even for fun, the sacred text advocates. Please your partner. Make the act enjoyable. Just limit your sessions to ones with your spouse. "Strike the adulteress and adulterer one hundred times." Abstain during certain occasions: fasting periods or when wives are menstruating, for example. And stay away from homosexuality. "If two men commit a lewd act, punish them both."

The arguments emerge on the areas not outlined, spilling over into mosque discussions and Internet chat rooms, *sheesha* tobacco pipe bars and street corners, podiums all controlled by the male voice. Egyptians are more than happy to talk about sex in public. The problem is that women rarely join the discussion. The only place Arabs don't talk about sex, locals joke, is in the bedroom.

As a result, the logic gets twisted. Just ask the women. Men in the cafés launch into lengthy debates on whether or not wives should be clothed while having sex or if good Muslims should engage in oral sex. Shiite men condemn masturbation, while some Sunnis advocate a more accomodating approach. Few sex topics are off-limits.

Egyptian men do this in a strident though tactful way, focusing on the issue in theoretical terms rather than lecturing their brethren about the practices they employ at home. When they do mention their wives on rare occasions, it is usually not by name, referring to "the mother of my children."

"You cannot look at your wife's breasts or her vagina if you are a good Muslim," said Esam, a goat herder from Edfu.

"I thought the whole point of having your wife wear a veil is that you alone get to gaze at her beauty when the curtains are drawn," I said.

"No, this is to prevent others from looking at her. Not for you."

"The Koran says you can't look at your wife's breasts?"

"Not Koran. Hadith."

Many of the bedroom restrictions preached by the clerics stem not from the Koran but from the follow-up thoughts and observations recorded by followers of Mohammed. Hadith.

So Egypt today has a Koran that touches on some sex subjects but leaves others up for discussion, clerics who differ widely on matters sexual, a raging debate that largely ignores the female voice, and a substantial generation gap, not to mention limited sex education in schools, and contrived Hollywood love stories in their movie theaters.

What's the result? Horrible sex, some locals say.

"Egyptian men do not respect the feelings of women," said Inji. "They feel sex is to please them. They don't know how to please a woman, and they don't try. Couples don't talk about sex. They don't tell each other what they want, even when they're married."

"We don't have the guts to talk about sex in detail," said Haila, referring to the communications gap between Egyptian men and women.

The movie *al-Naama wa al tawoos (Ostrich and Peacock)* struck a chord with many Egyptians. It told the story of an inexperienced fiancé who fretted about how to perform in bed on his wedding night. His solution: practice sex with prostitutes and hours of pornography. This, of course, stunned his wife on their honeymoon and killed their sex life.

We debarked in Luxor and sprinted away from the boat. For good. Kurt and I poured out over the country, to Mansura and Dahab, to Sinai and back to Cairo, cornering Egyptians on the topic of love. We had no problem finding the men, most sitting outside their work or beside a water pipe at the *sheesha* bars. We sat, they talked. And talked. My hand grew tired as I scribbled their words. Arab men do not hesitate to linger at the lectern.

In the villages and rural areas, they talked of the benefits and downside of having more than one wife. "This two mothers-in-law is no good. Very loud, very expensive." Many kept it secret, lying to the census takers when they come to count the broods. Younger generations and urbanites preferred one wife and smaller families. "Two kids—one boy, one girl."

Harder to find were forthcoming women. Try talking to a woman in public in the Arab world. Within five minutes you'll have several dozen male kib-itzers answering for her, then arguing among themselves about what she thinks. Kurt and I kept the talks with women far away from the village watch, in living rooms and backs of stores.

Still they sounded as if they were under surveillance. The unmarried ones spoke of marriage as the main road to happiness. They talked far more of the concept than of the man they'd like to join. It was as if they hadn't thought that part through. Their mothers and sisters preached the virtues of being wed—a partner for that battle called life, financial security, kids, kids, kids—while skipping over the man entirely.

We're fine, they said, sometimes convincingly. We don't need to mirror the West. We don't need your role model, a failed one, we might add. We're mak-ing progress, in shuffles more than strides. Things move slower here. We are gaining a greater say. While he sits in the coffeehouse, we run the real house. If the marriage goes sour, we can initiate a divorce now. The state will enforce child support. Our ranks and positions grow in government, media, life.

We're not the helpless creatures you make us out to be. Our strength is in-visible to you. It comes behind closed doors. We choose this lifestyle. Forget the veil. The West focuses too much on the veil. We choose to wear it. This avoids problems. It's easier for us.

We're content. Really. God willing. *Insha'Allah.*

For years I'd itched to see more of a fight, a massive uprising from women across Islam, out in the open, demanding equality and respect. I wanted protests, strikes. The Gdansk shipyards, Tiananmen Square.

Don't worry, assured the women of Egypt. The struggle is indeed taking place, though far from your eyes.

In the end, I believed them.

I'm freezing my ass off," said Kurt as we rode in the back of the pickup through the nighttime desert air.

"Abdul said a half hour," I said. "It's been a half hour."

"Is this his friend or something? The guy who's getting married."

"Seems like you're either a friend or a cousin of everyone here."

We'd met Abdul earlier in the day, a genial man from the endless line of male Egyptians who approach Westerners on the street and offer anything they can—rides, tours, meals, help. After several years on the road, I felt Kurt and I were able to distinguish between the hustlers and the hosts within a few minutes. Paydar, we called it, Kurt's antennae a degree more honed than mine. Abdul seemed sincere in his offer to escort us to a village wedding that night. I'm going anyway, he said; why don't you come along? It seemed a good idea at the time.

At last we slowed and pulled off the road to a half-finished village apartment complex. An old man rose from his crouch, smoking a cigarette and pointing to where we should park. He hugged us all.

"The father," said Abdul.

"Welcome, welcome," he said. "Thank you."

"It's an honor," I said. "Thank you for inviting us to the party."

"We hate George Bush, but we love Americans," he said, a mantra heard ad nauseam.

We followed him to the stairwell, a tube of rebar and stucco. What the strip mall is to America, the unfinished apartment is to the Egyptian skyline. It's as if the entire country defaulted on its building loan at the same time.

"Do they plan to complete the apartment soon?" I asked Abdul.

"Not until they are married, and the families have decided how to pay."

"Ah, I see."

In Egypt, you live at home until you are married, then move to your new home immediately after. Only then will the families open their wallets and complete the apartment. *Fatha* is a negotiated process, and at times an intense one, though there are standards and rules to prevent meltdowns. Much depends on the wealth. As in other Egyptian business dealings, whoever has more pays more.

Finances being equal, the bride's family traditionally pays for the kitchen, everything from light fixtures to silverware. His family would then cover the plumbing, couch, and dinner table. For the bedroom, her family would provide the furniture, but he would pay for the mattress. In Egypt, the man must always supply the mattress.

"And he will also pay for the television set," said Inji, a woman we met in Cairo. "To have a TV is a big dream for a lot of Egyptian women."

As best as possible, they try to fashion a fair split to keep everyone feeling good about the union and not griping about furniture costs on the big day. They also strive for parity in case the union doesn't survive. It will be easier to divide the belongings, knowing families explained.

Fathers have long constructed unfinished houses in the country, abodes to be filled by their married sons and daughters in future years. The roots of this practice extend to the days of child brides and prepubescent grooms too young to live on their own. By necessity, the process has always been communal.

K urt and I knocked on the open door.

"Welcome, come in," said a young man, rising from the couch to greet us.

Wiry and nervous, with a sparse goatee and a borrowed sports coat, the groom looked like he was on his way to a junior high prom.

"That's a nice television," I said.

"Thank you. My wife, she pick this one."

"You've been working on the place."

"My family, yes. I show you."

The Arab world may seem a dusty palette from the outside, but behind the doors is a love of the vibrant and bold. Their kitchen was awash in powder blue, their bedroom an amplified lime green. The walls had been painted before the windows were framed. Details, details. Everything at its Egyptian pace. The refrigerator must have cost a month's wages, I guessed. Boxes and dirt gathered at the bottom of the stairwell. I looked out the window to an open sewer line and dusty walkway and thought of the old Soviet apartments with neglected communal areas and no expense spared inside.

"Congratulations, my friend," I said. "I'm sorry I didn't bring a wedding gift."

"This is a gift that you are here. You will bring good fortune to my marriage."

"I don't know about that. My fiancée didn't show up to my wedding."

The young groom scrunched his brow, and I halted my explanation after realizing this might not be the most appropriate time.

"Just joking," I said.

"Please, sit," he said, pointing me to the couch in front of the television. "We will leave soon."

An uncle dozed in an easy chair as the Egyptian news flashed several clips of George Bush and camouflaged soldiers.

* * *

his wasn't our first wedding celebration. Kurt and I had attended a few in Cairo and Aswan. They didn't look too different from the American version. Over the last half century, Egyptian weddings evolved from village celebrations to hotel ballroom soirees. I liked seeing the horse carts out front or listening to the old women blare their ear-piercing ululations. The rest felt like a scene from *The Wedding Singer,* right down to the candy-coated almonds, satin bridesmaids' dresses, and 1980s cover tunes at volumes loud enough to draw complaints from Libya.

Egyptians scrimp for a lifetime, only to spend the bulk of their life savings within a two-week period—furnishing the house and paying for the wedding. Traditionally, her family picks up the tab for the engagement parties, while his foots the bill for the wedding festivities. The celebrations are as much a union of families as the joining of two. They're also not-so-subtle brag fests with invites to all and party favors like candles or figurines.

The Egyptian hotel weddings were boisterous and fun. And completely uninspiring. Like so many American weddings I'd attended, the happy couple at times seemed superfluous to the rigid agenda.

Just like yours. You had a ten-page time line, remember.

Abdul, Kurt, and I jumped back in the truck and followed the groom toward the music. I heard it as we drove down the dirt road. This was more of a drone, a reedy wail cutting its way around brick shacks and town alleys. We parked our car a few blocks away. Drums joined the percussion. Then a haunting, rhythmic voice above it all. Kurt and I walked toward the music, silenced by what we saw.

The singer, backed by players with hand drums and a ten-string mandolin, sat on a platform in the town square. All around them sat the town. The entire town. Hundreds of kneeling and reclining Arab men, women, and children, still and silent. They'd brought carpets and kilims from their homes and stretched them on the dirt. With the stillness and anticipation of an opera audience before a well-known aria, they leaned in to better absorb the words of the troubadour. The singer held the microphone like a glass of wine, his toast to them.

"He's written this song especially for the wedding," whispered Abdul.

Across the square, the groom took his place beside his future bride, holding his hand aloft toward the singer to acknowledge the lyrics. Aunts and well-wishers welcomed him with their eyes.

"This is a love song," continued Abdul. "He says they will soar through commitment and faith. It is the prescription of Allah."

I didn't feel Allah in our midst. I felt the town's commitment, and I felt honored to be among the entire population as they said, in body and word, they would do everything possible to support this union and ensure its success.

In America, we ask if anyone has an objection. It's an afterthought, a formality. Can you imagine someone actually standing up and saying, "Well, yes. I do. I just don't think her orderliness meshes with his lethargy." We get off easy. We're not asked to affirm, only to be silent.

This was a mass pledge of support. They'd spent days with the couple, verifying their assistance at every pause. This was real, all-encompassing community backing, the kind we used to provide long before the gated communities and drive-through windows and other "advances" that keep us in our homes and cars, afar from human contact. *We've lost that.* The band moved to another song and the crowd lined up to shake the couple's hands. *I don't know the names of my neighbors anymore.*

The camaraderie, the warmth—I'd felt them before. On my wedding day years ago, when my bride didn't show but my family and friends did. When I asked, they came. *We don't ask enough. It could be this way at home.*

Looking at the groom, in his buttoned coat and unbridled pride, I felt more envious than I'd ever been at a wedding. *They're going to be all right.*

Magued!" I said on our return to Cairo after three weeks in Upper Egypt and the Sinai peninsula. "We missed you."

"My brothers. Have you found love?"

"Personally? No," said Kurt.

"I wouldn't think so," he said. "It's okay for a Muslim man to marry a Christian. They assume she'll convert. Tougher for a Christian man to marry a Muslim woman. That could get violent."

"Noted."

We met at the café in front of the Cosmopolitan, a hotel as old-fashioned as the name. The tarnished bell on the front desk summoned managers from their catnaps; the waiters sported white dinner jackets; and it took me fifteen minutes to figure out I had to close the swinging glass doors on the elevator before the thing would work.

"C'mon," he said. "I'm taking you to an expert on love."

In the late afternoon, we dodged crowded minivan taxis sprinting workers to their night shifts. We walked past carts laden with towers of oranges and nectarines, fruit that never seemed to taste as good as it looked on display, and crowded apartments draped in drying clothes, men's trousers in front, dresses and undergarments tucked behind. Eventually we made our way to an upscale part of town. Magued rang the buzzer on the jewelry shop, and the guard let us in.

The owner, George, had just sold a large wedding ring. He grinned and rubbed his thick hands together, his body framed by a walk-in safe that remained from the days of British rule. He wore a loud mosaic sweater, a hand-me-down from the Huxtables.

"Beautiful," said George. "Just beautiful."

From his vantage point behind the glass counters and shimmering gems, George sees more than sales. He's an unofficial relationship prognosticator, priding himself on his ability to predict if the happy couple will flourish or not.

"For a couple to come here, this means they are getting serious," he said. "Most of the time, the woman will come several times before and get to know the inventory. Then she will come with her man and act surprised. In Egypt, the woman chooses. On average they spend about three to four thousand dollars here."

Or about twice what the average Egyptian makes in a year. You don't see stones on wedding rings outside the affluent neighborhoods in Cairo or Alexandria. Even the women who can afford them tend to wear jewelry only at big weddings or galas, upscale affairs behind electric fences and security details. For most married women in Egypt who can afford it, the unbroken symbol of their commitment is a simple gold-plated band with their beloved's name inscribed inside. A man is expected to purchase two rings. He and his fiancée will wear one each on their right hands, then switch them to their left hands during the wedding ceremony. In practice, most of the male hands in Egypt remain bare.

"I can tell if a relationship is going to last," said George. "If the woman lets me touch her hand a lot, there is a problem. Also with her eye. She should stare at the man as much as the stone."

Other red flags include when a man says he'd like to spend a set amount while his fiancée pushes for more. Or when the woman offers to throw in some of her own money to get a more valuable ring. Often women will return to the store and plead their case for a larger stone. If they disagree in public, his sales staff will fidget and smile uncomfortably. This is poor form in the Arab world.

"When a couple is fighting, we collect all the jewelry and ask them to take the fight outside."

A "good omen," according to George, occurs when the bride-to-be says things like "whatever you can afford" or "let's save our money for our children." If she holds her mate's arm throughout the process, the chances are high the couple will enjoy a happy life together, opined the jeweler.

Truth is, George likes the broken engagements. Either way, he profits. When the man calls it off, the woman keeps the ring. If the woman calls it off, the groom returns the ring and receives a 75 percent refund. George pockets the rest and sells the ring to someone else. This only happens about 5 percent of the time, he said. Just to be safe: cash or credit card only.

For all the happy moments he shares with his customers, George remains jaded. Too many men who cheat and too many families who meddle, he concluded.

"It's a business," he said with a shrug, though I couldn't tell if he was talking about the shop or marriage in general.

"The number-one thing in marriage is money. For rich people, they expect their kids to have a higher standard of living, a step up. The poor guys turn more poor. The rich guys want their kids to go the other way and marry up."

*A*rggggg, I said to myself as we walked outside. Does money ever have a positive impact on a relationship? Does sudden wealth solve any problems? Or has it done to love what oil has done to the Middle East—overpromised, underwhelmed, more often the exacerbation of problems than elixir.

"I need a drink," I told Magued. "Is there a bar nearby?"

"Yes. Café Stella. It's a writers' bar."

"Ahh, a place for the unemployed."

"Exactly."

I loved Café Stella. It was small, with just a dozen two-person tables and a water closet true to its name—a phone booth–sized bathroom with a wall-mounted urinal and a Wild West door that allowed patrons to relieve themselves while ordering another beer from the bar.

Café Stella teemed with its regular assortment of lapsed Muslims, thirsty

Christians, and those who couldn't care less about any god. You didn't see long beards or darkened patches on foreheads from pressing your head to a prayer mat multiple times a day. Egyptians called such marks "raisins," *zebiba*. Outside the bar they were a badge of honor, the darker the better. Infected? Better still. "That man is so pious, he refuses to alter his prayer ritual despite the sore."

Café Stella was honest. It was open, in all senses. It even came with a few women, a pleasant respite from the male-dominated settings throughout the trip. I realized how much I missed the mix. A young woman in black jeans and black caftan turned to talk, lighting a cigarette like everybody else. The stares end at the entrance, she explained. She came often. In here they don't care.

"Most Egyptian women will panic if they are twenty-five and not married," said Eamn, twenty-five and unmarried. "She's consumed with the home, the car. Then she gets it, and she discovers it's a disaster.

"She wants to be loved, to be treated well. But she married without knowing him. So she gives up, and throws all her love to her kids. If she's brave, she'll get a divorce. Or if she's afraid of the stigma of a divorce, she'll have an affair on the side.

"Everyone here is very, very, very jealous. That's why they carry cell phones—to check on their partner."

"Do you know anyone who married for love?" I asked.

"No. They marry for type. Many women here wait to marry a rich husband, wait until they are thirty. Four million people! This is a big problem."

Maybe coming to Café Stella wasn't such a good idea after all. I wanted to believe in the future of love in Egypt, to feel the optimism that surrounded the village wedding. I swiveled my chair to another table.

"There was no difference in love," said Yasser, a Cairo painter twice divorced, once from a British woman and once from an Egyptian. "Difference only in the culture and attitude. The Egyptian woman think for the house, mostly. She is waiting for the advice from the man. It doesn't even matter if she is intelligent. It is ingrained in the culture.

"English women are more free. You have to treat them as an equal. Men in Arab cultures always think they are higher."

Yasser said his marriage to his British wife dissolved because of her alcoholism, while his union to the Egyptian crumbled when he lost his job. He told me this at a bar during working hours.

"When poor comes to the door, love jumps from the window," he said, repeating an Egyptian saying. Still he believes, both for himself and his community.

"The world needs more love now," he said. "It is the only solution."

Kurt flagged me to the other side of the room, his arm wrapped around a bald grandfather with a cravat and thickets of dark ear hair. "Call me Prince!" the old man said. He was drunk. And in between the fustian ramblings and rants against Israel, he relayed the most lucid words I heard in the country.

"Love is to make love," he said.

L ove in the Arab world is like everything else in the Arab world—rigid, ancient, male-dominated, family-based, at times romantic and inspiring, often indecipherable to the outsider, draped in Allah, frozen in taboo. Egypt stacks the deck against love, forcing couples to come up with enormous sums of money before sanctioning marriage, yet giving them few ways to earn it. The fortunate ones with jobs make a handful of dollars a day. Egypt prohibits interactions between sexes and jails those who happen to be born gay. So many factors take precedence—dignity, appearance, tradition, money—how can love survive?

Through smile and prayer, answer Egyptians. Egypt, like much of the third world, is quick to wrap love in the cloak of their God. Love, as they see it, is a crucial part of the journey toward enlightenment. Ask a Muslim his thoughts on love and you'll likely hear a quote from the Koran. Love is heaven sent, they believe. It comes to the pious and faithful.

Over and over, Egypt told us love begins with God, moves to self, then to a partner, children, and beyond. Yet it can end at any step in the chain. Love is all-encompassing, Egypt emphasized. It seeps into every phase and fold of life if you allow it. When it's real, it's eternal.

And just as religion is most fervent in the poorest communities, so, too, the pull of love is strongest in the planet's poorest reaches. Their marriage ceremonies were the most crowded, their divorces the most devastating.

The happiest couples we met on the trips were ones like the newlyweds in the Egyptian desert—grounded in community, based in faith, consumed not by consumption.

Humor is the other instrument. Egyptian men do laughter well. They're warm, affable, frat-brother fun. The women, too, carve wit from the most dire of situations. It's what keeps us going, they say. Each Egyptian we met, no matter their lack of wealth or options, laughed and joked at some point during our chat. Every one.

In fact, if anyone at the world party could use a little loosening up, it's us, they chuckled. Couples talked of that special hour at the end of the day, when the chores were done and the kids put to bed, after they'd carried bricks or scrubbed laundry since sunrise, when they'd sit down, share a piece of bread, and laugh about the difficulties of being Egyptian.

A story relayed at Café Stella: George Bush, Tony Blair, and Hosni Mubarak end up in hell. Bitter and roasting, they ask to call their lawyers.

"No problem," says Satan. "I just need to charge you for the call."

Blair goes first, complaining that his current location is, in fact, hot as hell. When he's done, the devil sticks him with a million-dollar bill.

"Scoundrel," says the former British leader before paying the fee.

Bush goes next, pleading to Condi Rice to please get him out of yet another mess. The devil demands two million dollars after the call, which Bush grudgingly pays.

And despite his reputation as a spendthrift, Mubarak decides to phone home as well, telling his associates to do anything they can to free him. After a long chat and much argument, he hangs up and turns to Satan for the bill.

"Give me a dollar," says Satan.

"Hey!" complain Blair and Bush. "Why so little for the Egyptian?"

"His call wasn't long-distance."

Screen, Tests

Tracy had an audition in the morning for an independent film costarring Lou Diamond Phillips. The story line revolved around a cheap motel and a phony gold mine. I didn't remember anything else after she mentioned the nude scenes. "Can't they airbrush that stuff? Or use computers?"

The plan was to drop her off, then Calvin and I would run a couple of errands in Santa Monica. We wished her luck and hopped on the highway.

"I've got to go poo," said Calvin, thirty seconds after I pulled into the fast lane.

"Really?"

Never ask a kid, "Really?" What is he going to say? No?

"We're going to be at the bank in five minutes," I said. "Can you wait?"

"No."

Never ask a kid, "Can you wait?" What is he going to say? Yes?

He let out a slow, guttural groan, basso profundo.

"Okay, okay," I said. "I'll pull over right now. Just cross your legs. Think of England."

"What's England?"

I swerved through three lanes of traffic, crossing double line after double line, and made my way to the nearby McDonald's parking lot. Calvin sprinted while holding his haunches. He stopped at the front door.

"Can I get a Happy Meal?"

"What are you doing? I thought you had to go to the bathroom."

"Please."

"Calvin, don't stop. Go."

"But I really . . ."

"No."

Before I could finish the word, his eyes began to flood.

"No, don't cry. Don't cry. I'll buy you a Happy Meal. Let's just get you in the john before you burst."

"Who's John?"

His business completed, Calvin ignored the McNuggets and focused instead on the enclosed Tony Hawk action figure that skateboarded off the equivalent of a three-story building. Helmet included. This, of course, prompted Calvin to suggest building a ramp from the roof of his house to the street below. I nodded my head and told him we were late to pick up Tracy.

"Why do you always need to go to the bathroom *after* we get on the highway and not before?" I asked him.

"I dunno."

"We gotta work on that. Train your bowels to loosen in front of Amoeba Records or Skylight Books or someplace we could hang."

"Okay."

Tracy waited for us in the studio parking lot.

"Hi, boys," she said, getting in the car. "You have a good time?"

"Look what Franz got me. Tony Hawk!"

"Giving in to the devil already," she said.

"Doody calls."

"Hey, I got the part."

"Great. Congrats."

"Offered it to me right there. I gotta call my manager," she said, reaching for her phone in her purse.

"Yeah, that's fantastic. Did they say whether they'd shoot you upstairs and downstairs?"

She stared before answering.

"Just upstairs."

"I can live with upstairs."

"That's very big of you. Especially since your book is filled with sex scenes. Real sex scenes."

"But they're all fumbles, signposts to allow the reader to gauge my recovery after getting dumped."

"I'll probably do my signpost in the buff."

"My poor mom."

"Don't worry. This is an indie. Most never make it to the theater."

"Where does it shoot?"

"We're here in L.A. for a couple of weeks, then in Reno."

"What about Calvin?"

"His sitter Genielle usually comes on shoots. It's only for a couple days. Thanks for reminding me. I need to call her, too."

"I've got a brilliant idea. Why don't I go? I could move some things around and give you a hand."

"It's fine."

"No, I mean it. It'll give Calvin and me some more time to bond."

"Are you sure? The hours can be long. And boring."

"You can meet my folks. They live a couple hours from there, in Davis."

"Meeting the folks, huh? You don't waste much time."

"Quiet weekend with the family . . . and my twenty-year high school reunion."

Let me be clear about high school reunions. I am not antireunion. What discouraged me from attending them in the past wasn't the reunions themselves but the companies that organized them. You'd get these embossed invitations for themed parties featuring prime rib, photo keepsakes, and "once-in-a-lifetime" fun. $129.95? For a piece of meat that looked straight from liposuction?

At least this is how I justified discarding the invitation for my twentieth high school reunion when it arrived in the mail. That and the small fact I was single and my career consisted of sharing honeymoon suites with Kurt. I'd have to recount my getting-dumped-at-the-altar story five hundred times to five hundred people I hadn't seen in two decades. *No thanks. I'll pass on this one.*

Until now. Now, everything changed. With Tracy on my arm, I saw the reunion in a whole new light, one not shined on me. Of course. With Tracy by my side, they'd focus on her and forget all about my sordid life. Brilliant. Yes.

"Eww, reunions," she said. "I don't know. What about Calvin?"

"My folks will take care of him. C'mon."

"I don't have anything to wear."

"Now you're stretching it."

"You didn't get that until now?"

"Look, you're going to meet all my Davis friends at some point," I said. "Why not get it out of the way in one night? Either that or I'll arrange twenty get-togethers with my buddies."

This was a deft parry. Tracy avoided most social gatherings, and especially those with strangers. Plus reunions are torture for the significant other. You either hear too much information ("Damn, your wife was a party girl") or too little ("What was that look between you and the brunette?"). You feel like a gate-crasher at a *Star Trek* convention, struggling to understand the basics amid the junkies who know every beam-up. But if she said no, we'd take the water-torture approach with my friends and she'd answer questions from my mom all night. My mom likes to talk.

"Okay," she said. "I'll do it. Just not too late, all right?"

"Splendid. Did I tell you there's a Wisner family reunion at my parents' house that Sunday?"

"You're joking, right?"

Tracy and Calvin flew to Reno; I drove from Los Angeles to meet them. This was an independent film, which meant the hotel-casino would be well worn and on the outskirts of town. I passed about two dozen pawn shops and found it by the highway.

"Hi," she said, giving me a quick kiss. "They've changed my call time. I gotta go. Calvin's had a yogurt. And a banana. Needs a bath. I'll have my cell phone, but it'll be off if we're shooting."

"Banana. Cell phone. Bath. Got it."

"You boys behave."

"It's Reno, remember."

She grabbed her purse and hurriedly kissed Calvin good-bye as he waged a heartless war between Spider-Man and some poor Smurf. Spider-Man won, leaving the Smurf's blue body dangling from a curtain cord. Spider-Man often emerged victorious in Calvin's wars. The pecking order went something like this: Superheroes with bodybuilder physiques bested any action figure with an honest job, the firemen and cowboys and such. They topped the knights and other historical figures who conquered anything stuffed. LEGOs served as battle shrapnel. Upset the hierarchy with extreme caution and likely tears. His, then mine. This I learned early on. Usually I held teddy bears, and usually I lost.

"So what now?" I asked.

"I dunno."

"The Giants are on. We could watch the game."

"Nah."

"Do you like sports?"

"No."

"Wanna go swimming?"

"Nope."

"Hungry?"

"Let's make a fort."

I scanned the room.

"Umm, okay."

Calvin began to disassemble the rollaway bed, not to mention every article of clothing in his suitcase. I wondered where his mind wandered. The Alamo? The Bastille? Or maybe just to general anarchy now that he'd been freed of adult supervision. He had an epic story for each play session, taking ample time to explain the intricate alliances and nuanced motives of every plastic protagonist.

But as soon as I understood the rules and partnerships, he'd change them. R2-D2 decapitated General Custer one moment, only to have Custer gain his revenge later in the battle. I'd try to explain to Calvin this was implausible. Custer was cursed and R2 had better luck than Ringo, I'd aver. Plus the field medics rarely restored headless warriors to war. These rationales did not make an impact.

"I really want to go to China," he told me.

"Me, too. Maybe we'll all go someday."

"It must be great when you get off the plane."

"Probably looks like any other airport."

"But with toys everywhere! All my toys say 'China.' "

Calvin was sweet. Adults told him this and he said, "Thank you." So they told him again.

"Hey, chubby," he said. "Play with Jesus and Chad."

"What did you call me?"

"Chubby."

Ouch. I'd skip the buffet.

Calvin was also the only kid I'd ever met who could use the word "pha-lange" while using a phalange to root out a booger deep in his cranium. He had an unkid calm and a body stitch-free. At times, too many times, he talked about his mom's feelings, which made me feel even more strongly he needed a man in his life every day. *You can do it. Maybe you can.*

"I've got an idea," I said, pulling the mattress off the box spring. "Let's prop this up here, turn the couch on its side, and use the curtains as the roof. Do a *big* fort!"

"Yeah. And let's get these pillows and Mom's boots and make cannons."

"Thanks for letting me hang out with you, Calvin. You're a good kid."

"Thanks."

"I mean it."

"We'll show Mom when she comes back. She'll love this."

"The maid, too."

"Yeah."

Tracy said half of parenting was just showing up. And when Calvin and I spent time together I knew what she meant. Like signing your name on the SAT, you get credit for tackling the thing in the first place. I fumbled over every aspect—when to eat, what to wear, how to convince a four-year-old brain that asparagus is not cursed by a vampire because it makes your pee smell funny. Calvin didn't care about the missteps. I was there. The rest we'd work out. I wanted to express this in a language he'd understand.

"C'mon," I said. "Put down the pillows. We're going on an adventure."

"Yeah! Where?"

"Inside the hotel. Leave your shoes but wear your socks."

I had noticed the floors when I checked in, long and glassy and black. Somebody must have shined them every night with one of those big electric-toothbrush mops. The surface looked like a Formula One speedway cutting through the slot machines and flashing lights.

"Where?" said Calvin as the elevator opened on the ground floor.

"There. C'mon. Lean back and give me your wrists."

Ever cautious, Calvin did as I asked this time with only a slight pause.

"Hang on," I said. "Here we go."

Calvin reclined and grasped hold of my forearms like a trapeze artist, tilt-ing back, back, and straight into the performance. The elevator doors pinged shut and I began to backpedal, slowly at first to see how he maneuvered, then with building speed as we entered the main casino. By the time we reached the roulette tables, we'd quickened to a jog and then a dash, darting across the lambent marble floor, Calvin's feet fishtailing with every turn. Ding, ding, ding, ding. Clank, clank, clank. The jackpots and pulsating lights weren't for the gamblers. This was our arena, and we dashed around for more.

"Faster," he yelled. "Faster!"

"Okay. Hold on."

Blackjack players paused their hands and set down their drinks to witness the flash.

"Wheeeeeeeeeeee!"

Past the gift shop and around the slots we sped, the gray-haired speed demon and his towhead in tow.

"Yeahhhhh!"

Through the lobby and down the hall.

"Fasterrrrrrrr!"

At the starting point, I stopped, panting and sore.

"Do it again. Please, chubby."

"You think I'm fat?"

"No."

"Then why do you keep calling me chubby?"

" 'Cause you're silly."

"Ah, chubby means silly."

"Uh-huh."

"We might want to keep that one to ourselves, especially here among the casino crowd."

"C'mon," he said. "Let's go."

"Lemme just catch my breath."

"That was the best ride of my life."

I looked at his face.

"Me, too."

After several more laps around the casino racetrack, we ordered room service hamburgers with extra ketchup and watched a lightning storm on the back side of the Sierras. I didn't hear Tracy when she came home.

* * *

realized my good fortune immediately after entering my high school reunion.

"I've seen you in something," said a male classmate to Tracy. "The soap operas?"

"I didn't know you were a soap fan," I said.

"Oh, no. My wife. She has that stuff on."

The evening began exactly according to plan, starring Tracy as the world-class refraction. Every question about getting dumped at the altar—gone. Every inquiry about my job status—kaput. Not a ripple. This evening would be all about Tracy.

I retreated to a corner with a few of my close friends while Tracy sauntered to the bar. Oh, yes, this was good. In addition to Tracy's obfuscation of my shortcomings, the bullies were bald. The thwarted crushes wore muumuus. My football prowess grew with each drink. I didn't even mind the occasional nitpick. "I always thought you were gay." No, this would be a night of cheers, "Go Blue Devils," and . . .

Mark Blake? *No, no. Don't linger there. Move along.* You couldn't miss Mark in the masses, a flashing harbor buoy in his cowboy hat and handlebar mustache grin. He rested an elbow on the bar and pinned Tracy with his other. *Pick up drinks and go. See, me, thirsty.* I tried to wave. I tried to call. I saw him tip his hat back as they talked. Not a good sign. Mark knew my every secret from those days, probably ones I didn't know myself. I excused myself from the group and hurriedly waded through the crowd to reach her. *Please don't tell her about the time we got arrested for hustling beer and my dad made me spend the night in jail. Please, no prison love jokes.*

"Wiz," he said as I arrived.

"Howdy, Mark. I see you've met Mark, honey."

"We've been having a nice chat."

"Mark's a great guy," I said. "Don't believe a word he says."

"So what age is Calvin?" Mark asked.

"Four."

"Oh, I like four. They're still cute. At six they get a little bit poofy. You know."

"You guys are talking about . . . kids."

"Mark's got stepchildren."

"They're great, Wiz. They call me Dad, rely on me for everything. There's no difference. To them, I am Dad."

"What did you do to gain their trust?"

"Made 'em pick up dog shit. Day one. They were this pampered group when they came to live with me. I got 'em up at six A.M. and made them pick up every turd on my lawn. Set the tone right from the start."

"And it worked?"

"Hell yeah. Kids need order. They want a routine. Isn't that right, Tracy?"

"I guess I could try that with Calvin," I said, darting my eyes to Tracy as assurance we wouldn't be out before dawn with the pooper-scooper.

"Hey," said Mark. "Did Wiz tell you about the time we got arrested for drinking beer?"

"No. No, he didn't."

"You know, Tracy is a big-time actress," I said. "Done a ton of shows."

"Arrested?" she asked.

"What shows?"

"*Ally McBeal, 24,*" I said.

"I need to get my gal over here. She knows this stuff better than I do."

Tracy shot me a glance and mouthed, "Arrested?"

"Hey, honey!" Mark said, yelling across the room. "C'mere."

Tracy had help at the Wisner family reunion the next day. Low expectations. I'd spent a decade in a relationship that flopped and two years on a honeymoon with Kurt; I'm convinced my family would have applauded if I'd shown up with a Teletubby. My mother would have joined a support group. "Honey, it's perfectly fine to be with a furbie. There are dozens of people just like you out there."

Calvin jumped right into my nieces' world of princess and pink, suspending the action figure battles long enough for Spider-Man to join a Jasmine tea party. I stared at the kids and wondered what my parents must be thinking. I'd take their pulse later on, after the extended family had left. In the meantime, Tracy and I struck up a conversation with a friend of my cousin's on the patio outside.

"My mom started dating men when I was Calvin's age," he said. "I was such a butt to them all."

"When did you grow out of that?" I asked.

"I didn't. She stopped seeing people. Here was this poor, lonely woman just trying to gather some love and I buzz-killed the whole thing. I'm surprised she even talks to me today."

"She loved you," said Tracy. "I never understood that unconditional, all-giving love until I had a child. I can see her putting everything else aside."

"Well, I guess I did stop doing it."

"When?" I asked.

"College."

Just fourteen more years until you can relax naked in bed. By that time you'll have ear hair and gout.

I kissed Tracy and Calvin good night before walking back to the living room to talk with my parents. They started dating as sophomores in high school. My father enrolled at UC Berkeley as a math major, and my mother quickly transferred from College of the Pacific once she realized she couldn't stand to be an hour away from him. They moved to San Francisco after graduation, got married, and began medical school and nursing college. That's the way it was supposed to work, right? You picked a great woman early on and stuck with the plan. They'd been married for nearly fifty years. *Damn it.*

Their relationship was as frustrating as it was inspiring. I tried; I mimicked. And I realized each time I could never re-create the role models I witnessed growing up. Half of me didn't want to; the other half floundered to find an alternative.

As my dad played with the remote, switching between *Law & Order* and PBS's *Mystery,* I waited for my opening. Their approval meant everything.

"Honey, she's lovely," began my mother. "She's an absolute delight."

"I feel a bit guilty for making her do a family reunion and a class reunion in the same weekend."

"Everybody thought she was just great."

C'mon, Dad.

"Really, you picked a winner. And Calvin couldn't be any sweeter."

"I really dig her," I said. "I . . . love her. I'm just having a hard time getting my head around the whole kid thing. It's hard."

"Who said that good and hard are incongruous?" said my father.

Classic Dad. A scientist's full explanation of an affair of the heart. If there was a chalkboard nearby, he'd diagram it out. Subcircle A equals happiness. B equates to energy exerted. Aha. The circles can overlap.

"No, I'm not saying that they are."

"And when have you shied away from either?"

My father overthinks everything. Actions like buttering a waffle, for instance, consume oodles of brainpower and planning. For proper distribution and maximum flavor, each square indentation should be dabbed with room-temperature butter. Then syrup, hot Vermont maple syrup, should be applied evenly in a circular fashion beginning on the outside and moving in. This ensures proper distribution and equal coverage. An extra puddle of syrup, hot Vermont maple syrup, should be left on the side of the plate for sopping any stray areas that happen to be equal to or less than 36 percent saturated.

On this, he was 100 percent correct. I was the one overthinking. If I loved Tracy, nothing else mattered. If I loved her, I'd have to love all of her. Towheads, pound dogs, nude scenes, Joni Mitchell, Birkenstocks, and organic everything included. My father placed the chalk back on the ledge of the blackboard.

The following couple of months seemed without restraint. Except to Pluto, that is. The poor, dwarf-legged creature spent every waking hour leashed to the belt of a man who spent inordinate amounts of time doing crossword puzzles in the bathroom. As I sat there, he'd look up to me with those cloudy dark eyes as if to say, "Asian tongue? Four letters? Begins with *U*? Urdu. Now can we please go outside?"

Calvin, meanwhile, constructed a military-style obstacle course behind the hedgerows and up to the hill lookout in the back of the house. We bivouacked to escape the Huns and planned our raids on the Nazis. You're never too young to hate the Nazis. The regimen took on an added urgency when I introduced Calvin to the firepower of water balloons. The wars became a full-time endeavor.

As we hurled the aqueous projectiles toward evil tricycles and dastardly garden chairs, I decided I wanted to show Calvin the world, to take him on some of my trips. I wanted him to see firsthand that village laughter is as joyous as his own. In the interim, we went to the Norton Simon Museum to view the Hindu sculptures, the Japanese American Museum to learn about origami and internment, and Brazilian *churrascarias* to devour steaks and watch samba. From my travels around the world, I started a wooden mask collection for him—Nicaraguan skeletons, Nubian ghosts, Indian spirits.

He introduced me to SpongeBob. And Jesus. Calvin showed me the purity of a child's mind, and just how cynical the rest of us have become.

It struck me as we crafted chalk figures on the patio one afternoon. Many of the love lessons I'd picked up from the world, he already possessed. Like the Brazilians, he was open to love, and, echoing the Indians, he grew love through commitment. With each wrestling match and offer to play with superheroes, I felt him reaching closer. Here I'd conducted a world search on love, only to find one of the planet's most articulate spokesmen in the body of a four-year-old boy.

Tracy and I spent our summer hours taking Calvin to parks and museums, then stealing time together after he fell asleep. At the end of each day, I respected her more. Calvin was a good kid. He was her child. He was her.

I'd never dated a woman with a child; never thought it would appeal to me. Yet as the summer reached its sweet spot, I knew I would never be closer to anyone than to the woman in my arms. You know when you know, the world told me. And so I did. Every synapse pulled to connect with Tracy. You're striking, I thought as I stroked her hair. You're strong, I said, glancing around the house to inventory all she balanced. You're beguiling as hell, my mind said as she nestled into my embrace. *There's something incredibly sexy about a great mom.*

Honey," I said in bed early the next morning.

"Is Calvin up?"

"No."

"Then why are you waking me?" she said, her pillow muffling every word.

"There's something I want to tell you."

"Mmmm."

"I don't know if I can have children."

"Hmmm?"

"I have, umm, plumbing problems."

"You're constipated?"

"Wrong plumbing. Spigot, not the drain. I had a physical, years ago, where the doc gave me a hernia check."

"What's this have to do with kids?"

"He grabs your scrotum and makes you turn your head and cough."

"Why?"

"I don't get it, either. Anyway, he told me I had a lot of extra pipes and stuff in there."

She sat up.

"Franz. Sweetie," she said, now awake. "What's with the contractor's code?"

"Veins. I have too many veins. They make my sperm all funny shaped. Doughnuts instead of pollywogs. Mutants. He said I'd probably need to get an operation if I wanted to have children."

"But you've never tried to have children, so how would you know?"

"I've tried."

"Oh," she said. "Long?"

"Long enough to know I need an operation."

"So you get an operation. Big deal. I'll bring you an ice pack."

"Thanks."

"Or we'll adopt. I love the fact you're talking about children."

"I'm not talking about children," I said, straddling her. "I'm talking about sperm."

"It's nothing to be embarrassed about, having mutant sperm."

"Thanks."

"We'll get it checked out."

"We'll?"

Equability

As summer started to narrow, Tracy's inflatable pool morphed from cool oasis to West Nile mosquito breeding ground. Calvin kept asking about the "bugs that twitched." We drained it when he wasn't looking.

"I hate to do this," she said. "I really want him to learn how to swim this summer. My friends have pools, and your parents. I worry about him falling in."

"These inflatable pools aren't the best for learning, trust me. I taught swimming as a summer job in high school."

"It's got to be better than the swim lessons at the Rose Bowl. Calvin just doesn't do well in situations like that. Too many kids."

"He seems to raise his hand to go to the bathroom a lot."

"Maybe I can ask them to teach him how to swim without putting his head underwater."

"That's called dog-paddling."

"I just worry about his confidence. All those kids in his swimming school are diving down to the bottom steps to pick up those candies. You see how he looks when they come up?"

Yes. I had. And it killed me. The teacher would give him a token Starburst, but I could tell it didn't taste as good as the ones the other kids fished from the bottom.

"I'll teach him," I said. "We'll go every afternoon. Might take a while, but we'll do it. They keep the pool heated in fall."

"How are you going to teach him? You're going to New Zealand."

"We'll start tomorrow."

"We can't do that. It wouldn't be fair to Calvin, just to start a routine, then stop midstream. I'll talk to the teacher."

"I can do it."

"When you get back. Don't get me wrong. You're great when you're here, but I can't depend on you for stuff like this."

I paused to let her comment sink in.

"Then come with me. You and Calvin. Come to New Zealand. We'll continue the swim lessons there."

"It's winter in New Zealand."

"We'll find hotels with indoor pools."

"You're serious."

Kurt and I flew down first. We'd spend a few weeks on the North Island questioning Kiwis about love and rugby, not necessarily in that order. Tracy and Calvin would then join us in Dunedin, a city I hadn't seen since a family sabbatical at age twelve. I had no idea what to expect on any front.

On our first night in Auckland, Kurt asked where singles congregated, a place where we could talk to locals looking for love. The natives pointed us to a popular street with a name so long and vowel-laden they just called it K Road. That happened a lot with Maori names. The bar was indeed packed, and the exposed brick walls reminded me of my favorite nightclub in Rio. The similarities ended there. In fact, this was the anti-Brazil—no impromptu introductions, no perchance conversations, zero make-out sessions. We saw no hand-holding, hair-stroking, or heavy petting. Strike medium or light petting, for that matter. We witnessed, well, drinking. Pint after pint of it.

Kiwis claimed the urge to imbibe amply, rapidly, and without distraction was but cultural residue of the Six O'Clock Swill, the operating restrictions put in place by temperance unions during World War I. With jobs ending at five and the pubs closing at six, men would elbow their way to the bars for rapid-fire refills of ale. Chitchat with women? Friendly game of darts with the opposite sex? Ha! Bars were for imbibing.

The Six O'Clock Swill ended in 1967, but the effects remain. In New Zealand today, the "pickup bar" is something to use when bench-pressing at the gym, not the portal to the partner of your dreams.

"If I met a guy at a bar, chatted, and he asked me out, I would never go," said Rosalie, a patron that night. "The only time I dated someone from a bar was during a Latino dancing class. And he didn't speak English."

Beware the Latino dancer. Ever beware the Latino dancer.

The Swill rules remain, New Zealanders say. You go to bars to meet friends, never to scout or search. That night, patrons stared at their drinks and stole glances only when others weren't looking. When the eyes of strangers did meet, both heads quickly swiveled back in unison as if watching a tennis match with two balls. Bartenders left individual tabs rather than group checks at the counter.

"Only once have I seen a man send a drink to a stranger," said Edward, a gay rights leader in Auckland. "Everyone in the bar was shocked. The poor soul didn't know what to say. It threw everyone off their game."

Tempered codes of conduct extend beyond the pub. New Zealand is a tidy nation in area and attitude, contemplative and cool in all senses. It's an antitabloid culture. Rolex watches and exposed lingerie seem awkwardly out of place. Locals talk about Tall Poppy Syndrome: The longest, showiest flowers are the first to get whacked. To approach a stranger on a street or in a bar would be to expose oneself to a world of needy florists with sharp shears. Neighbors here prefer passive-aggressive kibitzing over confrontation. "I see the dandelions are back, John."

The size and intimacy of the island nation also play a role. Kiwis are careful to watch their comments to a stranger. They've had uncouth words come back to haunt them. Six degrees is an exaggeration.

"You don't meet someone through a bar," said Leecia, a South Islander. "Because New Zealand is such a small world, someone always knows someone you know."

The exceptions we saw, the alternatives to the bashful and the coy, were the Maoris. In many countries, native inhabitants have been silenced through force and intimidation and attrition. Not in New Zealand.

"It's because *pakehas*"—white New Zealanders—"are just guardians," said Tai, a retired rugby player from Otago. "We let them think that they're running the show while we do whatever we want."

Maoris are more than happy to engage strangers and go on dates, while *pakeha* New Zealand increasingly shuns one-on-one courting in favor of nights out with mates. If a couple "hooks up," it's casual, discreet, almost ancillary.

"There's not a dating culture here," said Amanda. "The whole courtship thing seems to have gone."

"I don't think I've ever been on a date in my life," agreed her friend Juliet.

School, work, and residences are where most New Zealanders find their partners. Common ground gives locals comfort, and a perception of risk avoidance. Otherwise, the trek as an individual can be painfully awkward and slow.

New Zealanders sprint from the spotlight, talk into their chests, and embrace the comforts of the known. They marry "longtime friends" and flatmates, fellow students at "uni," colleagues of their cousins.

G abriela's story is typical. We met her at an Auckland restaurant a few days later. She talked about her boyfriend, Chris, with whom she'd shared an apartment for a year without a hint of romance.

"I thought he was really boring," she said.

One night he brought a woman back to the flat.

"And I went septic. I suddenly realized I really liked him. I realized I loved him, and I had to tell him. So I said, 'I need to tell you something.' "

"What did he say?" I asked.

"He thought I was going to kick him out of the flat. Then I told him I had feelings for him."

"Did he reciprocate?"

"He said, 'I don't feel the same way.' "

Gabriela felt miserable. Living side by side, quiet and confused, she thought about evicting him. Instead, she moved on.

"He came back from Christmas and suddenly I felt okay. He was dating heaps of women. It didn't bother me."

"Good for you."

"Then he asked if I wanted to go away for Easter. And I thought, no, no. That I was way second choice. But he said, 'Do you remember that conversation we had six months ago? What would you say if I changed my mind?' "

"Did you change your mind?"

"I called my sister. She told me to relax. So Chris and I played cards for hours. And now everything is great."

They both believe relationships have a greater chance of succeeding in the long run if the couple starts out as chums *When Harry Met Sally*-style. New Zealanders we met agreed. They crave second opinions and nods from their social network. A step on your own is a walk into the wide oceans that surround. They demand confirmation, even if it's ephemeral.

"If you make eye contact with a woman at a bar, you'd never go up to her and ask her out," explained Craig, a North Islander. "But if you saw her the next day at the store, then it would be okay to talk with her.

"There's a prevalent insecurity here. With the men and the women. We tend to want everything right and in place before we can move forward and be happy. To do that requires the blessing of friends and family."

Bridget, a government statistician, summarized it this way: "Englishmen will put relationships first, mates second, and careers third. Americans would put career first, relationships second, and mates third. New Zealanders would put mates first, careers second, and relationships third."

But New Zealand is loosening up. Many credit *Sex and the City* for the incremental progress. They will tell you with a relaxed sigh and reluctant grin that Carrie, Mr. Big, and the entire cast helped them untie their tongues on matters sexual. The show gave voice to New Zealand's intimate questions previously pondered alone.

"Suddenly we talked about things that were taboo," said Jane, a friend of Craig's. "It empowered a lot of people. I liked the way Carrie would verbalize her thoughts, even though they were small. It empowered us to talk about sex and our bodies."

"Like what?" I asked. "Give me an example."

"Well," she said after a slight pause. "There was that show that focused on, you know, yourself. Sex with yourself."

"Masturbation," I said, possibly too loud.

"Yep, that's it."

"You can't say it, can you?"

"The point is we're talking about it."

The sexual revolution steams ahead in New Zealand, episode by episode, inch by excruciating inch.

"I admire the show," said Jane. "I have been inspired by it. But I still can't live like that."

Oh, New Zealand is dying to talk about sex. Behind the bulky sweaters and UGG boots, they're bursting to have a big ole Oprah session with a topic that's been largely deleted from public dialogue.

Maybe it's because they have sex so often. Yes, you heard me. Sweet little New Zealand. According to a Durex Global Sex Survey (and who wouldn't trust a condom company on such matters), two-thirds of New Zealanders said they have had a one-night stand, tying them for second place along with Finland and Sweden. The Norwegians topped the list at 70 percent. India, by comparison, ranked last with 13 percent, while 50 percent of American respondents copped to a quickie.

The poll also contended New Zealanders had the third highest number of sex partners, behind only Turkey and lusty Australia. Unfortunately the island nation was also fourth in the world in unsafe sex, with two-thirds admitting they'd had an unprotected encounter with a partner without knowing the person's sexual history. As a result, New Zealand has one of the highest chlamydia rates in the world.

So New Zealand's gettin' some. It's the international equivalent of the preacher's daughter. They have the hardest time talking about sex but are more than happy to partake once they leave the house. To use Kiwi-ese: There are scores of slappers (someone who sleeps around too much) and rooters (people who engage in sex) looking for a quick roger (one-night stand) or a dirty stop out (spending a night at someone's house).

Kurt and I found our seats and settled in to watch the most destructive force in New Zealand relationships today: the rugby match. We'd come with Tai and his fiancée, Yvonne. Under the lights at Eden Park, the Auckland Rugby Union squad prepared for battle against the Waikato team from Hamilton. Burly men stretched, spat, and tackled each other. That was just in the stands.

"Who are you rooting for?" I asked the large man with a large mullet in the seat next to me.

"Go on?" he said, pronouncing it *g'aow-on*.

"He means your squad," chimed in Tai at precisely the moment I realized I'd asked a 275-pound redneck about his sexual exploits.

"Auckland, mate," he said.

"Go Auckland," I replied. "Mate."

This wouldn't have been the first fight due to rugby (or my naïveté). The sport has long divided friends and couples. Never more so than 1981, when the New Zealand Rugby Football Union hatched a plan to invite the nation's toughest competitor to the islands for a series of friendly matches with the beloved national squad, the All Blacks. There was a slight problem. The guests had a racist apartheid government boycotted by much of the world.

New Zealanders sympathized with the plight of black South Africans. White locals bragged about their own policies of integration and support for indigenous Maori populations. Racism should be stomped out everywhere, they chanted—but what's the harm in a little rugby while we get these issues sorted out.

Kiwis weren't ready for this brand of controversy. They panicked. They ran out and purchased helmets and long batons for a police force that didn't carry guns. The protesters were equally inexperienced. They dressed in clown suits and motorcycle helmets, preached nonviolence yet carried the occasional Molotov cocktail, and massed in large numbers outside every match. In Auckland, a protester flew his small airplane over the rugby pitch and bombed the players with sacks of flour.

Both sides felt they needed to do something, though neither had any idea how to proceed. They clashed on occasion, and the protesters managed to scuttle a couple of matches by bum-rushing the stadiums. After fits and starts for two months, the Springboks concluded the tour and returned to South Africa. Final toll: a few scuffles and bruises, no deaths, no major injuries. New Zealand quickly tried to forget about the whole thing.

The reverberations came soon after. And they came from women. After the matches concluded, the men returned home and faced a barrage. "Do you think rugby is more important than everything else?" The protesters were right, they said. Rugby has gotten out of hand.

The international media backed them up. Can you believe this crazy little country down at the end of the world? Putting a sport few play on such a high pedestal? If it was soccer, okay. Maybe we'd understand. But this was rugby, a game where the guys give themselves wedgies trying to capture the ball.

And for the first time in New Zealand's history, rugby suffered. Its popularity declined. Rugby fans and nonfans stared at their feet in embarrassment.

New Zealand felt like that man in the bar who swore at the sporting event on television, only to turn around and see everybody looking at him.

Until then, rugby remained the unquestioned metaphor for New Zealand itself—workmanlike, rugged, a game of team more than star, tactical, played in a cold climate far from the rest of the world, clad in black jerseys, the ultimate nonfashion fashion statement. That rugby mentality has long spilled over into relationships, but after the tour a little less so.

New Zealand men have been socialized not to be vulnerable," said Diane, a minister living in Wanaka. "Many have a hard time communicating. This accumulates into not being able to love or to be loved. Women have been socialized to believe that men can't love. So they take what they can get."

"The men here aren't good at having women as friends," added Helen, thirty-four, a South Islander. "That's because they're taught to be tough."

The Springbok tour of 1981 spawned a generation of conversations. It gave women the opening they needed to question the rugby role model. Women began aligning themselves not by North Island or South but by rugby-tolerant or not.

"It used to be you got a lot of groupies," said Tai. "But now most New Zealand women don't love rugby players. They think they're too tough."

Women have gained power in relationships, added Yvonne. They've forced the men to compromise more.

"They still like to have their beer," she said, "but they have changed for the better. There's a lot more help for them."

After Auckland scored on a last-minute try to beat Waikato and the large man I'd propositioned nodded at the score, Kurt and I hustled to the other side of town to meet Craig and a group of his friends at an Indian restaurant. In many ways, he embodied the changes rippling through his homeland. Erudite and athletic, he'd watched the match on television after a session with his life coach.

"Guys are definitely changing," he said. "We tend to clam up. Don't like to communicate. But we're getting better."

As the men changed, so, too, the women.

"In the eighties, there was a missed generation," said Craig. "The women were taught to be corporate Gordon Gekkos. Then they hit their late thirties and realized they didn't have any kids. Now the pendulum is swinging back. They have much more balance."

"What do you like best about New Zealand women?" I asked.

"They're down to earth, relaxed. Outdoorsy. Levelheaded. Broad perspective, a global perspective. They're good conversationalists. Well rounded. They can be feminine if they want to. They can be really sexy if they want to. Women don't normally dress up, but when they do, they can look fantastic. They can be anything they want to be."

Several female friends of Craig's joined us at the table. They agreed that their lot is changing. More so than the men's, they argued. They pointed to Prime Minister Helen Clark and talked about the influence of the matriarchal structure in Maori culture.

"Craig isn't the typical guy," said his friend Jane. "He's much more sensitive."

Craig nodded his head before uttering, "Stop. You'll make me cry."

In that split second, he flashed the old and the new.

Lifestyles didn't evolve as easily when our family ventured to Dunedin in 1976. The biggest shock to the city then was the arrival of the fast food hamburger. Big John's. Residents whispered to neighbors and scribbled letters to the editor. Hamburgers? But what will happen to the meat pies?

Standing firm with the forces of change and the glories of fast food, I assured my classmates at Dunedin North Intermediate that McDonald's would soon follow suit. Then Burger King, Wendy's, and the coup de grâce, Taco Bell.

They in turn presented me with a Big John jumbo patty, which I devoured and pronounced fit. The golden stake. The beginning of a new era, I assured them. New Zealand was on its way.

"We fished it out the rubbish bin, Yank," they howled.

No, the city didn't exactly embrace change in 1976. Dunedin wore brooches and cardigans. They named their schools after Scottish ancestors and looked to Edinburgh as much as Wellington for guidance. The milkman left glass bottles each morning with a thick layer of cream, which we'd shake before pouring on our Weet-Bix. Ethnic food meant Italian. Shopkeepers accepted spare change and promises you'd pay tomorrow for that Cadbury chocolate today.

I couldn't see the Dunedin of my youth as I walked to the Octagon in the center of town. The new New Zealand leapt from neon signs and storefront menus. Minami Sushi, Curry Box, Thai Hanoi and Thai Over, Jizo Japanese, Galata Turkish Café, Barakah, Ombrellos, and Viva Zapata. Around each gathered uncles and friends, new countrymen with names like Singh and Nguyen and Fahad. The gray clouds blew through and the rainbow remained.

Meanwhile, New Zealanders grabbed their passports and hit the road in record numbers. As their economy globalized, so did they. Jobs in England, ashrams in India, surfing trips to Indonesia. New Zealand went out into the world, and the world came to them.

The confluence of cultures also influenced love lives, though the changes have been minimal so far, with New Zealanders of each stripe tending to choose the same. Members of the large and growing immigrant populations complain of separate worlds even when they've called New Zealand home for decades. The culture is as isolated as the geography, they say.

"You see people who have a circle of friends from university," said John, thirty-three, originally from Ghana and a resident of New Zealand for six years. "If you didn't go to school with them, you'll never be in that circle, no matter how long you've been with them."

Ms. Ruby wasn't around during my family's sabbatical. There were no Ms. Rubys in public Dunedin back then. Grant would have been around. He still is, running a bagel store just off the Octagon. We shared a cup of coffee with him at a table outside.

"What does a drag queen wear growing up?" I asked Grant.

"Rugby jerseys," he said. "Everyone in Gore wore them. Still do."

"Did you like the rugby jerseys?"

"Actually I did. They were loose, and allowed me to smuggle nudie magazines into my room without being noticed."

"And that's when Ms. Ruby was born."

"From Gore to the most prominent drag queen in Dunedin."

"And city council candidate."

"And city council candidate."

"What was the impetus to run?"

"The current council is so boring and staid. I want to get rid of the deadwood. Quite different people running this time—single moms, environ-mentalists, drag queens, people who are sick of business as usual."

"New Zealand has evolved quite a bit since I lived here and went to Dunedin North Intermediate," I said.

"That's where Destiny Church meets on Sunday mornings. They're the Pat Robertsons of New Zealand. Most churches don't give them the time of day. They organized a huge protest in Wellington to fight the civil unions bill but were criticized for using children."

"So my old classroom is now a gay-bashing headquarters."

"More or less."

Grant appeared more interested in branding Dunedin and promoting the region as a creative haven than in pushing gay rights. His brochures promised "People Focus."

"There are amazing artists down here, and the best designers in New Zealand. There's a lot of vibrancy down here. It just needs to be tapped into."

"Will Ms. Ruby show up at the meetings?"

"Maybe one or two. But in a three-piece power suit. She won't be wearing sequins. She has a fantastic seamstress."

The chic business suits remained in the closet for now. A few months later, Ms. Ruby failed to attract enough votes, and Grant returned to the bagels.

Gay New Zealanders we met on both islands boasted about their past and felt optimistic about the country's future. It's just the whole present thing that gives them fits.

"We actually have a rich history of tolerating and integrating the gay lifestyle," said Edward. "Captain Cook wrote in his diary about how some of his men were propositioned by Maori men. Another entry talked about two men having sex. Christians killed the buzz. The country didn't decriminalize homosexuality until 1986."

Indeed, Maoris had no problems including *takaatapui* in village lifestyles. The term loosely translates to "other sexuality"—gay, transgender, or celibate. Like fellow Pacific Islanders, Maoris allotted roles for their "others": caring for children, keeping the hut, reporting indiscretions to men returning from fish-ing expeditions or hunts. *Takaatapui* didn't mean stigma or avoidance or ridicule. They were who they were. Today most Maori are Christian.

"They still make the best drag queens in New Zealand," Edward averred.

New Zealanders legalized civil unions in 2004. They passed antidiscrimination laws and allowed gay couples to adopt, one of the first nations to do so. They shimmied a big ole rainbow flag up the pole and invited all comers. Nobody showed up to the party.

We met Edward on a Friday night at one of Auckland's best-known gay bars, a club called Urge, on K Road. Television monitors broadcast grainy gay porn. Orange flyers featuring bare-chested men advertised upcoming events. Techno music blared at a decibel level high enough to penetrate an enormous crowd. There were five men in the bar, including the bartender, including us. I felt awful for Edward, half wishing I were gay. This was Friday, after all.

"Behind the rainbow facade in New Zealand," he said, "it's a gray bureaucracy. Half the gay population here lives in Sydney. The other half lives in Bondi"—a Sydney suburb.

Not that a large crowd would change things.

"Gay Kiwis are just like Englishmen. They'll sit around in a bar not talking to each other because they haven't been formally introduced."

Gay men here tend to go to bars or restaurants with groups. They form dog-walking clubs and gardening groups to inspect each other's roses.

"What about sex?" I asked.

"Well, that's what the Internet's for," said Edward.

"Everyone knows each other," said Grant/Ms. Ruby. "It's quite a close-connected community. You meet a guy and instantly know who he's slept with. They want to be in a relationship, but it's a small ocean."

"We all sit around bitching," said Edward. "Single guys here tend to be more like brothers. Now they're all getting cats. The higher the number of cats, the less the probability of having a partner."

He brightened when I told him about the gay people we'd met around the world. The community is alive and well, I assured him. Growing almost everywhere.

"Well, we are seen as good husband material by men from other countries because we look beyond the next five minutes," said Edward.

If only they could meet one.

Kurt decided to check e-mail while I wandered on my own. Calvin and Tracy would arrive the next day. Pen and notebook in hand, I decided to conduct a few more interviews before they landed. The jewelry store caught my eye.

The cheerful manager wiped tuna from his mouth as he looked up from the counter.

"Sorry to interrupt your lunch."

"Not a problem," he insisted.

"Thanks. I've talked with jewelers in other countries. They've been insightful."

"Anything you want to know."

"Well, what's the typical wedding ring here in New Zealand?"

"Bands, mostly. Women prefer high quality—gold and platinum, but nothing too showy."

"How about diamonds?"

"Rarely more than a carat, carat and a half, if at all. Even wealthy New Zealanders prefer the understated."

"Do the couples come in together?"

"Usually the women come in first and ask a lot of questions about size and price and such. Then they come back with their fiancés and act surprised."

"That is a world phenomenon. The United Nations of jewelry ringers."

He spit out a laugh before rubbing his mouth.

"Do you ever work with guys who craft these elaborate proposals—things like rings in cakes or proposals on hot air balloons?" I asked.

"No. We've delivered rings to hotels, but New Zealanders don't really go for the elaborate proposal. Much more perfunctory about these matters."

"You have some beautiful rings here," I said, glancing at the display case. "What's the nicest one you have?"

"This one here, probably," he said, pointing to a singular, octagon-shaped gem on a simple platinum band.

"It's pretty. What are the specifics?"

Opening the case, he grasped the ring and flipped the tag.

"It's a one-point-three carat, G color, VVS clarity on a pure platinum band."

As he handed me the stone, it appeared to absorb all light from the room and shoot it straight back to my eyes. I looked at it from the side, and the refraction followed.

"How much do you charge for a diamond like this?"

"Let's see . . . thirteen thousand dollars. New Zealand."

"Thirteen thousand dollars New Zealand is about, what, eight thousand U.S.?"

He tapped a few buttons on the calculator nearby.

"Eight thousand four hundred and fifty."

"It's pretty."

"You're smiling."

"I'm just thinking, a guy walks into a big-city jewelry store in America and says, 'I want the best ring you got,' and he gets a bill for a quarter million dollars. He says the same thing here and he walks out with a wonderful ring without having to mortgage his home."

"We tend to think of things other than the ring."

"Oh, me, too."

"Are you done with that?"

"Sure. Thanks."

I handed him the ring, and he slid it back onto the gray velvet prong. Still the beams shot toward me through the glass. After a few more questions, the manager returned to his lunch and I walked outside. Raindrops began to ricochet off the surface of a courtyard fountain. I stood still.

Under the cascade, I concluded I was wrong to criticize New Zealand as the anti-Brazil. Every country is the anti-Brazil. No, I was wrong because I now realized it wasn't a criticism at all. If the world craves Brazil for inspiration, so, too, should it look to New Zealand. Ideally we'd all have a little of both.

Love here felt so grounded, lasting, real. Hear, hear for an affluent country that doesn't spend entire savings accounts on five-carat diamonds and liposuction. Three cheers for a dab of Tall Poppy Syndrome, because the rest of us don't suffer a lack of encouragement to boast. We could all use a dose of New Zealand humility and humor in our lives and relationships. I'm fine with a country where people don't wear dental floss bikinis to the beach, especially with the water this cold.

Yet New Zealand is sexy. There, I said it. Sure, it's easy to tweak the country for being cautious and gray. "What's the difference between New Zealand and a bowl of yogurt? One's got a live culture." They'll beat you to the punch line—and that's just my point. New Zealand has loosened up and grown comfortable in its skin, and that's one of the most attractive features of all.

In no other country on our journeys did I see women such equal partners as they are here. It's a product of their history as well as their psyche. Maori culture is matriarchal. White New Zealand granted women's suffrage before any other nation. Prime Minister Helen Clark is yet another stride. *Tracy will love it here*. The women are strong.

The result is an abundance of balanced relationships, even if they're not the most communicative ones. New Zealand's working on that. Still, it was inspiring to see partnerships of equal parts. "We're a nation of two halves," locals joke, both stating the obvious and paying homage to the two periods of rugby. They're more right than they know.

New Zealand had changed radically since my last visit, and for the better. Immigrant infusions gave the country energy, spice. More people turned outward to the world. The nation came out of its shell, all the while retaining the core values that make it so appealing.

"Yes, New Zealand's sexy," I repeated in the rain.

The lunch crowd began to gather up their takeout wrappers and cappuccino cups and return to work. I didn't have an umbrella but for some reason chose to linger. The water felt cleansing, clarifying even. Across the fountain and on the wall, I read the inscription. TO THINE OWN SELF BE TRUE.

To thine own self be true. This above all.

The rain intensified, and I turned and headed inside.

The minute Tracy and Calvin landed, I initiated Operation Towhead, a kid-friendly attack on the South Island. We visited yellow-eyed penguin colonies, explored the Te Anau Glowworm Caves, splashed around in Lake Wanaka, and cruised in the Milford Sound, the ship captain even letting an awestruck Calvin take the helm for a few minutes. We overindulged at the Cadbury chocolate factory in Dunedin and burned the calories during long walks in the botanical gardens. Calvin received his first tastes of rugby, billowy pavlova, and cheeky keas who crashed our picnics. If you count detangling the snarls in his sneakers each morning as knot work, then I'm quite certain we completed enough activities for Eagle Scout status.

All of this so he could declare, with assuredness and verve at the end of the trip, the "best part of New Zealand" was our motel room in Dunedin. Note to self: Next time, Econo Lodge, Barstow.

Actually, it was a nice hotel room, part of a remodeled series of townhomes complete with French toast *l'orange* for breakfast and a view of Kurt's elementary school alma mater, George Street Normal. Calvin's favorite part of the complex, though, was the private nook that housed his bed. Nooks, as any expert fort maker will tell you, provide the best possible setup for the garrison extraordinaire.

But as Calvin and I began the building process, I realized I'd forgotten something. Someone. Calvin's mom. I'd planned this entire trip around the whims and nap times of Calvin, remiss in carving out a little time for the two of us alone. With its Old West ruggedness and fireside bonhomie, New Zealand is one of the most romantic swaths on earth. I spent more time holding juice boxes and superheroes than I did holding Tracy's hand. If this upset her, she didn't show it, though I was beginning to realize single mothers rarely do.

Toward the end of the trip, I asked the front desk to recommend a babysitter.

My father, during our time in New Zealand, taught medicine at the University of Otago in Dunedin. He'd walk from our two-bedroom apartment on Heriot Row, down the hillside steps, across George and King and Cumberland streets, and onto the campus near the center of town. Strolling to dinner with Tracy that night, retracing his daily steps, I felt as if I'd never left the town.

"That's where I learned to play rugby," I said. "We had maroon jerseys and metal cleats. I thought that was so cool, hearing them clank on the bathroom floor. I'd screw them in and out for hours.

"And here's the fish and chips shop where we ate after each match. You'd slap down whatever money you had in your pockets and the man would serve you up a newspaper full of hot, greasy French fries."

"I'm hungry," she said.

"And here, here's the entrance to the university. They didn't have these modern buildings when we lived here. Only the old stone structures."

"Calvin would say it looks like Hogwarts."

"My dad would say the new glass buildings look like wart warts."

We crossed over the creek that halved the grounds and strode past the only other couple on the plaza as they rehearsed lines from a play. *Hamlet*? I paused in front of the gray and white stone Clock Tower, the university's beacon. The fading spring sun highlighted the oxidized green copper roof and Gothic spires for a final time that day. *It does look like Harry Potter's school.*

Now.

"Yeah, beautiful," she said. "Stunning."

You've been here before.

"Honey," she pleaded. "Can we see it from the restaurant? I'm starving." She turned to go, and I grabbed her arm.

"Um, ah, you'd never dump me, would you?" I asked.

Shit.

"What did you do?"

"Nothing."

"You did something."

"No."

"No man asks for assurance without having done something first."

That's true.

"I love you," I said.

"What . . . is . . . wrong?"

Breathe. There are no assurances, no guaranteed results, but the world has showed you how.

"Will you marry me?" I said, struggling to find the gray velvet box in my pocket.

"Oh . . ."

Answer? Please answer. Oh, right—the ring.

"I'll be a good father to Calvin. I'll give him everything he'll ever need," I said, giving her the ring.

If she tries on the ring, that's as good as a yes, right? Wedding rings are like underwear. You don't really want to return them.

She stared at the ring. Silent.

Say something. Yes. No. Just not maybe. I can't take another maybe.

I ducked my head to see her face. Never, in the disoriented path I called my life, did I imagine I'd be here, in a town of my youth, proposing to my polar opposite, my beautiful opposite.

They restored your faith. They showed you it wasn't as gone as you imag-

ined. You would have never proposed to this woman had it not been for the world.

She slipped the ring on her finger and smiled.

"You're smiling. That's a yes, then?"

"Yes. Yes!"

"Really?" I exhaled. "Great! Let's go eat!"

"Wait," she said, laughing. "Kiss me. Hug me."

"As long as you want."

And I did.

The restaurant had no champagne. The salad sprigs had brown spots. The tablecloth hadn't been changed from the previous diners. And I left the waiter the biggest tip of my life.

Throughout dinner, I waited for it to come, my order of rosemary lamb with a giant side dish of *What the hell did you just do?* I'd known Tracy a grand total of six months. Her mother's maiden name, her bank account balance, her childhood home, I knew them not. I didn't need to. I *knew* Tracy. This was at once the best decision of my life and the most reckless.

I would have never married Tracy prior to the honeymoon with my brother. Those days I made my decisions on logic and minimized risk. I rose each morning and made my to-do list, adding things like "14. Put newspaper in recycling bin," just to boost the sense of accomplishment. In a greater sense, life proceeded as a to-do list. It wasn't about opening my eyes and embracing opportunity or striving for a Buddhist-like focus on the present. It wasn't living. It was execution. I already had the plan. My days, I decided, would be spent seeing it through. Vice president at my company? Check. House on the beach? Check. Marry a sensible woman who met the criteria? Almost.

Here, at the end of the world, in an empty restaurant, I tore up the relationship checklist and stared at a single mom, an opinionated actress, a pain in the ass, a woman who just happened to be my most compatible partner all along.

The World's Ten Worst Places to Be Gay

1. **JAMAICA.** At least that's the verdict of *Time* magazine, which cites strict anti-sodomy laws (ten years of hard labor), the murders of gay rights leaders, and frequent beatings of homosexual tourists and local "batty boys." Even reggae gets in on the act. "Mister Fagoty," sings Bounty Killa, "wince in agony," leaving the rest of the world longing for the "One Love" days of Bob Marley.

2. **THE REAL AXIS OF EVIL:** Saudi Arabia, Sudan, United Arab Emirates, Yemen, Mauritania, as well as parts of Nigeria and Somalia. Go to these countries and you'll see men walking arm in arm, kissing each other, sharing beds, spending their days intertwined. That's fine, according to the governments. But do something in that bed and face a different reaction—the death penalty.

3. **IRAN** recommends death as well. But no need to worry, declared President Mahmoud Ahmadinejad on a trip to New York, as "we don't have homosexuals like in your country." Are theirs more flamboyant?

4. **GUYANA** is the only country in South America where it's still illegal to be gay. "Everyone who commits buggery with a human being or with any other living creature shall be guilty of felony and be liable to imprisonment for life," proclaims their law. Guyana is also a favorite touring spot for Jamaican reggae singers, by the way.

5. **MALAYSIA.** You know a country has gay-tolerance issues when the opposition leader is jailed not for corruption or sedition but for alleged sodomy. Anwar bin Ibrahim, a married man with several children, was convicted of homosexual acts with two men and sentenced to nine years in prison. After several years behind bars, Ibrahim convinced the courts to overturn the conviction, while continuing to criticize the ruling party. The result? Another arrest for supposed sodomy and a potential twenty-year sentence behind bars.

6. NORTH KOREA. Hennessy and Hollywood-obsessed President Kim Jong-il swears he's done away with homosexuality in North Korea. Even the word is banned. This may come as a surprise to the million-plus soldiers in Kim's military. According to commanders who've fled the country, about half partake in gay sex while in the barracks. "It's not like homosexuality in the West," explained former lieutenant Kim Nam-joon, as quoted in *Under the Loving Care of the Fatherly Leader.* "It's just that there are no women. A young guy with soft skin may feel like a woman."

7. GAZA. How gay-intolerant is this Palestinian-controlled territory, with penalties of up to a decade in prison for homosexual acts and strict antigay laws that have been on the books since British occupation? Gay men frequently flee to Israel.

8. COOK ISLANDS. Pacific Islanders have a long history of integration, affording homosexuals positions of authority, respect, and acceptance. Captain James Cook and fellow Western colonizers began to change the gay-friendly atmosphere, bringing with them cargo loads of Bibles, structured law, and good ole Western venereal diseases. The result in today's Cook Islands: fourteen years in the brig for sodomy or five just for being gay.

9. UGANDA. Churches organize antigay rallies, newspapers "out" suspected homosexuals, and nine in ten Ugandans disapprove of homosexuality. President Yoweri Museveni says homosexuals don't exist in his country, but, should they emerge, he'll jail them for life.

10. WASHINGTON, D.C. The laws are fine, but the clothes are miserable.

Insta-Dad

Calvin treated us to several bouts of the croup on the Wednesday night after we returned to Los Angeles, at 1:35 A.M., 3:14 A.M., and 5:39 A.M., to be precise. The LCD numbers from the electric clock etched themselves into my dreams during the short shifts when I did sleep. Did every parent operate like this? How could they perform their jobs when they sleep like soldiers in a DMZ? Shouldn't we keep everyone with a child under five away from heavy machinery? After Calvin's last session, I gave up on sleep in favor of coffee.

Ugg. The coffeemaker smells like cardamom. That's one immediate change. The room, and the house, looked different to me now, still foreign yet somehow mine. Like how new clothes feel until you've worn them a few times. I filled the coffee carafe with water and poured it on the plants. I'd never watered the plants. I sat where Calvin ate his breakfast and looked at the walls.

What would you think if a strange man walked into your house one day and said he planned to stay? For good. You'd never met him, never knew he existed until that moment. You and this stranger shared nothing in common. He chose to stay up late; you went to bed early. His sense of humor seemed cutting and sarcastic, while you preferred a more slapstick approach. He ate your food, monopolized your television, and occupied most of your roommate's time, hours you used to control.

Worst of all, the stranger began to boss you around. Little things, at first. "Don't tilt your chair back" or "quit spreading peanut butter on the dog."

With time, he nagged more, venturing into uncharted territories like syntax or personal hygiene. Before you knew it, he ruled every inch of your life.

My response would be hemlock or asphyxiation. Better yet, stoning. I'd want something gruesome and noteworthy, enough to make the evening news and convince any other would-be stranger to stay away.

I decided to make Calvin pancakes. No, not just pancakes, monster-cakes, with banana eyes and blueberry mouths, scowling and twisted and mean. For such a soft-spoken boy, he sure loved the morbid.

To compensate for the cardamom flavor remnants, I made the coffee strong. Too strong. I felt the shakes after a cup.

"Whatcha doing?" said Tracy.

"Shit! Don't sneak up on me like that."

"C'mere. Give me a hug."

"I'm sleep deprived."

"My baby," she said, stroking my back.

"I know that's facetious, but I'll take it anyway."

Then, as if on cue, Calvin stumbled into the kitchen and shot straight to the space between our legs. With all his strength, he pushed us apart so that he could hug Tracy's waist alone. He did this often. The Hug Killer of Tipton Way.

"You CB'd me," I said.

"What's CB?" asked Calvin.

"Never mind," said Tracy.

"Calvin block," I said.

"Calvin," said Tracy, "you don't need to push Franz away. Just join in the hug."

"I want my own."

I started to add up all the times Calvin threw a wet blanket on intimacy. The croup and the bathroom breaks, the barge-ins and mandatory fort-building sessions. "You need to get creative," my friend Andy counseled. Creative? You need to fight. Did married couples ever have sex?

"I made you pancakes, Calvin. Want one?"

"No."

"Blow your nose, honey."

"Here, take a look at these guys. Straight out of *Scooby-Doo*. The scariest pancakes on the planet. Scooby-Dough," I said, poking my fork into the blue-berry eyes. "It's a vampire pancake, with blood pouring out."

"Cool," he said, still clutching Tracy.

"And if you cut the bananas like this, you can make fangs."

Slowly he turned.

"Rarrrrrrrrrr. I vahnt to suck your blood!"

"Can I try?"

I moved the plate through the air, like Dracula floating through the halls. Fork in hand, I ranted.

"No, Count of Phlebotomy! You shall be avenged for all your hickeys. Take that! And that!" I said, digging my utensil into the dough.

"Dad! Stop it. Lemme eat that pancake."

"What did you say?"

"Stop it."

Dad? Dad.

I stared at Calvin, silent. Tracy and I had told him about our engagement the morning after. She showed him the ring and explained we'd all live to-gether. His new family. Dad? Calvin paused before asking, "Can I have a ring, too?" Over the following days, I saw him process the change with increasing requests to hold my hand and more aggressive tackles in bed.

Tracy told me she'd given him a bath the night before. They talked about his new cousins in Sacramento, especially their ages and action figures.

"What should I call him?" he asked.

"What do you want to call him?" she said.

"Dad."

Dad. Six months prior I had shared honeymoon suites with my brother in far-flung locales. Now I was arranging fruit fangs on pancakes to please a four-year-old. I saw then how a week's worth of frustrating, selfless, runny-nose par-enting could be wiped away with a single word. It made it all worthwhile. Dad.

"C'mon," said Calvin. "Make another one. Really scary."

"How about one with scars?"

"Yeah."

"And bloodshot eyes. We'll carve the veins into the bananas."

"And blood."

"Always blood."

* * *

Later that morning I fulfilled a promise to Tracy, sneaking from my car to a nondescript medical office building in Century City. A Mexican grandmother looked up from her *People en Español*.

Good. Don't know her. Nobody else in the waiting room.

Above her, straight from the supermarket parking lot art sale, hung an etching of a muscled whitetail buck, a ten-pointer. Atop a crag, he surveyed his forest dominion and, no doubt, the bevy of does worthy of his virility.

Rub it in, why don't you.

It could have been worse. The fertility clinic could have lined the walls with those corporate inspiration posters, the kind with words like COURAGE and EXCELLENCE plastered across giant waves and snowcapped peaks. Then I really would have felt pressured to perform.

"Franz Wisner?" the male receptionist blurted.

I sprang from my seat to quiet the blast.

Couldn't we do this in sign language?

"You're here for a sperm test," he announced.

"Mmm-mmm."

"Have you been here before?"

I turned to see if the Latina grandmother understood any of this.

"No. I'm fine. Healthy."

"Fill out these forms, then I'll bring you back."

I glanced around the room again, then shot back to the reception desk.

"Excuse me," I said. "Do you have anything other than *People en Español*?"

"*Men's Journal, Redbook*. Whatever's out there."

"I was hoping for something, you know, a little stronger."

"Everything's in the bathroom. Paper towels, magazines. Men and women. Just make your deposit in one of the cups and bring it back to me."

You think I'm gay? Do I look gay?

"Thanks," I said.

The Latina smirked.

I'd smirk, too. You're a thirty-nine-year-old man, foraging for pornography, about to make a "deposit" and hand it in like a final exam. "Here you go, professor. Worked really hard on this one. Had lots of practice."

"You can go back whenever you're ready," said the nurse, the male nurse.

* * *

The bathroom appeared as expected, with a squat low-flow toilet and peeling vinyl wallpaper, metal handrails, and just enough elbow room to maneuver. *Handrails?* A dripping, supersized bottle of Vaseline Intensive Care Lotion sat underneath a plastic dispenser with a partially torn paper towel hanging out. *He must have been in a hurry.* The Glade PlugIn bullied any odors of onanism. Berry Burst. *They must be so proud at Glade headquarters. This would make the newsletter.* Thankfully, the door locked firmly, muffling most sounds outside.

I sat on the toilet seat and assumed my first task: library inventory. The well-worn magazines sat in the bottom of a wicker basket, a few draped on the handle. *Did the last guy in here think this one would be my best bet?*

The buzz from the fluorescent lighting grew louder as soon as I focused on it.

"I can't do this," I mumbled to myself.

I stuck my hand in the pile, and instantly my body went limp. The dog-eared pages and the oil stains on every third photograph, those I didn't mind. But there, at the bottom of the heap, sat a *Playboy* pictorial I owned in college, the cover model practically winking at me.

Ah yes, Shannon Tweed. So we meet again.

The envelope came within a week. Sperm count: 27 percent.

Khaki Fever

A warning, guys. Just forget it. Someday you might be able to hold your own with an overly aggressive Italian Romeo or a sunburned Santa Monica lifeguard. But under no circumstances, in any conceivable scenario, will you ever be able to top the romantic allure of the African safari guide, especially on his home turf. Sorry if this stings. I want you to know the truth. Celebrities, models, rock stars—these folks have nothing compared to the men who make their living escorting tourists through the sub-Saharan bush.

I got an inkling after befriending Rudy, a South African game tracker who'd moved to Los Angeles. At a dinner party I rambled on about being thrown from a horse with an aversion to gringo riders.

"Interesting," he said, struggling to appear amused. "That reminds me of a time we had to track a sick bull rhino who hated the sight of all humans. I fired one tranquilizer into his rear, and he immediately spun around and charged our group. Barely got that second shot off."

The women swooned. A bachelorette shuffled her chair closer to his. I made a mental note to never open my mouth at group gatherings with Rudy.

During a tour of South Africa, I saw why. It's called Khaki Fever, and it's lethal.

"Women in the U.S. see men in suits with briefcases," said Gillian, a safari-goer from California. "Here, you see men in khaki uniforms holding rifles to protect you. Of course you're going to fall for that."

To begin, tourists give guides their lives. Literally. The minute they leave their air-conditioned cottages to stray into the wild for an afternoon game drive or a walking safari, the only thing that separates their existence as they know it and their existence as a three-course meal are the men in khaki. The guides know exactly where and when that pride of lions sleeps, hunts, and mates, knowledge they'll subtly reinforce after every growl from the bush.

During treks in rugged Land Rovers, guides invite single women to sit in the shotgun seat. On safaris it really is a shotgun seat. Riders straddle one. Each time the guide spots an emerald-eyed leopard or a toothy lion, he'll kill the motor and position the vehicle at the precise distance where tourists in the back will feel safe, while his front-seat companion will feel the overwhelming urge to bury her face into Savanna Ed's hairy chest.

"Don't worry about a thing," Ed will assure his maiden. "Just a few more minutes here to make sure everyone gets a photo. Video? Anyone need to shoot video?"

Around the dinner table, guests relay trifling stories of meager sightings. The ace guides will humor them before entering the discussion.

"That same leopard you mention, the one we saw at the top of that tree? I once had to give him a root canal. Sans novocaine."

It's after dinner and after after-dinner cocktails when Khaki Fever can really be potent. Monkeys scurry across footpaths, hyenas cackle, beasts rustle, all within an arm's distance of guest cabins. Of course, you'll need an escort to your room, an armed escort. Retired guides told me they waited until the loud game appeared before offering chaperone service. I can see how it works. At the sight of a wayward hippo one evening, I, too, felt like hugging my guide's hulking torso.

Closing time, and the opportunities abound. Guides relate many a tale about women begging them to share a bed, "strictly for protection." Some camps even have campout policies. If a guest wants to sleep outside, a guide must sleep nearby. Camp rules don't specify how close nearby.

For the industrious guides and willing partners, there's always the legendary "private evening drive." They'll pack up the Land Rover and head out into the wilderness, driving far enough into the bush to make a return trip that evening seem pointless.

"Better to wait until first light," he'll say.

"Will we be safe?"

"Actually, the safest place for us to be is on the roof. Make sure to hang on tight. And leave any clothing with a scent inside."

Sometimes Khaki Fever can be a lifelong affliction. Just ask Paula, a graphic artist from Chile who decorated her apartment with zebra-covered chairs and saved her money for an African safari. When she finally set foot on the continent, what took her breath away wasn't a majestic elephant or a sprinting cheetah but a species far more familiar. *Homo sapiens guideus.* She wished her English were better.

Sometimes Khaki Fever is just as strong in reverse. Just ask Craig, Paula's guide on the final trek of that two-week stay in the South African bush. He described his reaction to the sight of Paula for the first time with one word—paralysis.

They shared a drink after dinner, and he shooed the pesky baboons from the veranda in front of her room.

"When he touched my arm," she said. "That's when I felt my body start to wake up."

They swapped phone numbers the next day before she headed back to Santiago.

"I had a knot in my stomach when she left," said Craig. "I wanted to stop the bus and tell her how I felt."

He tracked her down in Cape Town.

"She's out right now," said the hotel clerk. "Would you like to leave a message?"

He paused and felt his entrails, still entwined.

"Yes," he said. "Tell her I love her."

The phone calls between Chile and South Africa started as a biweekly occurrence, then every other day, then daily. His friends said he was crazy. Hers told her it would never last. Everyone except her mother, that is. She talked about the power of love to bridge oceans. The following year they married.

They now work together. He leads guests on safari drives; she serves as a camp greeter and concierge. She can't imagine a life anywhere else, though she misses her family and Chilean shellfish. She calls Craig her "milk man." They plan to raise their family in the wild.

Optimism

BOTSWANA

I felt better while on safari during the first half of my trip to Botswana. The vervet monkey ruffians who stole my breakfast and the eight-thousand-pound hippo who decided to make the grassy area outside my tent his nightly buffet had distracted my attention. Hungry eight-thousand-pound creatures tend to do that. The lonesomeness sank in when I reached the dusty town of Maun.

I love Africa. Under any other circumstance, I'd jump at the chance to come. But I'd just proposed to a woman who'd actually said yes. I didn't want to do anything to screw this up like before. This was a life-changing decision, one that demanded dedication and long hours. I'll be there for you, Tracy. To love and to hold. I'm your man, your rock. Now I just need to go to Botswana for a month.

With ample guilt and SPF 50, I wandered the streets of Maun wishing at every corner I were home. For the last several years, the road had been my partner, my healer, my muse. I'd throw on a backpack, traipse around a foreign haunt, and feel secure, whole. Now, suddenly, the trips lost their allure. No longer did I long for adventure. Now I dreamed of routine. I fantasized about eating the same cereal in the same bowl every morning.

I'd been away from Tracy before, missing her more and more each trip, but this one was different, torturous. Burning cauldrons and stretch racks and such. Here in Africa, I felt like I *had* to be with Tracy. *Saudade,* as the Brazilians said. And then some. Every impulse within said, *Go. Cancel the rest of the trip and go home. She needs you.*

* * *

Maun is the former haunt of the great white hunters and the current jumping-off point for the upscale safari camps, today owned by corporations and hotel chains a world away. It's remote, resourceful, and chock-full of offbeat characters who've been raised in the bush or escaped to it. The city had its Wall Street–style heyday in the 1980s—the elaborate parties, the all-day drink fests, sex with anyone who'd oblige. AIDS stopped the music.

"Tarred roads also killed the party," said Map, a legendary local wilderness expert. "Before the roads, people were rugged individuals, happy to be on their own. They wanted freedom, which meant sexual freedom as well."

Activity slowed to a shuffle in the afternoon heat. Women in long cotton dresses carried tattered umbrellas to shield their bodies from the sun's attack, a cast of Mary Poppinses on a stage of crimson dirt and sun. Indoors there were small farmers and big idlers, peasants who sold hurried carvings, large families with no father in sight, Zionist Christian Church followers with their khaki uniforms and ZCC stars, teenage boys trying their hardest to look and act like 50 Cent, most of whom had never left the city.

I paused for shade under a tree next to a group of women waiting for a ride. The youngest of the group approached me.

"You've got an African bum," she said.

"Um, thanks," I said.

I'd been in Maun only a couple of days but already knew this to be high praise. A trip to the African nation is the perfect remedy for anyone feeling aware of his or her derriere. Lose the diet pills and leave the Zone. Go to Botswana and watch your ample caboose morph instantly into an object of pulchritude.

"In the Setswana language, if you tell a woman she's fat, that's a big compliment," said Peter, a Maun local. "We like Western women. But deep in our hearts is a love of large women."

He told a story about walking around town next to a woman with a large backside.

"Massive by Western standards. The men stopped and stared. They ooohed and ahhhed. Some came up to her and rubbed it. She loved, *loved* it all, protesting only for show."

There are practical considerations as well.

"The men here will tell you a large woman is good for a cold night," added his friend Paul.

Size 2s and 4s are considered unhealthy, infertile, not a load of fun.

"Thin women love their bodies more than their man," said a bus driver in Gaborone.

Views are changing, though. In 1999, Gaborone's Mpule Kwelagobe became the first black African to win the Miss Universe contest, in the country's first attempt. Her image and her causes are plastered on billboards throughout the nation. Along with a growing influence of American media and fashion magazine tastes, Mpule is forcing Botswana to reassess.

"I like fat women, but just not too fat," said Yaone, a university student. "I'm having now an interest in thin women. This is because I'm watching much television."

"On behalf of the ample-buttocked," I said, "allow me to offer a heartfelt and loud 'Don't!' "

"Love in American movies and television is much better than love in Botswana," added Gorata, a fellow student. "Most of them marry for true love. I think this is the way it is in America and some other countries. It is better than Botswana."

Thank God cable and satellite in Botswana frequently break down.

Parched, craving Tracy yet feeling better about my backside, I stopped at a chicken and chips restaurant for a Coke. A thick-necked businessman with a loosened tie invited me to his table.

"We have full respect for our parents," explained Fred. "This is number one. You are always thinking about what will please them."

This means introductions through family ties, romance within tribes. It also means many parental consultations before commitment, including those of the heart. *Morero,* as the locals call it, is an essential component of doing business. Dating rituals are still carried out with the thoughts of Mom and Dad in mind. Botswanans tend to meet at parties, at extended family gatherings, or through introductions from sisters and cousins.

"We have discos and other Western meeting places," he said, "but we prefer to meet through family and friends. There is still a stigma attached to bars and discos. With most of my past girlfriends, I have been introduced. It's a matter of comfort. Whoever introduces you, you trust them. I knew my wife's family, so I was comfortable."

"A girl from a decent family would never approach a man," added Moses, an elderly man at an adjoining table who entered our discussion. "Only prostitutes approach men. The older generation believes a man needs to fight for what he wants. The ones who come to you, you don't think much of them."

Family desires also shape courtships after the couple connects. They frown upon overt displays like holding hands or kissing in public. The younger generations, only a shade less conflict-avoidant and shy, usually acquiesce.

"It's disrespectful for couples to do this," said Moses. "Especially in front of parents in the old days. Parents don't want to see this."

Geography also plays a role in the dating ritual. If New Zealand has two degrees of separation, then Botswana maintains only one.

"The population here is very small," said Fred. "There are dangers with talking to a woman. Maybe she is your neighbor. Maybe everyone knows her. There are fewer tribes and fewer dialects in Botswana than in other African countries. There are fewer borders."

Manners go arm in arm with family. Botswana, an amiable land in the sweet spot of Southern Africa, a nation of *dumela,* hello, a place where avoidance is unacceptable. *Botho* is the concept of desert hospitality, respect and compassion for others. The Setswana greetings are clear and honest, the handshakes soft but unfailing, often with a grasp of the forearm to signal added respect. Botswana is a nation of whisper and shadow. They are soft-spoken here, quick to agree, rarely wishing to offend, often with true feelings tucked far away. Sure, rides can be arranged. Of course, introductions can be made. "No problem, *mma, rra,*" madam, sir. "Pleas-zahhh," they'll sing with a colonial lilt.

Botswana today ambles along the path to love, through sky-high AIDS rates and tribal customs that applaud promiscuity, in discos and bars they cannot afford, with bighearted yet stubbornly traditional partners striving to improve their lot in a land with little opportunity to do so.

Ask Botswanans about their ideal characteristic for a loved one and they'll say things like "a provider for my family" or "someone who works hard." Love here often sounds like a business proposition, and to many it is. Rarely did I hear a local talk about physical appearance initially, though the tall, dark, and handsomes abound.

Bolstered by introductions from family and friends, Botswanans make contact with a potential love interest at parties or village gatherings. The men are expected to take the lead. They start polite, then move fast. Whiplash fast.

Polokano met her love at a village party. She felt safe with him since their families knew each other.

"He was handsome," she said. "We enjoyed the party together. At the end of the evening, he told me he loved me. I said I loved him, too."

"The first night he told you he loved you?"

"Yes."

"Talk about a living hell for commitment-phobes," I said.

"Not so," said Moses. "In your world, 'I love you' means 'I want to marry you.' In Botswana, the words mean something different. 'I love you' and 'I like you' can be said the same. *Ke a go rata* is 'I love you' and 'I like you.' We still use it if our feelings escalate."

There's a less heartening reason Botswanans, and many other Africans, are quick on the "I love you" draw. AIDS has sliced life expectancy rates to less than forty years.

Cecilia is a large woman with cloudy eyes, a widow from Ramatlabama whose black dress matched her mood when we met at a town square. She had lost her husband of ten years, the father of her three girls aged nineteen, eighteen, and thirteen. Her face cleared for a spell when she talked of him.

"I found my love at the football," she explained. "I went to the playground, shouting at the players. 'I like how you yell,' he said."

Right then he told her he loved her.

"I told him I will think about it. I was thinking, 'Does that guy really love me, or is he a playboy?' I decided he loved me."

When the year in black expires, she hopes to find love again.

"But I would only want a widower. I don't want a divorcé."

Janet is twenty-one and from Mmathethe. Her boyfriend told her he loved her on their second outing as they watched television at his home. She wasn't shocked.

"In most cases, the man has to say it first," she explained. "I don't know any women who have said the 'love' word first."

Long walks, shared meals with family, and couch-potato sessions at home are common dates for newfound loves. Few can afford the malls and chain restaurants that have popped up in Francistown, Maun, or Gaborone. While salaries inch above those in most sub-Saharan nations, and the economy is relatively stable, Botswana remains a poor country with savanna-sized gaps between the haves and have-nots, and those so far away they don't know the difference.

"Sorry about the smell," said Ericka as I ducked into her threadbare Toyota. "I was delivering chicken last week and forgot about it."

In her blue halter top, black shiny satin pants, and oversized sunglasses, she seemed better suited for the Miami nightclubs than the Okavango bush. On the dashboard she placed a small Bible. A perfumed air freshener clung to the air-conditioning vent, filling the car with Freon, jasmine, and eau de KFC.

"I thought you'd be older," I said.

"Really."

"Somebody says they're going to introduce you to a minister, you think middle-aged white male, hair parted on the side."

She matched the white part, but nothing else. Ericka grew up in South African boarding schools and Botswana villages. Her life meandered as she bounced between the two.

"Then my cousin died," she said. "He fell down a sand pit and broke his neck. And I decided to go to Bible school in Dallas. Not to become ordained but to clear my soul. I wanted to see other people restored."

"What brought you home?" I asked.

"I didn't want to come back. Africa is extreme. But two prophets came to me in Texas. God told me to come back."

She did, without a penny. To support her new Breath of God ministry, Ericka types documents at a local safari company and cares for an elderly woman a couple of hours a day. She earns enough to deliver meals and encouragement to a never-ending list of locals who need both.

"Sometimes it just takes a bottle of cold water to make a day," she said as we made her rounds.

Over dirt roads we bounced, pointing the Toyota toward lean-tos and one-room homes of cinder block and thatch. A young woman in a blue V-neck dress patted her hair and met us outside.

"Ericka," she sang. "I was hoping you'd come today."

Pungi is twenty-five and already a widow with a parting gift of HIV.

"How are you doing?" asked the minister.

"Better. I couldn't get out of bed for a few days."

"Ericka!" screamed the twin boys as they barged outside. "What did you bring us?"

They wore aloha shirts with matching patterns, one with Diamond Head framed in orange, the other in royal blue. Ericka handed them water bottles and bags of food, which they promptly gave to their mother. A younger sister shuffled behind, making her way to the space between her mom's legs. She returned my smile with one sans front teeth.

This could be Calvin. They're about the same age. Only this is Africa. You don't gain parents here. You lose them.

Ericka explained the reason for my presence, and Pungi jumped to comment.

"The men," she said, as her boys listened in. "They want many women. They don't want to stick to one partner. That is why we see the HIV in Botswana. The women, they like to stick to one partner."

Hearing the conversation turn to an issue they knew too well, the boys excused themselves and darted back to the dirt mounds.

"The Botswana man, they don't like to condomize," Pungi continued. "I want a man who likes to use a condom."

"What about the type of man?" I asked.

"Any. It doesn't matter. Just not too short."

"You believe in love."

"Yes. One love. I don't want to spread the disease."

After we'd driven away, Ericka pulled the car to the side of the road and killed the motor. I stared at the open space ahead, a large field with hundreds of flimsy metal frames and tattered fabric between. They looked like homemade chicken cages, and I'd seen them in unexpected areas, near homes, beside shops, on the roads out of town. I saw them often.

"They're there to keep the hyenas from rooting out the bodies," she said. "It takes nine months for the bodies to sink into the ground."

Nine months. Nine months of fending off scavengers to allow a loved one to rest in peace in a land where even the cheapest coffin and burial costs a month's salary. Botswanans make far too many trips to the cemeteries. They know the grounds too well. They know the killer.

Commentators are quick to point out that AIDS victims don't die of AIDS, they succumb to things like pneumonia or meningitis because they don't have enough lymphocytes or T cells to wage the war. They are more than familiar with the terminology in Botswana. The distinctions don't lessen the pain.

Roughly one in four Botswanans carries the HIV virus. Those are the ones who've been tested.

Yet Botswanans are far more knowledgeable about the disease than the world believes. Gone are the days when most locals swore you contracted HIV by using a condom or cured it by having sex with a virgin. Slow to educate, like the rest of Africa, Botswana rallied and spread the word about prevention and cure. Safe-sex billboards in the major cities plead with people to ABC— Abstain, Be faithful, Condomize. "Know Your Status," advise the campaigns. The United Nations, churches, and relief organizations poured hundreds of millions of dollars into the peaceful country with hopes of brightening its story. They've succeeded only in moving Botswana from the top position on the world's HIV/AIDS list to the second slot.

They've misspent the money. All the condoms and the billboards and the pleas have yet to change the most important factor—Botswana's addiction to infidelity.

For all their knowledge of the virus and how to prevent it, Botswanans re-fuse to halt the affairs. Prostitutes here charge two prices—regular rate for sex with a condom, more for sex without.

Botswana grew up watching Dad and Mom stray. It didn't see the conse-quences. The stories sounded fun. People didn't "cheat." They weren't "un-faithful." They were "with a friend." *O ratana le mongwe.* "He's going with someone else." Even today, Botswana doesn't have a word for infidelity.

Despite the crowded Christian churches and open-air sermons, Botswana has never cloaked itself in the concept of sin. Churches are for prayer, not re-pentance. It's grueling in the land of the Okavango. Please, Lord, let us have a little money and a little fun.

Botswana knows the lethal hangover of its ways. People bury their family members and vow never again. Greater numbers use protection. Scores are screened for HIV now that the government requires it. Those who test positive receive their medicine on the spot, free of charge. The methods evolved, but the party remains in full swing. Botswana cannot stay faithful.

Infidelity. It's the number-one gripe you'll hear from women in all parts of Botswana. They'll describe their dream man as "loyal," "someone who is content with me," "not a playboy." Loyalty trumps all on the wish list, they say, including appearance, family, money.

"They are the most selfish creatures in the world!" said Priscilla, a married woman from Francistown.

Remember, there are a lot of creatures in Africa.

"The men are not in love with the women, they're in love with the land," said Rosie, a longtime Maun resident. "Botswana will test your relationship. These are harsh conditions. You need to put up with that. Plus nobody can cuddle 'cause it's too damn hot."

"They're so irresponsible," said Lolly, a student in Gaborone. "Cheaters! Liars! Most of them. All ages."

Their counterparts downplay the transgressions. It's cultural, the men plead, an ingrained component of *botho*. It's how we saw our fathers behave. Relationships fray like everything else in the desert. Your divorce rates are higher than ours, are they not?

"They're not all cheaters," said Moagi, a fellow student who interrupted Lolly. "The problem is the girls. Women focus on money and cars. They just want money. I wish they didn't always look for money."

I heard his words often from male Botswana. With a shrug, men admitted they'd cheated on their girlfriends or wives. It's how it's always been, they stated. The women do it, too. What they recoiled at is the fact the sex here often comes with provisos and costs, either stipulated or expected. They railed against *go becha,* money paid to keep a lover. They talked about it being common for women to take paramours to cover various expenses—a lover to pay the cell phone bill, another for petrol.

Botswana's hope for change isn't in the earnest relief programs or the cartons of antiretroviral drugs. It's in the schools. It's in the hands of girls.

"African women have been far too tolerant," said Map. "But more and more are taking a stand. Look at the class valedictorians. They're girls. And they're not going to put up with this forever."

Janet is part of the change. A calmness masked her eighteen years. Janet is

Christian, and a virgin. I'VE TESTED, HAVE YOU? proclaimed her black T-shirt. She'd spent the morning at a Maun health fair, screening countrymen, dispensing education.

"I'm going to wait until I'm married to have sex," she said matter-of-factly. "Most people won't wait. They're afraid they will die waiting."

S o you want to marry a Botswanan? Well, you'll need a close-knit family. A brother or cousin who can negotiate would be helpful as well. Most important, you'll need a good cattle rancher. In Botswana and throughout much of Africa, marriage is all about the beef.

For centuries, village customs required the groom to give the bride's family a small herd of cattle as a way to honor them for allowing their daughter to be married. Critics, mostly white, characterize the practice as bride price for the amount of a few hamburgers. Botswanans counter that the tradition, known as *bogadi* or *lobola,* is a way to strengthen bonds between families and a necessity to apportion wealth.

The number of cattle depends on several factors, including the wealth of the families, the age and health of the bride, past marriages or children by other men, and the reputation of the tribe.

"Bangwato tribe members don't have to pay *lobola* if they marry another Bangwato," said Dimpho, from Molepolole. "But if someone from another tribe marries a Bangwato, the *lobola* is eight cows. Balete tribe, *lobola* is five cows. Bakgatla from Mochudi, they pay only two. Maybe this is because they are known to be very rude. It is believed you will have problems."

Most countrymen belong to the Tswana tribe, but there are several dozen smaller ones. Take notes. Oh, and you could also use a good accountant, because there's been inflation in the *bogadi* biz. What used to be a cow or two is now up to six or ten or twelve.

"In Maun, it's six or seven cows," said Callastus, forty-one, a man who would know the price to the exact hoof and horn. He's been planning to marry his girlfriend, Mary, for several years. "But I've been very good to her family. So maybe they ask for two or thee cows."

H alf of all potential grooms cannot afford *lobola,* choosing instead to live with their partner without an official marriage certificate. Wealthier urbanites frequently offer cash in lieu of cattle.

In some villages, the bride's family demands payment in full before they allow the couple to cohabitate, a custom known as *go ralala*. Other village customs require a little good-faith livestock up front—a single cow or a goat, for example—with the rest of the booty to be paid after the official ceremony.

You might also want to bring along a copy of Emily Post's latest tome, because bad manners could hike the price. If the groom's family is a bit tardy on the delivery, the bride's brood can up the ante with another cow or two. Locals call this *kgomo ya tlhagela,* the cow that has broken into the family's corral. If they're rude to their future in-laws or address them too informally at first, more cows. If the groom-to-be or his brother even walks by the future bride's house, the bovine wish list grows.

Nowadays, the wannabe groom will relate his marital intentions to his uncle, who will then break the news to his father. Once both parents have given their approval, the negotiating process, or *patlo,* begins with all the diplomatic nuances of a United Nations peace treaty. Dusty jeans and work skirts are discarded in favor of suits and Sunday dresses. The father will assemble a small group to plead on behalf of his son. This could include his wife, a brother, good friend, or neighbor, but only if that person is betrothed. Unmarried locals are rarely seen as relationship experts.

Family members gather up food, clothing, trinkets, and alcohol as gifts to smooth the schmooze. Without the prospective groom, the clan will travel to the home of the bride's family. Not to enter, to wait. In some villages, they're required to arrive before sunrise. In others, *patlo* means sitting on the side of the road until they've been summoned inside. The insolence continues even when they're allowed in, with the groom's family addressed as hyenas, scavengers.

The family will play along, knowing the game will end soon. In most marriage negotiations, the two families will know each other. They'll go through the motions more for the sake of ceremony than the sake of steak.

Of course, nothing will be settled during the first meeting. There'll be a lot of introductions and posturing. That's because men are involved. The real decisions are made in the days following, when the women get together to hash out the specifics—the time and location of the wedding, who pays, and, the most favored topic among the Botswanan better halves, how the women do all the work while the men sit around and talk. This chat session is referred to as *go tlhatswa puo ya banna,* washing the words of the men.

A couple of weeks after the initial *patlo,* the bride's family summons the groom's clan to announce their decision. Usually this is a foregone conclusion. If there were real problems, the parties would find a way to end the discussions with as little embarrassment as possible. This includes not being asked back as a way for her family to say no.

When they do request an audience, it means one thing: Let the celebration begin. The prospective groom can now visit the house, with gifts, of course. He and his family are treated like equals. Food will be served, the men will huddle together to give advice and ridicule to the young man, and the women will go about running things like they always do.

"This whole getting on one knee, this is tedious," said Dimpho. "We don't get on one knee. It embarrasses her, and it embarrasses me. We just say, 'Isn't it time we get married?' You buy her a dress, shoes, a shawl. Maybe also a handbag, a necklace. Anything she wants.

"In the old days, the man did this on his own. Most couples now purchase the gifts together. You put the clothes and items in a bag, and she pretends she doesn't know they exist."

After the wedding day is set, it's time to round up the herd. Witness a procession of eight or ten cattle being led on the side of the highway or driven in a truck, odds are there's a happy bride and even happier father-in-law at the end of the journey.

This is a problem for city dwellers. Where do you store eight cattle in a one-bedroom apartment? What will the neighbors say? Fortunately for the rest of the building, there are businessmen who will take the cattle once they've been presented to the bride's family and sell them right away. In Botswana, there are businessmen for everything.

Thinking about my own wedding, I rose early and made the five-mile walk to the district commissioner's office outside Gaborone. The civil ceremonies took place on Thursdays.

That's exactly how it should be done. None of the frilly accoutrements of the last one. Your invites were wrapped in sea grass. Sea grass. Talk to Tracy.

On the gray-brown lawn in front of the government building, antsy couples mingled with their families. The men wore borrowed business suits and sports coats, often a size too big or small. Their brides adjusted their Sunday church dresses, some bulging with babies on the way. Brothers and moms smiled. "Welcome." I adjusted my camera and took a few pictures.

The announcement from the official quieted the crowd and sent the couples inside to a fluorescent conference room with a long table. He pulled the red curtains over the windows to discourage onlookers and to cool the room.

"Close family only," he said. "Please. The room is too small."

As I made my way back outside with the friends and second cousins, a large woman grabbed my arm.

"Stay," she said. "You are with our family."

"I don't know if they'll believe you, but thanks."

A young commissioner with a tailored jacket entered the room, acting like young people with power in any country do—smug, speaking loudly enough to obfuscate any insecurity. The elders forgave him his disposition and waited patiently while he finished a rambling speech.

"What did he say?" I asked the woman.

"Nothing," she said.

"Malcolm and Bamouni?" he yelled.

A woman in one of the room's only white outfits, a retailored skirt and jacket with a netted pillbox hat in cream, rose arm in arm with her fiancé. He wiped the sweat from his shaved head and looked down at his feet. Their small contingent murmured muted catcalls and words of encouragement. Several others joined in.

The commissioner asked them to recite a list of vows as dry as any government document, the couple nodding after each promise. At least I think they nodded. It's hard to nod when your chin is glued to your chest the entire time.

"Do you have a ring?" he asked.

They did. Most did. Many returned them to others after the ceremony. Those wealthy enough to afford their own produced gold bands inscribed with their names. Botswana is one of the world's most abundant sources of diamonds. I didn't see any here.

"Okay," said the commissioner. "You may present this."

Lifting his head a couple of inches, the groom turned to his bride.

"This is for my love for you," he said, placing the band on her finger.

"To our future," she said, giving him a similar ring in return. "Loving you . . . forever."

Then the room changed in tone, as guests milled and chatted. The bride licked her lips; her groom wiped his hands on the sides of his coat. The audience reminded me of one at a weightlifting competition, encouraging the participants in waves, first when they approach the bar, then when they hoist it to their shoulders. Now they readied to cheer the climax.

"The state pronounces you man and wife," said the commissioner. "You may kiss."

Now, Botswanans are courageous. They will walk for hours through lion- and hyena-infested bush. They'll move to Johannesburg or Nairobi to find employment in the world's most dangerous cities. Such things scare them not. But having to kiss someone in front of a room of strangers? That's another story.

As the audience quieted, the couple leaned into each other without touching. Their lips met for a millisecond, with their heads darting back just as fast. This didn't matter to the audience. The insta-peck gave them more than enough ammunition to hoot and cackle, the lady standing next to me among the loudest. In Botswana, elderly women with headscarves are often the loudest.

"I am so much content," said the young groomsman after the ceremony.

"For the marriage or that the kiss is over?" I asked.

"Both. Just to give her that respect."

Next the real weddings begin, the multiday, multivenue celebrations, starting at the bride's home. An unlucky member of the *bogadi* herd will join the party as boiled *seswaa,* paired with *morogo* (a mixture of spinach, tomatoes, and onions) and served to all. As a stereo system blasts African pop music, the women will huddle with each other and the men will huddle with their beers, often homemade brews distilled from sorghum or corn. Villagers may not even know who got married until the party is in full swing. The laughs, lights, and soca music are clarion calls for all to join. There's no such thing as a party crasher in Botswana.

The festivities continue through the night, which is a good and bad thing for the revelers. Wedding celebrations encompass more than just the joining of two people. They're family and community fests, a time to embrace the people who shaped the couple's lives.

The downside comes when the party shifts to the groom's quarters, a customary part of any wedding celebration to symbolize the bride accepting a new life, a new home. Wedding guests often help in this process by carrying the bride's belongings with them as the party moves. Imagine having to drag a credenza across town after having partied all night. There are a lot of dented pieces of furniture in Botswana.

* * *

The Gallup International Association asked the world a simple question a few years ago: "Will next year be better than this?" They sampled thousands of people across sixty-two different countries and uncovered some fascinating facts. Europe answered with the highest number of noes, citing war and the economy as chief justifications for their gloom.

The world's most optimistic continent? This happened to be the land with the least, an area with every ill known to man—genocide, plague, corruption, curse. Africa. More smiles. More can-do spirit. More belief in life, in love.

Cynics dismiss these results and similar ones as proof only of Africa's dire situation. Things can't get any worse, they snarl. Yet anyone who's been to Africa, *really* been to Africa, anyone who's left the tour buses and the *Condé Nast Traveler*–approved safari camps and ventured to the villages and felt Africa like you'd feel a long-lost relative in a long-overdue hug, will dismiss this skepticism without delay. Africa is one of the few places on our planet that can penetrate you, change you, and stay inside you.

If you allow it full access, Africa will cause you to shed your every pretense and false god. Its inhabitants, buoyant despite the sea of pain around, speak to the vibrancy and resilience of love. The young widows and orphans remind us of its brevity. Africa confirms we are alive, ready to love.

Things are ugly here, and cruel. Warlords turn their terror on innocent tribes, Robert Mugabe and other thuggish leaders pillage their homelands, and the biggest killer of all, the tiny mosquito, claims a million lives a year. Optimistic about next year? There's no reason to be optimistic about tomorrow.

But Africa is, which makes Africans' brand of love the most inspirational of all.

Want to teach a kid not to gripe when he gets PlayStation for Christmas instead of a Wii? Exchange the video games for a few plane tickets and let him hear the laughter in an African village. Think your relationship has problems? You and your partner at wit's end? Do yourselves a life-changing favor and stop by Africa on the way to the marriage counselor.

How they smile, I'll never know. Only that they do. And each one I saw buoyed my hope in love.

After two weeks on safari and the dusty streets of Maun, the cool waters of the Gaborone hotel pool felt sublime. I could feel the burn and grime exit my body. Down. Down. For an eternity down. I slipped to the bottom of the deep end, sometimes remembering to come up for air.

From the depth I saw the legs: chubby, tiny, and bowed. The toddler splashed on the top step while her mother hovered by. *Please don't pee in the pool.*

"Sorry if we ruined your silence," said the woman in her American accent.

"No, no," I said. "The water's nice."

"Are you here on vacation?"

"More like a research project."

"About Botswana?"

"Here and a few other places. How about you?"

"Oh, my husband is with the American Embassy. But we're getting ready to move back to Virginia. Our stuff ships in a few days."

"You must be sad. Botswana's an amazing place."

"Yes. But it's time."

"You have a beautiful daughter," I said. "Cutie."

"Thanks," she said as her infant continued to splash around.

"Your first?"

"And last."

"Aw, you're young."

"It took us ten years to have her. There's no way I'll go through that again."

"Took my folks about that long to have me. My mom was on so many fertility drugs, I came out with hair all over my face and body. The wolf baby. They declined the free photos."

"I can relate," she said. "What saved us is that my husband was stationed in Malaysia. The treatments were a fraction of the price over there."

"In vitro?"

"Drugs, in vitro, artificial insemination. The works. Finally he had to get an operation."

I loved this brand of American openness, how you could talk to a stranger about intimate body parts without either party thinking it odd.

"Really? Pardon me for being so nosy. I might have the same thing. Varicocele?"

"Yep. We didn't figure that out for a long time."

"Please don't tell your husband you talked about his plumbing with a stranger."

"He's had to talk about his plumbing with strangers for years."

"I don't want him to put me on some State Department blacklist or anything."

"Have you been tested?" she asked.

"Yes."

"And?"

"They said I need an operation. If I want to have kids."

"You should get it sooner rather than later. The longer you wait, the harder to conceive."

"I'm not even married yet. So we have some time."

"Still."

"If you don't mind me asking, how much does an operation cost?"

"We spent about a hundred thousand dollars on all the treatments over a decade."

"Wow."

"It would have been several times that if we weren't living abroad."

In the morning, her night, I purchased a batch of calling cards and phoned Tracy.

"Hey," I said.

"Heeeeey," she said with a warmth that made me feel the word.

"I miss you."

"I miss you, too, baby."

"No, I *really* miss you. I've been having these dreams the last couple of days, strong ones. It's hard to describe."

"I really miss you, too."

"It's not that. I dunno. It's like I'm supposed to be with you now."

"You are supposed to be with me now. Calvin misses you. He keeps asking how many days until you're home."

"I saw this little girl here and I wanted to cry. I wanted to pick her up and rock her back and forth and kiss the back of her chubby neck."

"That would get you arrested."

"Her dad has the same stuff I have. Varicocele."

"See."

"It took him ten years and a hundred thousand dollars."

"Don't worry about it."

"What's happening with the election?" I asked.

"They're still voting, but Bush is going to win. The Democrats are losing everything."

"It's nice being away from all the ads and cheap shots."

"Daschle lost."

"Wow. That's a big one. They must have poured a ton of money up there."

"Yeah."

"You don't sound that upset."

"I love hearing your voice."

I pulled the phone away from my ear to stare at the receiver. I knew. Despite the distance and the odds, I knew.

"Franz?"

"Are you pregnant?" I asked.

"Why would you say that?"

"I dunno. It's just I've never felt anything this strong. Like I'm going against every impulse in my body being away from you."

"I miss you, too."

"You didn't answer me."

"Damn it."

"Are you?"

The line clicked.

"Tracy?"

"I just took the test. Yes. I'm pregnant."

"I knew it!"

"We're going to have a baby."

I crouched to the floor.

"I started feeling it, about a week into the trip," I said. "Then more each day."

"I'm sorry not to tell you in person. I wanted to see your face."

"Plus we just saved a hundred thousand dollars. Forget the operations. All we needed was one good swimmer, a champion from the healthy twenty-seven percent!"

Never had I wanted to hold someone as much as I burned to embrace Tracy. I thought about that hug every single minute for the next several days, on the crowded bus from Gaborone to Johannesburg, during an overnight stay at the Westcliff, through the air to Atlanta and on to Los Angeles. I sprinted through the terminal and down the escalator to baggage claim. A confused tourist hovered at the bottom of the steps.

"Excuse me," she said. "Do you know how I get to the United terminal?"

"There," I said, dashing past. "That way."

Tracy stood by the automatic doors. She stood alone. I dropped my bag and wrapped her body in my anxious arms. Feeling her sobs, I stroked her hair and embraced her even harder.

"This is," I whispered, "the best hug of my life."

Love's Embrace

The first and most important thing about love on our planet is that the world believes in it. Now, with Tracy in my arms and my child in her body, I felt my faith renewed. Embraced, in love, waiting for my backpack at the LAX baggage claim, home at last, I thought about their words over the previous year.

"It's a really, really strong feeling," said Mario. "So strong you will give up your friends."

I laughed and kissed a tear from Tracy's cheek.

"Life is a sailboat on the water," said Magued. "Love is the wind. The rudder is the mind. Sometimes when you have just wind, you'll crash. And without wind, you won't go anywhere. You need both."

"Without love, life would be vacant," said Ajit. "Your heart would not exist. Love is that yearning that is not of this world. It fills the space. Nothing else makes any sense."

When their words failed, they turned to their countrymen.

"When you're in love, a person will take the rock from your hand and it will taste sweet," an Egyptian man proclaimed.

"The depth of a man's heart and the depth of the ocean are unfathomable," related Jonas, a student from Gaborone.

"Where there is love, there is life," quoted a taxi driver in Goa.

It's a feeling, they agreed. One that starts within, then spreads. One without par. I cupped Tracy's cheeks and stared, just stared.

"Love is like the wind," said Rana. "We can't see, but we can always feel."

"Love will always come to you, but you need to dedicate time to feel it," said Anna. "It starts with your eyes, then with your feelings. If couples don't have this, there is no love."

"But how do you capture it?" I asked her.

"You don't. You create it."

The world nodded in agreement. Love is something that grows, but only if you labor and behave. Love will come. Love will grace couples who work hard and treat each other properly, God or Allah or Buddha willing. Love isn't the force that brings people together. It's never at its apex when you first meet. They see it as a reward for people who stay committed to each other. It's the end result of being a good provider, a caring husband, an attentive parent.

Things are significantly different in the United States, where more people fixate on love's wane, the "loss of love" in a relationship, on trying to recapture some of the envisioned reservoir of love that existed when the couple first connected. We spend millions of dollars on self-help books and counseling sessions trying to "rekindle" love. The third world didn't talk to me about rekindling. In their eyes, love flourishes in a successful relationship, dies in a bad one.

Let's build, Tracy. I'm ready.

"Love is simple, pure," said Dr. George. "The more you analyze it, the more complicated it becomes."

I kissed her again and felt every muscle ease.

"If you want love, live the love," said Yorda. "You take a partner to live, love, and be happy. Don't take a partner to fight. That's not love."

Yorda told me this from the front steps of her two-room wooden shack on Big Corn Island, Nicaragua, a home without paint or a yard, a place where she raised twelve kids. She'd never attended school, and I smiled at the simplicity and brilliance of her answer. "If you want love, live the love."

Or as the "Prince" of Egypt said with a shrug, "Love is to make love."

As I stared at Tracy's smile, my mind went blank. Where did the questions go? There were so many on the plane, ones about doctors and ultrasounds and that pregnancy class with the French name.

Tracy reclined against my chest, and I leaned over the crown of her head. *My unlikely queen.*

Love on our planet is alive and well.

Love Lessons from Abroad

The global community shares each of our relationship woes. They are every bit as petty, jealous, unfaithful, conniving, selfish, sappy, and forgetful of birthdays. Plus they've had a lot more experience at this stuff. They've built up their rituals, and flaws, over millennia, not just over a couple hundred years.

They also have much to share.

MAKE IT A FAMILY AFFAIR. I'm close with my family. Yet as my relationship with my previous fiancée showed signs of a breakdown in the days and months before our wedding, I never asked my parents or siblings what they thought. I wish I had. They could have illuminated problems and helped fashion solutions. In our family, and in many others, there's a don't ask, don't tell mentality when it comes to relationships. We tend to fend on our own.

This isn't the case in much of the world, from arranged marriages in India to negotiated ones in Africa to the heavy involvement of Jewish mothers everywhere. I never thought this approach was healthy, or even possible for families like mine. I've changed my mind.

Family involvement doesn't have to mean ceding control. It just means seeing relationships in a larger context than one-on-one. The problem with "you and me against the world" is that when the "you and me" becomes just "you," you're stuck in a fix on your own.

If your family cares about you, they're going to have thoughts about your relationships. If your family is functional, those thoughts might even be valid. Why not channel them in a productive fashion? Let them try to fix you up like locals do in Asia or help settle a dispute like in Africa. At the very least, talk with them. Look back to their judgments of past romances. They weren't that far off, were they?

LISTEN TO THE MASTERS. We ask rich people for stock tips and fit friends how to get in shape. Yet for some reason we don't think to ask longtime couples how to stay together for a long time. We think their advice couldn't possibly have any relevance to our modern world. We couldn't be more wrong.

There are many reasons why foreigners seek the advice of elders more frequently than we do. In some corners it's cultural, with older generations afforded a more prominent role in society. Sometimes it's economic. Grandparents in other countries live with their offspring far more often than grandparents do here. They remain an integral part of family life.

And sometimes it's just a matter of verve. I love the African weddings where newlyweds are asked to stand before a group of elders and receive their counsel for a successful marriage. Those are the times when Aunt Beya will tell the groom to give his paycheck to his wife and not blow it on card games. You'll see all the heads in the room nod in agreement. They know.

Around the world, the advice of longtime couples is surprisingly similar. Commitment, they say. Compromise. Understanding. Younger generations often forget to apply these lessons in their rush to the altar. Of course, marriages are failing at record rates. Increasingly we're a world of instant gratification and short attention spans. Nobody wants to work.

ANCHOR YOUR RELATIONSHIP. There's a reason why churches and mosques are packed in the third world. In countries decimated by wars or corruption, diseases or natural disasters, the religious centers provide a refreshing respite from chaos. They give messages of hope when so much else disappoints.

Couples in developing nations know that love is fragile. They understand, better than Westerners, that love can fray or end at any moment. In a world that crumbles, they look to bolster their relationships with forces that do not—faith, family, community. They use that support to strengthen their partnerships.

Those support systems are there for us, too. We're just less likely to ask.

SEE LOVE IN THE FUTURE TENSE. I was amazed by the calm demeanor of young adults on the verge of arranged marriages in place like India. "Aren't you scared you're going to wake up that first morning on your honeymoon and see the syringes, the gambling receipts, or the Megadeth tattoo on his back or hers? Aren't you afraid you won't love each other?"

No, they said, unruffled. We trust our parents. We will work to make this work.

The concept of learned love/earned love is one of the world's greatest secrets. We tend to see newlyweds at the peak of love. Indians and others see them at the bottom. Many other Indian couples told me without hesitation that they did not love their spouse when they got married. "How is that possible?" they asked.

Do you want to help your relationship succeed? See it like the Indians see a new relationship. Envision it as a vacant lot rather than a finished house. That way, you'll pick up a shovel and go to work rather than relax in the La-Z-Boy and assume love will come automatically.

INVEST IN APPRECIATING ASSETS. Ask Africans about their ideal qualities in a partner and they'll use words like "hardworking" or "faithful." Arabs talk about piousness and Allah. South Americans stress the importance of family. All are appreciating assets. The world invests wisely.

TAKE AWAY THE TRAPPINGS BEFORE MAKING DECISIONS. That's a lot easier for the developing world. They don't have the trappings to begin with. They know exactly how their potential mate is going to react in times of poverty or setback. They see it every day.

We tend to hide our emotions behind our possessions and give the appearance that our world can never be shaken. All too often we fall for the lifestyle rather than the life behind it.

I agree with the suggestion that the best way to witness your partner's true character is to travel together. I'd add a couple of twists. Travel with nothing more than a small backpack. Go somewhere remote, challenging. Volunteer together for a project in the third world. Live with locals. Stay as long as you can. Then watch hidden personality traits appear, the good and the not-so-good. By the end of the journey, you'll know. Bon voyage.

LOSE THE GAMES. It's dizzying, trying to keep up with all the rules of the American dating game. Only date once a week. Don't call him and rarely return his calls. And heaven forbid men or women express their true feelings. The laws are so intricate and cumbersome we've created entire industries to help us keep up.

Why, asks the world. What's wrong with common sense? If you want to meet someone, introduce yourself. If you'd like to see them, ask them out. If you like them, say you like them. The planet, and especially its poorer stretches, prefers a more direct approach. They don't have the life spans, money, or mind-sets to play our games.

FORGET LOOKS. Or at least move physical appearance to the bottom of the priorities list. Only a handful of people around the world mentioned looks when I asked about their ideal qualities in a partner. Beauty is fleeting and does nothing to help a family prosper, they said in a matter-of-fact fashion. If anything, good looks can be a problem.

"The beautiful are better off marrying a mirror," said a taxi driver in Botswana.

Instead of spending their time searching for that supermodel, the planet takes a more practical approach. A retired factory worker from Calcutta summed it up for me.

"My wife, in the eyes of others, she is ugly," he said. "But to me, she is Mumtaz Mahal"—the favorite wife of Shah Jahan and the inspiration for the Taj Mahal.

If you want to marry a "ten," the world counsels, simply declare your partner a "ten."

Plan on It

So let's have a baby," I said, stroking Tracy's leg as she drove us home from the airport.

"Let's get married first," she said.

"Deal."

"I don't want to be a cow in my wedding dress."

"Cows are important in Botswanan weddings."

"Thank God you asked me to marry you before I got pregnant. I would have worried for the rest of my life you were just doing it for appearances."

"You know what they do in Botswana? Just a simple ceremony at the government office."

"I'm not saying—"

"Then they party for a week."

"I can't think of anything worse than to watch other people drink champagne for a week while I down pregnancy vitamins and herbal tea."

"We don't need to do that. Family only. Put the savings toward the kid. Hey, we're going to have a baby!"

I looked to her belly to see if it had grown since the airport.

"I can't tell you how great it feels to be home," I said.

"I'd like a wedding."

"We'll have a wedding. A small one without all the brouhaha."

"I'm not one of those girls who dreamed of this big to-do her whole life."

"I know. That's one of the eight million three hundred and seventy-five thousand reasons I'm marrying you."

"But I am a girl."

"Woman."

"And I feel like I want a little of that girly stuff."

"Sure," I said. "What kind of girly stuff?"

"Where do you want to have the wedding?"

"My family goes to Kona Village each year. It's this great old-school resort on the Big Island. No phones, televisions, computers. You sleep in these private bungalows. I was thinking we'd do something there with our immediate families."

"Sounds nice."

"It's amazing," I said. "Or we could get married at Sea Ranch."

"You want to get married at the same place where your fiancée dumped you?"

"It's beautiful over there."

"But isn't that your place? Together?"

"Honey, she didn't show up. How could it be our place? Besides, it's too pretty to cede it to her. We could take it back!"

"No. It's too weird. I don't want to spend my wedding talking about your Runaway Bride."

But of course we did talk about my previous run at the altar, or, as Tracy labeled it, "the practice wedding." How could we not?

Suddenly, I felt horrible for Tracy. Could there be a worse lead-in for a bride? Not only had I completely messed up this drill before, I had written about it.

The easiest solution, I decided in Botswana, would be a quick ceremony in a quiet place. Not that I was nervous. *Okay, a little nervous*. I just didn't want my past screwups to dampen Tracy's day.

"Let's start on common ground," I said. "When do you want to get married?"

"I think we should get married in the next month or two, while I can still fit into a dress."

"How about New Year's? We don't have any plans."

"Others do."

"So we'll save some money."

"That gives us five weeks to plan a wedding," she said.

"We won't need that much. Trust me, I've done this before."

She exhaled. Deeply.

"For a writer and a former press secretary, you sure say a lot of dumb things," she said after catching her breath.

"I'm sorry. I didn't mean it like that."

"It's okay."

"What do you want?"

"A nice setting, my immediate family and close friends, and the best non-alcoholic champagne you can find."

"Okay."

"Serious?"

"Just a few caveats."

"What caveats?"

"Like no tuxedos."

"Great. Wear a nice suit."

"And no floral arrangements with wheat or dandelions or anything you'd normally scrape off your shoe."

"I'm not that hippie," she said. "Fine. And no gifts."

"You're right. We don't need any more toasters."

"No. I just hate writing thank-you notes."

"Okay. Here's another. No music with adjectives—hard rock or new age or modern jazz or anything like that."

"No music with adjectives. You've got problems."

"And now they'll be all yours," I said, hugging her from the passenger seat.

"Back," she said. "I can't concentrate on the road."

"Most important, we get a first-class resort and let them do all the work."

"Deal."

Within three days, we'd secured a minister and a caterer, called and e-mailed seventy-five guests, arranged music and wine, purchased a suit for my best-man brother and a dress for her maid-of-honor sister, ordered simple wedding bands, and booked a honeymoon suite at the Mandarin Oriental in San Francisco for two days, the longest Tracy had ever been away from Calvin. Along with things like save-the-date cards and wedding-planner consultations, we'd also eliminated most of the stress and all the arguments with mothers-in-law over arrangements.

After a few phone calls and a quick visit, we chose the Carneros Inn in the southern Napa Valley, a modern resort with a homey feel nestled amid the vineyards clipped bare for the winter. The individual cottages had wood patios and bright white rocking chairs, and the bathrooms were as big as the living quarters, with heated tile floors and indoor-outdoor showers. Calvin liked the cowhide chaise lounges. Best, they could accommodate seventy-five people on late notice.

It's amazing how many details just fall into place without having to lift a finger at the nicer hotels and resorts, things like chair covers or passed hors d'oeuvres. Centerpieces, they appear. Champagne flutes, too. The great ones will never let a table go bare.

The venue settled, the guest list finalized, we started to call our friends. Then something odd happened: They said they'd come, even on short notice, over a holiday, across the country or from abroad, and with my history of these things not going through. Our conversations went something like this.

Me: "So I'm getting married."

Friend: "That's funny. But I'm not going to fall for that one again."

Me: "No, for real."

Friend: "A Brazilian."

Me: "Tracy. The hippie actress from L.A."

Friend: "Well, congratulations, Wiz."

Me: "You can congratulate me again. We're pregnant. Or she is."

Friend: "Congrats, congrats. Is that a shotgun I hear in the background?"

Me: "We got pregnant ten days after I proposed to her in New Zealand. It's a short romance, long story. Mutant sperm and such. I'll tell you over a beer."

Friend: "When's the big date?"

Me: "January 2."

Friend: "A year from now."

Me: "A month from now."

Friend: "I think that's a land speed record for going from vagabond to dad."

Me: "What are you doing New Year's?"

Friend: "Some god-awful office party. Mumms champagne and tuxedos."

Me: "Can you ditch that and come drink good wine in Napa for a couple of days?"

Friend: "Gladly. Can I use the wedding gift I got you last time?"

At the end of the calls, almost every person who attended my practice wedding would be there. With refundable airline tickets, they added. Just in case.

All the Love in the World

Of course, I didn't follow a word of the planet's advice. Or so I concluded as Tracy and I unpacked our bags at the Carneros Inn. Outside, the rain pummeled the corrugated roof for a fifth straight day. I looked at Tracy as she laid out her makeup box and wondered what in the world I'd done. In so many places, marriage is a practical decision, a business venture, a union of families. There was nothing practical or prudent about what I was about to do.

You saw her mom and sister for ten minutes. What if they're in the witness protection program? Or Gypsies who parade their pretty daughter to hoodwink bachelors?

I had no idea of her caste, sign, tribe, debt, religious standing, medical history, shaman curses, dowry, *lobola,* ability to plow a field or hold a secret, or any other preunion prerequisite the planet uses to help ensure the success of the marriage. My journey to the altar was not what they prescribed. Only a fool would get hitched this way.

And you haven't even met her father. He's from the South. They bring shotguns to shotgun weddings.

I flopped my road-worn body on the chaise longue and grabbed the television remote to check the football scores.

"I'm going to take a bath," Tracy called from the other room.

We'd brought Calvin's babysitter, Genielle, for the weekend to help entertain him and the dozen children whose parents would arrive soon.

"Did you hear me?" she said.

"Yeah. Have fun."

Was that an are-you-ignoring-me "hear me" or a come-in-here-and-make-love-in-the-water "hear me"?

The rain got louder, and my mind drifted away from the Chick-fil-A Peach Bowl. The marriage I'd crafted went against the world's grain.

Or did it?

Beyond caste and tribe, what the world most sought in a partner, it seemed to me, was strength. Not chiseled shoulders or endurance-runner legs for working long and hard days, though those were certainly important. Internal strength. Fortitude. People sought to marry strong, to attach themselves to someone who could rise each morning and tackle the myriad of problems they'd encounter along the way. Women craved men who stood firm in the face of rejection, who scrapped for opportunity, who didn't fold at the temptations of the bottle or the flesh. Men looked for women who would be active partners, vociferous advocates, great moms. Choose wisely, they said. Pick someone whose qualities will last a lifetime.

I heard her turn off the water and saw wisps of steam from under the door. Tracy would be a great mom because Tracy already was a great mom. That surety pulled me closer to a woman than I'd ever dreamed possible. It made Tracy seem so compelling, attractive. *Sexy?* Sexy! It was as if my DNA had sent me a giant text message: "This is your job. This is why we are here. Get to it. Follow that blonde over there. She knows what she's doing."

No, I didn't know every detail about Tracy's past, but I knew the ones that mattered. Like the way she held Calvin when he had a cold. Or how she'd buy him twenty outfits before one for herself. I knew she hurt when I hurt, laughed even when my jokes weren't funny, and gave and gave until she was vulnerable. The rest didn't matter.

India and the Arab world (and Calvin) sold me on the concept of learned love. Forget about fantasized soul mates and wedding days crafted as your love's crowning achievement. Choose wisely, they said. Toast each other among family. Then get to work. I was ready. I wasn't before. Only after the world treks did I commit to the process. Now I'd do everything possible to make my relationship succeed. Now I'd surrender, to paraphrase our hosts in Delhi.

In the Czech Republic, I marveled at love amid chaos, often the only sane course. Tracy worked intermittently as an actress, and my ATM card considered me unemployed. Calvin's costs compounded with each day, and we had a baby on the way. Our used Volvo needed new tires and brakes, and we wanted out of our rental home in Los Angeles now that it had been yellow-tagged by the city because of the slope failure next door. If you had to pick the least prudent time to get married since the day I'd reached puberty, this would be it. It doesn't matter, said the Czechs. Love first, plan second. Use your Golden Hands. You will find the way.

Tracy and I wrote a note to the minister who performed the ceremony, describing our union as "a testament to the wonderful unpredictability of life" and the "importance of embracing unplanned splendor when it unfolds." I could see the Czechs nod.

Nicaragua reemphasized the importance of love and family over forces outside our control. Latin America often did. "We have a full-sized partner in this venture," we further noted to the minister. "This wedding is also his wedding. This marriage is his marriage. And we thank him for showering us both with open arms and heaps of love." The baby would stand at the altar as well. "The child is yet another of life's unforeseen wonders and, in many ways, a miracle child."

In a roundabout way and far from the shores of Ipanema, Brazil showed me allure of a different ilk. Her attraction stemmed not from the bikinis but from her strut; her attitude more than her shape. Brazil also showed me her less secure side. She hurt and hoped and summoned her courage anew. Brazil bared her *saudade*. Of course, this made her all the more attractive.

On the other side of the world and the spectrum, New Zealand expanded sex appeal to include the subtle and centered. And after I'd witnessed women as the lesser partner in many parts of the world, New Zealand showed me how attractive equality can be. It's only fitting I proposed to a strong woman there.

And Africa. Always Africa. Every lesson from the birthplace of humanity seemed a roller coaster of low and high. Until I set foot in Africa, I'd never laughed and cried at the same moment. Then a smiling, malnourished child hugged my knee. Africa changes and inspires like no other.

In the poorest stretches of the globe, amid those with limited means and opportunity, I learned to act with my heart. They showed me the crucial importance of passion over plan.

Without making a sound, I opened the bathroom door and joined Tracy in the tub.

*　*　*

Our wedding didn't go according to plan. Do any? Maybe we wish them to stray. Perhaps we're so ruffled by the seating charts and cake cuttings that we do everything possible to wreck the staged elements and see what emerges. Family's dirty laundry? Disapproval? Love?

My friends, many of whom had yet to meet Tracy, arrived a few days early. We met Ben and Jessica Johnson for lunch. He'd been there before. My room-mate for several years in Orange County, Ben, along with Kurt, had helped me call the 150 guests coming to my Runaway Bride wedding, then convinced me to go ahead with the festivities. I'd introduced him to Jessica several years earlier. They'd recently moved to Maine.

"Thanks for coming all the way out," I said.

"It's minus fifteen in Brunswick," he said, his Boston accent restored. "It wasn't a hard sell."

"You guys seeing family while you're out here?"

"My folks," said Jessica. "And we spent the day with my brother and his wife. You remember Jack."

"You'd never believe these two," said Ben. "They've got their kid sleeping in bed with them. He's three. So now they can't go anywhere alone."

"Attachment parents," I said.

"Nightmare."

Tracy squeezed my leg with one hand and reached for the bread with the other.

"Here's the kicker. He's not circumcised."

"Actually, half the kids in Los Angeles aren't circumcised," I said.

"Half the kids in L.A. aren't legal, either."

"More and more doctors are advising against it," I said. "And the insurance companies are refusing to pay for it. They're all concluding there isn't a medical need."

"Wiz. Do you know what you're saying? Tell me if your kid is a boy he's going to be snipped."

I looked at Tracy with pumpernickel going into her mouth and nothing coming out.

"I can't believe it," said Ben. "You, of all people. Knock some sense into this guy, Tracy."

"I'm trying," she said.

* * *

The forecasters said the rain would stop. In a week. I couldn't remember a deluge like this since the Amazon. Rain on your wedding day is supposed to bring fertility. But what if you're already pregnant? Should we make plans for triplets? We'd hoped to get married in a courtyard overlooking the vineyards, drenched in noonday sun. The area now looked like an aquarium. We had no Option B.

Unfazed, Tina, the affable events manager, suggested we remove the sofas in the resort entryway and exchange vows in front of the lobby fire. I hoped it would work, the seating and everything else.

In the lead-up to the "practice wedding," I handled most of the arrangements. This was a red flag, as anyone who has seen me fumble while ordering Chinese takeout, let alone plan an elaborate weekend for 150 people, can attest. The harder I worked, the more I felt my fiancée distance herself from the process. Or maybe it was the other way around. I chalked it up to her detached nature. *She's aloof. She's not anal about chintzes and prosciutto-wrapped melon. That's a good thing.* Down deep, I knew it was more. If I didn't orchestrate the festivities, there would be none.

Tracy and I had two or three conversations with Tina about food and arrangements, then turned the weekend over to her. So in the weeks prior to the wedding I didn't have to think about seared ahi crostini. I thought about our relationship, thought about love. I thanked the world for showing me I believed all along.

In the snare drum solo of the morning rain, as Tracy slept in a separate suite with Calvin, I woke in a haze. Literally. I'd left the front door open and opened my eyes to find my room occupied with Bay Area fog from stem to stern. I pulled on an overcoat, turned on the fan, and waved pillows at the thick fog bank in my abode.

Kurt arrived about the time I'd thinned the clouds from cumulus to cirrus. A room service tray of eggs and coffee came shortly after. Caffeine laden, barometer dropping, I began to see in focus.

If you're out there, God, I want to thank you for the day. I've been bugging you about it for a long time. I appreciate you not getting mad.

The guests, the same ones as at my practice wedding, now had kids, divorces, 401(k)s, parents who'd passed away. They'd grown up, it seemed, while I Peter-Panned with Kurt, traveling, escaping. In a few minutes, I'd adopt their lifestyle and go from vagabond to family man in a flash. Several friends told me they wished they could have honeymooned for a couple of years as well, before their commitments made it difficult. They're probably right, I concluded. But it's time now.

Calvin and Tracy's stepfather, Jay, were knocking on my door. I put a towel around my waist and emerged from the bathroom.

"Dad, guess what?" said Calvin. "Grandpa Jay let me ride in the front seat."

"Just in the parking lot," said Jay.

"Calvin, you look great."

He'd gotten rid of the facial scars crafted the day before with Tracy's mascara and had swapped jeans for a blue pinstripe suit, with sneakers.

"And look," he said. "You don't even need to tie this tie. You can just clip it on."

"You nervous?" asked Jay.

"You know, I thought I'd be. But I'm really not. I kinda feel like a bystander, if you want to know the truth. Like this whole thing was supposed to happen this way."

As I said the words, I felt a surge of verification. I hadn't thought about it until Jay asked. Over the last five years, events, crazy as they might have been, followed each other in a quasi-logical fashion. My fiancée didn't show up, therefore I'd have a wedding without her. I'd already purchased the tickets for the honeymoon, so I brought my divorced brother instead. The honeymoon felt meaningful, so we extended the trip. It wasn't until now that I saw how far my orbit had gone . . . and how far it returned.

With a dark suit on the bed and a mash-up of emotion, I stood in the exact same place I'd been five years ago, nearly to the day, and just a coastal range away. *It's been a strange ride.* Suddenly an enormous weight of realization drained me. I felt like a hiker sitting down for the first time after a strenuous climb. *A long way.* I excused myself and turned the shower on high to drown my tears.

Over the past several years, I'd met and heard from a lot of dumpees, including many who had been left days before their wedding, a population far greater than I'd imagined. I suspected this was due to our tendency to focus on the event rather than the relationship itself. Once the date has been set, weddings go on autopilot. We spend the preceding months talking about crab cakes and peonies rather than the bond between the couple. You were lucky, the dumpees told me. Your bank account was lucky. What if you had kids?

The point is, no matter how and when they'd been left, despite the pain they had suffered and the time it had taken to recover, not one of the dumpees wished their relationship had gone forward. Not one. Wiser, stronger, they'd moved on to more compatible partners and enriched lives.

I couldn't agree louder. Prior to the honeymoon, in an old life that seemed not mine, I would never have married Tracy. I was incapable of seeing her appeal. I suspect I wouldn't have seen her at all. She sat beyond the periphery, far from my blindered view. Had we, by some accident, met each other back then, we would have both looked away. A single mom? A terminal bachelor? An actress? A political spin doctor? Someone who, gulp, likes to talk about things? With a man who prefers to gloss over? I think we'd best be going now. Have a good life.

Tina was now Saint Tina. In the vast outdoor courtyard, the small crowd would have appeared, well, small. But here in the entry lounge, with an inviting fire behind me and a drizzle outside, the room felt abuzz. When I worked for the governor of California, we used to find the smallest rooms possible for our events to make the media use phrases like "packed house" and "standing room only" in their stories. Tina pulled off the same.

Best of all, the crowd sat close enough that I could see their every expression, feel their thoughts. *This is exactly the same cast as before, hopefully with one change.* Kurt, my best man, fidgeted next to me. The marriage to Tracy meant the honeymoon with my brother was over.

I remembered calling Kurt five years earlier to tell him the wedding was off; he caught the first plane from Seattle to help. I chuckled at the thought of him asking to be carried across the threshold in our Costa Rica hotel, and I remembered the moment he agreed to continue the honeymoon for a couple of years and a handful of continents. Soccer at Maracanã; the silk tailors of Hoi An and the steel drum bands of Trinidad; fresh hummus from the Syrian markets and pilsners in Prague; hikes up the Inca Trail, Table Mountain, around Angkor Wat; new friends and unlikely messengers; those talks, those back-of-the-bus talks; the power of family and faith; poverty and awakening; love; and the world's worst cabdriver—I relived it all. *Thank you, my friend.*

My sister and her husband, Doug, sat in the first row. *Don't cry, Lisa. You'll make me do the same. You, with your beautiful family, inspired me as much as any country or location. Your role model is the one to which I aspire.* Glancing over at my mother and father, I thought Dad's tie looked similar in construction to Calvin's.

In my four decades, I have seen my mother silent only twice. The first came after a Davis City Council meeting when a town rabble-rouser hurled an unkind word at her.

"I'm going to kill him with kindness," she announced at the breakfast table after mulling over the confrontation. "The next time I see him, I'm going to pretend he has a brain tumor."

The second came when I blurted out that Tracy was pregnant and we planned to get married in a month. Maybe it was my delivery, something along the lines of "Mom, guess what? There'll be three of us at the altar." Perhaps she envisioned a polygamist cult wedding. Frozen, the only sentence she could muster was "Who will take the pictures?"

On select few occasions, children wrap a special moment in life and present it to their parents. "Mom, Dad, I got into Yale!" "It's a girl!" "I've decided against the Elvira tattoo." I'd taken two such packages, my baby and my wedding date, crammed them in a brown paper bag, and thrown them at her feet.

But just as before, she rallied. She would have a new grandchild, and a mate for her oldest son who had a hard time seeing weddings through. With her salon permanent and consignment-store dress, holding my father's hand, my mother beamed large and true. *Or maybe she's envisioning you with a brain tumor.*

Guests plaster grooms with the word "lucky." Lucky in love. Here's the lucky man. Lucky SOB. At that moment I felt anything but. *I wasn't supposed to marry Annie. I was supposed to be here today. I see that now. I feel it amid the rain.*

A parade of children made their way down the improvised aisle, some spreading flowers, some fleeing to their moms with sudden cases of stage fright. *You look so handsome, Calvin. Suit pressed and hair parted. You look proud. I promise to be a good father to you.* A guitarist filled the room with classical Spanish chords. *Here we go.*

My brain, fueled with five years of circuitous turns and too much caffeine, zoned to the end of the aisle and out to the vineyards. *This all worked out.* I daydreamed about a new life, one less far-flung yet even more adventurous. This was full circle, and so much more. This was, from my four-decade perspective, the most randomly perfect moment on earth.

"Hey, Wiz," Ben yelled. "She's late."

Huh? I glanced at my watch. Ten minutes past the scheduled hour.

The audience started to laugh, prompting Ben to continue.

"Don't worry about it," he said. "If she doesn't show, there's your sequel."

"Keep that backpack handy," said another.

Shit!

I tried to laugh along, pushing my face muscles into their required positions and emitting a noise that could be construed as a guffaw, a sweaty, nervous guffaw. This was awkward, and ever more so as the minutes ticked by and Tracy remained AWOL. The laughter morphed to nervous cackles, then silence, awkward, painful silence.

The human brain contains a hundred billion neurons capable of processing a hundred trillion calculations per second. The most powerful computers cannot match its ability to create, improvise, and feel. Never does it spin faster than mine did at that moment.

Shoes, it's always the shoes. She's still fussing over her footwear. No, it's her mom. Probably trying to talk sense into her. Wait a minute. Even though I'm not a dog person, Mom's fine with me. Plus she's sitting right here. Maybe it's that comment I made about disliking lace dresses. A setup question if there ever was one.

I love you, Tracy. I wish there were a more meaningful way to say it, but I can't think of one right now. Everything, I love it all. Like the small of your back and the breadth of your smile. The way you cradle babies and your poise among strangers. Your preference for Chinese takeout over Hollywood-scene bars.

Relax. Breathe deep. Bend the knees. It would make a good sequel. Right? Two more years on the road with my brother?

Tracy?

Kurt interrupted the mental montage.

"Ladies and gentlemen," he announced. "Don't worry. Tracy *is* coming!"

They laughed en masse while letting out a collective sigh.

And there she was, my answered prayer at the end of the room, holding the arm of her father, Robert. The audience faded away, as did the rest of the world. My brain downshifted to a single, powerful, all-encompassing thought—*Wow.* I'd never seen a human being that stunningly gorgeous, let alone married her. Tracy's dress was lace. I now love lace.

I do.

Tracy's Oscar

LOS ANGELES

The Wisners are doctors. My grandfather, uncle, cousins, father—all physicians. My mother is a retired nurse. I spent family gatherings asking them about the rare and tropical diseases listed in my father's gory medical journals, the ones that would make Stephen King retch.

In my late twenties, I tore the ligaments in my knee playing weekend football. Make sure to get the right specialist, they emphasized. The attending physician recommended ACL replacement surgery. Instead of getting a second opinion, I brought the X-rays to the next family get-together and passed them around.

My father, a pathologist with a lifetime behind microscopes, looked at them upside down.

"If it doesn't involve bullets, I can't help you, either," said my cousin Dave, an emergency room surgeon.

At night's end I tossed them to Dave's brother Erik, the veterinarian.

"Sure," he said, holding them up to the light. "This black spot here is a clean tear. And you have some meniscus damage as well. See the discoloration. You need surgery."

"Thanks."

"Do you want me to do it?"

My parents spared no expense when it came to health. I grew up seeing the best doctors, the area specialists, receiving top-notch care. So when Tracy told me her preference for childbirth, to say I was acquiescent would be a stretch. No, a lie.

"Promise me you'll keep an open mind on this," she said.

"Of course."

"Home birth."

"No way."

"In a birthing tub."

"If you gave birth in a bathtub at home, I'm the one who'd need the epidural."

"Statistically, it's safer than a hospital birth."

"No kid of mine is going to come into this world breaststroking."

"They're in water for nine months. They're fine for that extra two seconds."

"If they have gills."

"It's about comfort. It's where I feel grounded. Childbirth is emotional more than anything."

"Calvin was born in a hospital."

"That's only because I had complications at home."

"See. He turned out just fine."

"Will you at least come with me to the midwife?"

"No."

O*pen mind, open mind,* I told myself the whole ride over to Shelly's office. Up we drove, to the top of the hill in the blue-collar neighborhood of Mount Washington. *This is a partnership.* The handcrafted sign asked that we remove our shoes before entering. I placed mine next to a pair of clogs. *Open mind.* Tracy knocked, and nobody answered. We entered with a "Hello!" A parrot squawked from the kitchen. On the walls and outside deck I saw dream catchers, wind chimes, paintings of Native American chiefs, and feng shui fountains.

"This looks like a place you'd come for a séance," I said.

"Shhh."

Within a few minutes, Shelly appeared from a back room, dressed in a yoga tank top and Indian sarong. She was the most tranquil health care provider I'd ever met, gliding across the wood floor as if on skates. She was also the first doctor I met whose first words weren't "Sorry for being late."

Like a parent, knowing and comfortable, Shelly wrapped her arms around Tracy, then slipped her hand down to my wife's swelling belly. Immediately I sensed they knew each other, caregiver and baby. Shelly continued rubbing and mumbling words not meant for me. *The womb whisperer.*

"Shelly, this is my husband, Franz," said Tracy.

This shook her from the private conversation.

"Hello," she said with an embrace and a smile. "You're a blessed man."

And you're the first doctor I've ever hugged.

Shelly's cheerful partner Seannie introduced herself as well, and the four of us walked back to a room with an examination table and file cabinets, looking very much like a private practice. *Okay, there's a stethoscope. Good.* I quit looking for similarities and noticed a few differences. Like the Christmas cards and thank-you notes on the walls, mementos from families who'd birthed at home, giggling people with clear-skinned kids. I looked for clues in the photo backgrounds to bolster my argument later, a rainbow afro or a commune sign, but didn't see any.

Shelly and Seannie didn't so much examine as they conversed. They took Tracy's blood pressure and asked her about her diet. Greens, they said. Dark greens. Kale and chard. *Shouldn't there be more prodding and poking?* I glanced to the clock and noticed we'd already been there a half hour. "And Calvin. How's Calvin?" *So this is what happens when you take the lawyers and the HMOs out of the picture.*

From the back of the room, silent, I realized their conversation included another. See you soon, they said. There's a world of love for you here. Keep growing. Enjoy the kale.

"Why don't you come and listen to the heart," Shelly suggested.

Me?

"Say hello."

For the first time, I did. Sure, I'd rubbed, kissed, and talked to Tracy's belly every day since I'd returned from Botswana. The belly, not the baby. So when they called me to the examination table, I felt a wave of nerves, like a chorus singer who suddenly finds himself alone onstage. Introducing . . . your baby.

Um, hello. Nice to meet you. I have no idea how I did this. I mean, I know how-how if you're talking about process. The why part is where I'm stumped. Fortune, I guess.

No, I don't believe that. Not now. Not after this long and crazy road to get here. I'll explain it all to you someday. Honeymoons with siblings and mutant sperm and such. You're not happenstance or coincidence. You are supposed to be here.

You look beautiful, even though you're a bit covered right now. You're still beautiful. You'll probably get acne like I did in high school. And premature gray hair. I'll love you even more. Don't dye your hair or worry about pimples. Men don't know how to dye their hair, and women do it too much. It has nothing to do with beauty. The world helped show me that. I'll tell you someday. Oh, and please don't hit your brother.

Tracy turned on her side, and the midwives continued their exchange. I returned to the chair, though now a full participant in the conversation. This was my baby, our baby, a person, not a mound. I sat back and absorbed the spiritual link between mother and child. The way Tracy placed a hand on her hip, her stretches and shifts, the deliberate, yoga-type movements of every action, now seemed the work of a duo.

"It's going to be a big baby," said Seannie.

"I gained forty-five pounds with Calvin," said Tracy.

"I think you'll gain even more this time."

"No worries," I said, trying to be helpful. "It'll be like dating a different woman every month—a size two, then a size four, then eight, then twelve."

Thankfully Tracy didn't hear me as she arched her head back over the side of the bed.

She's the one who's going to do the work. Not you. Like pulling your lower lip over your head, according to Carol Burnett.

On the way to the car, I told her I was fine with home birth.

"And the tub?" she asked, grabbing my hand.

"Does it have spa jets?"

L et's go somewhere for a night," suggested my wife. "Just you and me. My sister and mom can look after Calvin."

"Sure. Where do you want to go?"

"The Ritz Carlton."

"You're about ready to birth a kid at home, with a midwife, in a birthing pool, and you want to go to the Ritz days before? Don't the two cancel each other out?"

"I'm a walking contradiction. You'll get used to it."

In the topiary-and-chandelier confines of the Ritz, Tracy and I took a three-hour nap and a long walk around the grounds. We ate steak fillets and finalized the names. She sipped a glass of champagne, and I lit up a cigar. After years of quick turns and changes of plan, everything fit. I inhaled and pronounced all right with the world. We went to bed late, and at 4 A.M. I heard the voice from the bathroom.

"Honey," she said, "my water just broke."

"You're kidding."

"We're going to have a baby today."

Now, any man who's been through it knows the whole "we're having a baby" thing is a ruse perpetrated by women to keep their counterparts quasi-focused. Here's the "we" in our childbirth: I ordered breakfast and packed the bags. Tracy braced to endure the highest amount of pain a body can take without passing out. Childbirth took time, everybody said. No need to panic. I ate all my bacon and called for the car.

"Everything's going to be just fine," I said on the ride home.

"The electricity in your car doesn't work," she said. "I can't roll down the windows or turn on the a/c."

The radio announcer forecast temperatures in the hundreds. We opened the doors at each intersection for ventilation, suggesting to the neighboring motorists I was about to force a pregnant woman into a Chinese fire drill.

Tracy's mother and sister met us at the front door. Tiffany, a midwife in training, flew down to Los Angeles for her only four days of vacation that summer, willing her sister to deliver during the short stay. She guessed right.

In the middle of the room, I saw the blue birthing tub, now full and beckoning. We really were going to have a baby that day. Calvin, I suspected, should be credited for the rubber duck floating in the middle. He roared to greet us, bounding over in blue silk karate pajamas with gold dragon embroidery and a Rising Sun headband to complete the outfit. Clearly one family member was ready for battle. In the rest of the room, disposable hospital sheets covered couches and chairs, making me wonder if some births were projectile. I didn't remember that from the birthing videos.

Seannie came shortly thereafter, taking Tracy's pulse and giving her an antibiotic IV.

"It's going to be well over a hundred today," said Linda. "You're going to need more than this fan."

"You okay, Tracy?" I asked.

"Fine. My contractions are weak. It's going to be a while."

"All right. Linda. C'mon. We're on a hunt. Seannie, any more stuff we need?"

"Something sweet. Cookies."

"For Tracy's blood sugar?"

"For me."

Within an hour we'd accumulated two shopping carts full of SmartWater, Gatorade, ice, sandwiches, deli salads, herbal teas, fruit tarts, cookies, and anything else Linda suggested; a full wardrobe of onesies and pajamas even though we had no idea of the baby's sex; and a giant air conditioner on wheels that blasted frost strong enough to shake the windows.

"How's it going?" I asked once back home.

"Seannie gave me black cohosh and castor oil," said Tracy. "And Tiffany and I have been walking those stairs."

"Any good?"

"I won't need a colonic anytime soon."

"We're trying to speed things a bit since her water broke," said Tiffany.

"Let's go for a hike," said Tracy.

"Wow," I said. "You're a badass."

For the rest of the afternoon, we trekked through the arroyo near the Rose Bowl in Pasadena. *I'll bet none of the football players have gone through this type of workout.* First came the pauses, every ten minutes or so. She'd close her eyes and see the pain through. Then the double-overs, clutching Tiffany and me for support.

"Should we head on back?"

"Just a little bit longer. I don't want Seannie to measure my dilation until I'm far along."

"Baby, I hate to be the pushy father before I'm even a father, but this kid might be born in UCLA tailgate territory."

By the time we'd convinced her to end the aerobics and return home, Tracy had already dilated six centimeters. Her groans for most of the day had sounded like a painful inconvenience. Now they sounded like Chewbacca channeled. Calvin heard the new tone and fled outside to the safety of his fort. And he's a *Star Wars* fan.

Tracy's mother tried to drown them out with a New Age CD. This made the room sound like Enya being attacked by a starving grizzly bear every five minutes. Now every four.

"Honey, do you want to get into the birthing tub?"

"Mmmmmmmmm," she groaned, her face frozen in grimace and smile.

"Okay, not yet."

Seannie glanced at her watch, cool and calm. Calvin's curious face and mangled yellow hair popped up and down against the window outside. He'd lost the samurai bandanna.

Tracy had told us earlier in the day, at a time when she spoke a language resembling English, she wanted to wait as long as possible to enter the tub. A reward for the "hard part." *This isn't the hard part?* I looked at my wife in awe as she worked through long, deep sighs. Pick strong, the world said. *Oh, you picked strong.*

Then, with a jolt of consciousness, I spoke fluent Wookiee.

"Mrrrreeemmm!" she moaned.

"All right, people, she's ready to get in the tub now."

"Arrrmmmeeeggg."

"You want me to get in with you."

"Rrrrhhhhhgggg!"

"Just not naked. I'll put on a swimsuit."

Tracy nestled up against my back as I slid into the water, using my body as a brace for the contractions. The others chanted the Ten Centimeter Chorus, crescendos of "you're doing great" and "almost there."

"I can see the head," said Seannie, holding a mirror in the water.

"What color is the hair?" I asked.

In a history of dumb questions at horrible times, that was quite possibly your worst.

I have never loved a human being more than I loved my wife in that tub. Big, goopy, *Steel Magnolias*–watching love. For the first time I could feel, physically feel, her Herculean odyssey with each clenched grip and stiffened push. *And I love this water. Makes you feel part of the process.*

"Arrrrraaaaa!"

A distant part of the process.

"Okay, Tracy," said Seannie. "Just one more big push and you're there. Through the pelvis, forcing down."

And there, from the bottom of a white trash Jacuzzi, with pan flutes and

Moog synthesizers in the background, in front of a towheaded brother who'd mustered enough courage to come indoors, popped a baby, stunned and grunting, eyes swollen and closed. Calvin rushed in to examine this foreign creature and to present him with a wrapped box of new orange socks from Sears. Guys can always use new socks.

"Hello, Oscar."

Kurt's Afterword

Okay, I know what you're thinking: "But what about Kurt?" Or to quote e-mails from our readers: "What about 'the brother'?" Good question. Franz was kind enough to give me this space at the end of the book to answer. This came as a welcome surprise to me. Usually he doesn't let me talk. Big brothers tend to do that.

To answer the most frequent question I receive: Yes. My dogs are fine. You can see for yourselves on our Web site, at www.honeymoonwithmybrother .com. Fritz, the Jack Russell, doesn't take as many long runs with me these days, but he still has enough energy to drive me crazy each time he barks at his food before eating it. Shih tzu Riley doesn't seem to mind when everyone refers to him as "she." I don't, either, because I know he's really one ornery pack leader. Those two guys have helped me through many a tough time, and I wouldn't trade them for the world.

These days, I'm an early-to-bed homebody living in a hipster part of Los Angeles, and yes, I'm still single. I'm sure Franz hoped to fix me up with someone on our travels for this book. Would have made for a nice final chapter. That didn't go so well. The whole non-Muslim thing wasn't a big seller with the Arabs, and India didn't see a jobless, forty-year-old divorcé as a catch. Don't worry, Mom, I'll get there. I've been married before, so I don't feel the need to hurry anymore. Mrs. Right just needs to have a valid passport, enjoy both one-star and five-star accommodations, and love to explore new places.

While Franz wrote this book, I earned my California real estate license and starting selling and listing homes again. I work about half-time and try to do good-karma transactions only, getting a great deal for that first-time home-buyer, representing people who will take loving care of an old house. The media say this is a horrible time to be in real estate, but I've managed to do okay. If anyone needs a real estate agent in Los Angeles, by the way . . . kurt@honeymoonwithmybrother.com. The honeymoon business is fun, but it's not the best for bank accounts.

Outside of real estate, I'm still a professional brother. Franz and I do a lot of speaking engagements, charity fundraisers, and corporate events to spread the word about *Honeymoon with My Brother* and all the powerful lessons the world has to offer. We urge them all to chase passion, to strengthen family ties, to embrace and explore. Like our grandmother LaRue said, "You don't regret the trips you take, only the ones you decline." I miss LaRue.

The book business is difficult. Unless your name is Grisham, Patterson, or Rowling, the literary world can be a frustrating place. We've sold books out of the back of my old van, hawked copies at state fairs, and even tried to move product on the beaches of Southern California. But the minute we meet someone who has been inspired by our book, the aggravations evaporate. That's what fuels us.

I get a huge rush when someone tells us something like "I read your book, and I called my brother whom I haven't seen in years." Or when they say the book inspired them to take a trip or helped them get through a tough breakup. One lady even e-mailed us to say she'd read the book and decided to dump her fiancé on the spot. Probably for the best, I decided.

When *Honeymoon with My Brother* first rolled off the presses, we caught a few breaks. The *Today* show asked if we'd tell our story on air to Matt Lauer. I was excited, until I realized seven million people would also be listening. We flew with our parents to New York and told each other, "Don't be nervous." This, of course, made us exponentially more nervous. I slept for six minutes the night before the show. The in-house beautician used a mason's trowel to scoop pancake makeup under my eyes to hide the bags.

"Are you okay?" Franz asked as we waited on set with our faces terra cotta orange.

"I'm a little nervous," I said. "You do most of the talking."

That's when I saw on the television monitor a soundless shot of the crowd outside, waving.

"Uh-oh," I said. "Do you see that gray-haired woman in front?"

"Where?" he asked.

"There," I said, pointing. "Behind Al. The petite woman with the huge sign that says HONEYMOON WITH MY BROTHER."

"Mom?"

We froze as Katie Couric walked over to our mother. Still we couldn't hear any sound.

"Uh-oh," I said. "This could be really good, or really bad."

The show went to commercial, then returned with a shot of Katie, arm around Mom, both smiling. Our mother is not shy. She'll gladly reveal to any stranger who asks the exact date Franz stopped wetting his bed (later than you'd think, by the way) or the fact that my head was so big when she gave birth she had to sit on an O-ring for a week.

"Maybe the corporate gig isn't so bad after all," Franz said to me.

But Mom didn't talk about pregnancy stitches or hygiene milestones. She said she was very proud of her boys, and *Today* extended our interview by several minutes. Love Mom.

More than moms and media, what fueled the success of *Honeymoon with My Brother* was word of mouth. And nobody has more words or better mouths than the book clubs.

We received hundreds of e-mails from book clubs who said things like "If you're ever in Huntsville, Alabama, we have a literary club that meets at a beautiful old church." Or "We have the world's greatest pie shop in Jefferson, Texas. Come on by if you and your brother are ever in town. Meet with our book club." They had no idea how far we'd go for a good slice of pie.

So for the paperback tour, Franz and I sent an e-mail back to everyone saying, "Guess what? We're coming to Huntsville, and to Jefferson, and to anywhere you want us to go." We loaded up my Volkswagen van, found a sitter for my dogs (a woman who got arrested for stealing our identities, but that's a story for another day), and spent three months crisscrossing the United States, doing events and book club appearances in coffee shops, beauty salons,

independent bookstores, bars, malls, libraries, and private residences. The
book clubs decorated their homes as if they were having a wedding, complete
with flowered trellises, champagne, and wedding cake. They had parties with
foods and wines from around the world. Some asked detailed questions about
structure and alliteration; others talked about their own failed loves and never
got around to the book. We loved every second.

Franz and I raise a glass to them all. Our only word of caution is that they
think twice before inviting us over for this book. We're likely to accept.

Sources

LOVE IS DEAD

World Bank statistics, www.worldbank.org.

The Penguin Atlas of Human Sexual Behavior. Judith Mackay; Penguin, 2000. (This is a much more interesting book than *The Human Atlas of Penguin Sexual Behavior.*)

Ending Violence Against Women. Lori Heise, Mary Ellsberg, and Megan Gottemoeller; Johns Hopkins University School of Public Health, Population Information Program, December 1999.

"Maldivians Like to Marry Over and Over." *Taipei Times,* October 27, 2003.

"For Many in Cuba, Marriage Is for the Birds." Tracey Eaton; *Dallas Morning News,* July 3, 2004.

Civil Code of the Islamic Republic of Iran, book 7, chapter 2, articles 1133 and 1134.

"Porn in the U.S.A." Steve Kroft (reporter), *60 Minutes,* CBS, September 5, 2004.

BRAZIL

A Death in Brazil. Peter Robb; Duffy and Snellgrove, 2003.

The Masters and the Slaves. Gilberto Freyre; Random House, 2000 (1933).

How to Be a Carioca. Priscilla Ann Goslin (author), Carlos Carneiro (illustrator); Livros TwoCan, 1992.

The Brazilians. Joseph A. Page; Addison Wesley, 1995.

Rio de Janeiro. Ruy Castro; Bloomsbury, 2004.

INDIA

The Complete Illustrated Kama Sutra. Lance Dane (editor); Inner Traditions, 2003.

The City of Djinns: A Year in Delhi. William Dalrymple; Penguin, 2003.

Holy Cow: An Indian Adventure. Sarah Macdonald; Broadway, 2004.

Seduced by the Beauty of the World. Iman Bijleveld (photographer), Don Bloch (author); Harry N. Abrams, 2003.

India: A Wounded Civilization. V. S. Naipaul; Vintage, 2003.

WORLD COURTING: THE GOOD, THE BAD, AND THE UGLY

African Ceremonies. Carol Beckwith, Angela Fisher; Henry N. Abrams, 1999.

"Abduction, Often Violent, a Kyrgyz Wedding Rite," Craig S. Smith; *New York Times,* April 30, 2005.

"Gender, Sexuality, and Marriage: A Kaulong Model of Nature and Culture." Jane C. Goodale; in *Nature, Culture, and Gender,* ed. Carol P. MacCormack and Marilyn Strathern; Cambridge University Press, 1980.

Vanishing Beauty. Bérénice Geoffroy-Schneiter (author), Bertie Winkel and Dos Winkel (photographers); Prestel, 2006.

NICARAGUA

The Country Under My Skin: A Memoir of Love and War. Gioconda Belli; Anchor, 2003.

The Jaguar Smile: A Nicaraguan Journey. Salman Rushdie; Viking, 1987.

Blood of Brothers: Life and War in Nicaragua. Stephen Kinzer; Putnam Adult, 1991.

Moon Handbooks Nicaragua. Randall Wood, Joshua Berman; 2nd ed., Avalon Travel Publishing, 2005.

Rubén Darío: Selected Writings. Ilan Stavans (editor), Andrew Hurley, Greg Simon, Steven White (translators); Penguin Classics, 2005.

Clemente: The Passion and Grace of Baseball's Last Hero. David Maraniss; Simon and Schuster, 2007.

CZECH REPUBLIC

The Prague Orgy. Philip Roth; Vintage, 1996.

The Good Soldier Svejk and His Fortunes in the World War. Jaroslav Hasek (author), Cecil Parrott (translator); Penguin Classics, 1990.

The Metamorphosis. Franz Kafka; Waking Lion Press, 2006.

The Unbearable Lightness of Being: A Novel. Milan Kundera; Harper Perennial Modern Classics, 1999.

Laughable Loves. Milan Kundera, Harper Perennial Modern Classics, 1999.

New Catholic Encyclopedia. Berard L. Marthaler (executive editor); Catholic University of America Press, 2003.

TEN GLOBAL THREATS TO LOVE

The State of the World's Children: Excluded and Invisible. The United Nations Children's Fund (UNICEF); 2005.

EGYPT

The Yacoubian Building: A Novel. Alaa Al Aswany; Harper Perennial, 2006.

Whatever Happened to the Egyptians? Changes in Egyptian Society from 1950 to the Present. Galal Amin; American University in Cairo Press, 2001.

The Koran. N. J. Dawood (editor, translator); Penguin Classics, 2004.

NEW ZEALAND

Way of the JAFA: A Guide to Surviving Auckland and Aucklanders. Lee Baker, Benjamin Crellin; Hachette Livre NZ Limited, 2004.

Storm Out of Africa: The 1981 Springbok Tour of New Zealand. Richard Shears; Macmillan, 1981.

THE WORLD'S TEN WORST PLACES TO BE GAY

"The Most Homophobic Place on Earth?" Tim Padgett (reporter); *Time*, April 12, 2006.

Human Rights Watch, www.hrw.org.

International Lesbian and Gay Association, www.ilga.org.

"Ugandan Government Accused of State Homophobia." Reuters; August 24, 2007.

Under the Loving Care of the Fatherly Leader: North Korea and the Kim Dynasty. Bradley K. Martin; Thomas Dunne Books, 2004.

"Anwar's Return." *Economist,* August 24, 2006.

"Police Seize Leading Opposition Figure in Malaysia." Seth Mydans; *New York Times,* July 17, 2008.

BOTSWANA

Culture and Customs of Botswana. James Denbow, Phenyo C. Thebe; Greenwood Press, 2006.

The No. 1 Ladies Detective Agency. Alexander McCall Smith; Pantheon, 2005.

Voice of the People End of the Year Survey. Gallup International Association, Zurich, 2005.

Culture Smart! Botswana. Michael Main; Kuperard, 2007.

Acknowledgments

A warm thank-you and a chilled beverage to:

HOSTS AND HELPERS: Jonathan Terra, Iveta Živná, Šárka Dohnalová and family, Paul Swart and Natural Migrations (www.naturalmigrations.com), Map and Kathy Ives, Ker and Downey (www.kerdowney.com), *familia* Laura Davidson (www.ldpr.com), Erika Masiero, the mighty Lacayo clan of Nicaragua, the Nicaragua Tourism Board, Chris Berry and Pelican Eyes—great place, great karma (www.piedrasyolas.com), Casa Canada (www.casa-canada.com), Chez Schaible, Justine Amodeo, Doug and Natasha Rowan, go-go Gina Greblo, aptly named Incredible India (www.incredibleindia.org), Priya Parker and her bighearted family, Paul Campos and the Kippery, Kelly Lorson, Dana Valenzuela, Courtney Smith, H. D. Palmer and Co., the Fridens, the Youngs, the Clyburns, Diane Reverand, Maestro Larry Thomas, and Magued Abdel, our man in Cairo.

HOMES: Pasadena Central Library, Swork Coffee in Eagle Rock, the Westport Public Library, and the beautifully restored Pequot Public Library in Southport, Connecticut, with special thanks to Dan Snydacker and Robyn Swan Filippone for their hospitality and toasty fires in February.

HAND-HOLDERS: Elizabeth Beier, John Murphy (thanks for the shower cap, too), Stephen Lee, Michelle Richter, Frances Sayers, and Julie Gutin at St. Martin's; Kris Dahl and Laura Neely at ICM.

And the heartiest toasts of all to Robert and Joyce Wisner; my brother/ honeymoon partner Kurt; Doug, Lisa, Elizabeth, Eleanor, and Eddie (Pirate) Menzmer; the Middendorfs, Dietrichs, and Vogels for lowering their standards and allowing me in; and to Tracy, Calvin, and Oscar for the best trip I've ever taken.

"If you could completely change the course of your life, where would you go?" *

"Franz Wisner's funny, endearing, and breathtakingly
detailed journey with his brother Kurt is a timely reminder
that sometimes we have to travel the globe in order
to find ourselves and the places and people we call home."
—Jodi Picoult*

St. Martin's Griffin   www.stmartins.com